Soldier's Fight

Veteran's Vote

Or

How I Radicalized a General

Our country, may she always be right; but our country, right or wrong. Lucius Fairchild, Commander in Chief, Grand Army of the Republic, 1887.

Printed in the United States of America

ISBN-10: 0-9768832-0-1

ISBN-13: 978-0-9768832-0-3

For Mona,

whose unwavering support had made this work possible.

Foreword

This work is not meant to be objective. It was written with a purpose; to show how the political culture of today is merely a reflection of events which took place 150 years ago. It is not an in-depth study of circumstances but rather a glimpse into the past and explains how radical politicians had manipulated events and the American people which resulted in the needless loss of hundreds of thousands of American lives.

Using the Civil War as a timeline this book reveals how politicians were willing to spill the blood of this nation's youth for their cause and in the interest of party preservation. Although slavery was the foundation on which this war was fought I cannot assign blame for the entire bloody conflict solely on the slave powers of the South for northern political leaders were also to blame. There is no doubt that certain elected officials welcomed the impending war and viewed this, in the words of Secretary of State William Seward, "irrepressible conflict" as a ways to a means; to achieve their own goals. Tactics such as manipulation and coercion were used to convince soldiers, veterans, and the public into accepting and endorsing a radical agenda.

The Joint Committee on the Conduct of War had obstructed and interfered with Lincoln's plans regarding the conduct of the war. By relieving the professionally trained officers in favor of those less competent who accepted this ideology, committee members admitted that defeat was preferable to victory until their goals were achieved. Their methods had no doubt been just as responsible for the death of many of our Union soldiers as rebel bullets.

At the end of four bloody years of war, when the nation longed for peace these same politicians waved "the bloody shirt" to ensure a harsh reconstruction and a continued division between the North and the South, thus prolonging the long, overdue healing process.

Although time was a factor I had made the decision not use footnotes or cite my sources. With so many fascinating and intriguing stories which surround this monumental event, it is my intent to induce the reader to turn to the bibliography for further reading.

Throughout this work the reader may recognize events and sentiments similar to those of today. Over the years politicians had connived, obstructed, investigated and even threatened to overthrow the government when diplomacy failed. All in the name of patriotism and with no regards to consequences. The price paid for this attitude has been ghastly and it is for this reason that we must remember our history lest we are doomed to repeat it.

Acknowledgements

To name everyone who had been instrumental, directly or indirectly, with this writing would be impossible but there are those whose names do bear mentioning. My interest in the American Civil War began nearly five decades ago when I would accompany my father to his competitive matches of the North-South Skirmish Association. The sights and sounds of these events were mesmerizing. I had since inherited my father's library of which the core of my research was derived from.

Over the years I have had the good fortune to encounter teachers, professors, reenactors, living historians, and ancestors of those who had fought in that bloody struggle; all of whom were willing to share their experience and knowledge.

As always, the staff at the Dormann Library deserves mention. Their ability to locate elusive research material was uncanny. To Samuel Washburn whose extensive knowledge is unequaled, thank you. I may not have followed all your advice or suggestions but I am grateful for your willingness to assist. Marie Hannan-Mandel, what can I say? Even with your busy schedule you gave me so much of your precious time and for that I am grateful. To Tasha Ferris and Ralph Begeal at Multi-Media Services, your patience seemed endless. But most importantly, I must thank my wonderful wife Mona for your support in this endeavor was immeasurable.

Table of Contents

Chapter 1

No More Compromises

Raising an army to wage war is as old as civilization itself. Whether it was for personal, political, religious, or social purposes, man has always been to ready and willing to shed the blood of their fellow human being in the name of their cause. And the monumental experience which took place in our own history during the mid-19th century was no different.

This curse was never mentioned in the Constitution by name but it was referred to directly. Its principle was detested; its necessity tolerated. By skillfully burying it in the text of the document our forefathers, unable to agree on the issue had unknowingly cursed this fledgling nation with a system which they themselves could neither embrace nor discard. Two sections of the country were at odds over this issue. Northern abolitionists detested holding another human being in bondage while in the south, it was an accepted practice. And whichever side had more representatives in Congress could technically control the status of the institution.

In order to gain political power, 30,000 people were needed for one representative. Since slaves outnumbered whites in many of the Southern states, slave owners wanted them to be counted as citizens. To the Northern abolitionists and the anti-slavery crowd this was absurd. If Southerners considered their slaves as property and yet demanded they should be counted as citizens, then the Northern crowd insisted on using their property such as horses, cattle, mules, and furniture to be counted towards representation as well.

A solution was offered by James Wilson of Pennsylvania; a free person would be counted as one while "all other Persons" would count as

3/5 of a person. This brought the number up to 50,000 for each representative.

As *Manifest Destiny,* the belief that the expansion of the nation was both justified and inevitable, took hold across the young nation, pioneers began their westward journey. Others, hoping to break away from the traditional roles they would be fated to should they remain in the East, sought to settle down on their own land. But some insisted on introducing the practiced tradition into the new lands against the opposition of others who contested its intrusion. This challenge would set off a chain of events which would promote sectional conflict, party division and ultimately the division of American people themselves, and lead this country to its most defining moment, the effects of which still reverberate today.

Young America was coming into its own, and by the mid-19th century it was well into an age of individuality, an age of the self-made man, an age where there were no limits as to what a man could achieve if he chose to apply himself. But as these brave Americans ventured westward to forge for themselves a new life, there were sectional factions at home who saw the expansion west as a way to expand their own way of life.

The *1820 Missouri Compromise* was one of the first in a series of compromises which allowed the problem to grow and fester. The compromise had allowed Missouri, the first state west of the Mississippi notched out of the Louisiana Territory, to be admitted into the Union as a Slave State with the stipulation that future states and territories north of Missouri's southern border which fell on the 36° 30', would enter as Free States. There was now an equal number of Free and Slave states, twelve each. To the Southern politicians, this meant that future admission of territories in the West would ultimately tip the scales of power into the hands of the anti-slavery Northerners thus threatening the continuance of their way of life.

The *Donation Land Claim Act* of 1850, later known as the *Homestead Act,* was another bill of contention between the North and the South. Based on the premise of Jeffersonian democracy, the government proposed settlement of lands acquired through the *Mexican Cession* and *Louisiana Purchase.* As the anti-slavery movement gained momentum in the New England states, anti-slave advocates began pressuring their elected officials to halt the expansion of slavery into these areas. In an attempt to prohibit this expansion, the *Free-Soil Party* advocated settlement by independent or yeoman farmers only, in order to deny the slave-owning planters of the South access to these lands. Their fear was the wealthy, non-resident speculators of the South would force the independent farmer onto inferior or marginal land. The Southern Democrats opposed the bill, believing it denied their states the right to land which they helped to acquire. The war with Mexico had been won by two Southern generals with an army made up of two-thirds Southerners under a Southern president. As John Randolph of Virginia had stated thirty years prior, "The question of slavery is to us, a question of life and death." Since the institution of slavery was under the control of the state and not federal authority, the government was denying them their state rights.

But the South had other grievances as well. They objected to Congress' attempt to pass the *Wilmot Proviso* which would deny the expansion of slavery in land acquired from Mexico and the lack of enforcement of the *Fugitive Slave Act* in Northern states. Also, the proposed protective tariffs and the use of national resources to construct a transcontinental railroad system, they felt were designed to promote northern industrialism and to aid northern manufacturers. These issues led up to slave owners in Mississippi calling for a convention of like-minded planters in Nashville in June of 1850 to discuss the option of secession. This was not a novel idea. Delegates of the Federalist Party of New England met at the *Hartford Convention* in Connecticut in 1814-15 to discuss concerns over the increasing power of the federal government. The more radical at the convention even proposed secession. The demands of the Nashville convention had led to yet another compromise.

The *Compromise of 1850* drafted by Henry Clay would again temporarily shelve the issue of slavery in the territories. The final outcome would be California admitted as a Free State and retain its current boundaries while Texas would be compensated ten million dollars to pay off its national debt if it dropped its claim to land north of the 36th parallel and to the west. The relinquished land would now become Utah Territory and New Mexico Territory and popular sovereignty would decide its fate regarding free or slave state. The slave trade in DC would be abolished over strong opposition of Southern representatives, but not slavery itself which would remain intact. A strengthened *Fugitive Slave Act of 1793* was also passed which allowed for all federal officials to actively assist in the return of escaped slaves. Law enforcement officials were also mandated to arrest anyone suspected of being a fugitive slave, even if only on sworn testament of the claimant. The slave would be denied a trial by jury also. Furthermore, anyone caught harboring a fugitive slave was subject to six months imprisonment and $1,000 fine. The officials of course would be compensated for the efforts.

Several of the northern states did not agree with the last passages. To counter the Fugitive Slave Act, many northern states passed personal liberty laws which could question a petitioners' claim of an alleged fugitive. It also guaranteed the rights of alleged fugitives by offering trial by jury. Additionally, states were authorized to mete out severe punishment for illegal seizure and perjury for the claimants. But, in the western states, Black Laws were passed in which some states banned blacks from migrating within their borders while others restricted their civil liberties.

Both sides had concerns over the compromise regarding the size of the states and how many states would eventually be free or slave states. Overall, the concessions were accepted by both sides and the smoldering crisis was again dampened down.

As social change swept the country in the early 19th century, fortunes in the North were made in manufacturing and relied on tariffs, banking acts and internal improvements which favored their interests. While in the South, cotton, tobacco, and rice were the prize commodities and plantation aristocracy, built on the backs of slaves, reigned supreme. During the 1850s cotton was selling at a premium and the price of a slave was at an all-time high. Now, the western movement, which offered new lands to be exploited, was being denied to southern slave-holders.

As more settlers headed west where there were no laws or regulations it wasn't long before settlers asked for intervention from the government in the form of territorial officers and recognition as territories of the United States. The response was the Kansas-Nebraska Act, introduced by Illinois Democratic Senator Stephen Douglas, chairman of the Committee on Territories. The bill would allow for popular sovereignty to decide if these territories would be admitted as free or slave states. Of course, this would also be the cause of many heated debates.

On March 5, 1854 the *Kansas-Nebraska Act* became law thus rendering the Missouri Compromise null and void. Within weeks, there were protests across the north from the New England states to the Mid-West. Resolutions against the bill were passed while thousands marched in loud protest. Abolitionists in the north, aroused by Harriet Beecher Stowe's recently published *Uncle Tom's Cabin* now had a cause in which to rally around. Hailed as one of the greatest piece of propaganda, its publication in March of 1852 gave the impression that all slave-owners were evil and vicious. The South responded in kind with propaganda of their own, extoling the virtues of the slave owners as they tended to every whim and need of their property. From free medical care to housing, their slaves, they said, were better off than the poor whites that were free.

Both factions quickly recognized the need for Kansas to be settled by their like-minded compatriots. In New England, emigrant aid companies were formed to raise funds and recruit settlers to migrate to Kansas while pro-slavery elements also sought to take advantage of the cheap land and "save" Kansas from the abolitionists. As a result, Bleeding Kansas would be making headlines as these two sectional groups sent more people to the territory to help tip the scales in their favor. Thousands of pro-slavery Missourians would cross the border resulting in bloody confrontations as they vied to make Kansas a slave state. Even the clergy would become involved. The Reverend Henry Ward Beecher, the brother of Harriet Beecher Stowe had arranged shipments of "Beecher's Bibles" to the territory. These crates contained Sharps rifles which Beecher said was more efficient to ensure morality than bibles. In the end, Kansas would be admitted as a Free State.

The Kansas-Nebraska Act had other implications as well. The Whigs, the Know-Nothings, and the Democratic Party were now divided by pro and anti-slavery factions and, as a result, a new party was born; the Republican Party. But this new party would also be split into two factions. Both factions, to some degree or another, opposed slavery; either its existence or its expansion. On the right was the anti-slavery faction composed of moderates, conservatives, ex-Whigs, Free-Soilers and anti-slavery Democrats. They could foresee the economic and social complications of a full and hasty emancipation. At this time one could say Lincoln was more aligned with the moderates. He hated slavery, he said so time and again. But he also knew it was something which could not be cut away immediately, at least not where it already existed. But, he could work towards preventing its expansion.

On the left of the party were the extremists, a small group of radicals who took their orders from the fiery abolitionists. Fanatical, aggressive, and vindictive, the group was headed by Senator Benjamin "Bluff Ben" Wade of Ohio. Joining him was Senators Zachariah Chandler of Michigan, and Massachusetts' Charles Sumner. The lone House Representative was clubbed-footed Thaddeus Stevens of Pennsylvania. It was these four who John Hay, Lincoln's private secretary had dubbed the Jacobin Club, named after the radical political club instrumental in the development of the French Revolution. Some believed the Jacobins were motivated by policy and party rather than the well-being of the Negroes. By denouncing slavery, the Radicals could claim the moral high-ground as they fought to secure political and economic control upon the South. To many of the Northerners, the institution of slavery was one of a morale issue and a threat to free labor. To the Radicals, it meant party preservation and ideologies over the wants and needs of the people.

The South had their own radical faction called the Fire-eaters. Spawned by the Nashville Convention, this pro-slavery advocacy group watched the election of 1860 with great concern. The Democratic Party had been in power for most of the young country's life. Now, with the rise of the new Republican Party, with their dangerous and fanatical ideas, most Southerners viewed it as a threat to their way of life. Although the new party's platform made no outward mention of war on slavery where it had already existed, they did intend to halt its expansion into the territories. But southern newspapers continued to agitate the issue by claiming the mission of the "Black Republicans" was to destroy slavery altogether. Soon, the *Dred Scott Decision,* the savage bludgeoning of Charles Sumner by South Carolina's Preston Brooks, and John Brown's Raid would aid more fuel to the fire.

Individually, the South's list of grievances was not enough to be divisive or destructive, but collectively, and coupled with sectional conflict the long smoldering embers were now being stoked. Just as each individual component of a wheel is useless on its own, when put together it makes the device effective. The same was true with the grievances of the South. In this case the grievances were the spokes; rigid and inflexible. The spokes gave the wheel structure and strength. The felloes were representative of the Southern oligarch, made of very few long, narrow slabs. Thin yet strong; strengthened by its arched shape and made to incorporate every aspect of Southern tradition and way of life. Joined with other felloes they completely enclosed the entire perimeter of the wheel. However, these components were useless unless anchored securely to a fixed object; a center in which the other elements could be securely fastened too which would complete its being, a hub. And in this case, the hub of the wheel was slavery. For, without the hub, the felloes and spokes would lack relevance and usefulness.

Since this was the age of individuality, the day of the self-made man, the time was ripe for the fanatics and extremists to now fan the growing flames. While the agitation of the abolitionists failed to unite the North against slavery it did cause the South to rally in its defense of the institution. All that was needed now was a gust of wind to turn the whole affair into a blazing inferno. And Abraham Lincoln would be that gust of wind.

There is no doubt Lincoln knew the role he was about to play, for good or bad. The country was facing war or, as some in the North called it, a revolution. In the South, their leaders referred to their own actions as a counter-revolution. In any event, Lincoln was about to inherit a hornet's nest and no matter what action he took it would no doubt leave an indelible mark in the annals of history. Like every other politicians of the day, he could not ignore the storm clouds which had been gathering since before America began its westward expansion.

The election of Lincoln came as no surprise to the Fire-eaters for they had caused it. At the Democratic National Convention held in Charleston in mid-April, fifty delegates walked out when the Democrats refused to accept a slave code platform which demanded slaves be allowed in new Territories and the high seas. When Lincoln received the nomination in May for the Republicans, Democrats held another convention in June. This time 110 delegates walked out, leaving the remainder to nominate Douglas. The Fire-eaters held their own convention and promptly nominated John C. Breckinridge, vice president under James Buchanan. They knew that by splitting the Democratic vote, Lincoln would win the election, and thus, give them sufficient reason to secede. Consequently, the election of Lincoln crushed any further chance of compromise. The Fire-eaters and the Radicals would make sure of that.

The debate over the expansion of slavery into the national territories was the fuel which fed the fire of secession but it would be the Radicals who would make the destruction of the evil institution of slavery itself as the overall issue.

The day after his election, as Charlestonians burned his likeness in effigy, Lincoln composed his list of those he desired for his Cabinet. For the top post of Secretary of State Lincoln had selected William H. Seward. Fiercely anti-slavery, the Radicals would object to Seward's attempts to avoid the war. Two months later the newly appointed secretary would propose provoking Spain, France, and Britain for their interference with Mexico. Seward believed this would unite the country against a common enemy.

Simon Cameron, a corrupt former Democrat, had secured the appointment of Secretary of War for his patronage to Lincoln during the election. Again the Radicals were disappointed. They had wanted abolitionist John C. Fremont or former Kentucky Representative Cassius Clay in that position. Slave-owner Edward Bates would be the first Cabinet member to be selected from regions west of the Mississippi. As Attorney-General, Bates did not care for the growing power of the Radicals. Salmon P. Chase was anti-slavery and a political chameleon, joining various parties which fit his ambitions throughout his career. As Treasurer, Chase recognized the shifting winds and was quick to throw his support to the radicals. Lincoln had chosen Seward, Bates, and Chase, who all lost their presidential bid to him, for their skills and abilities to the top positions in the government.

To help balance his Cabinet, Lincoln appointed Montgomery Blair to be the Postmaster-General. Vindictive and critical of others, the former Democrat's father was a close friend of Lincoln's and his brother Francis Jr. was head of the Republican Party in Missouri. Mutual distain between the Radicals and the Blair clan would be a constant source of grief for Lincoln. Gideon Welles was appointed Secretary of the Navy. Although he did not always agree with Lincoln, he did give the president his full support. Of course, the Radicals could not approve of him. Caleb Smith would be appointed Secretary of the Interior for also helping to secure Lincoln's nomination. Lincoln had a reason for choosing such a diverse group; he wanted to present a united front to the nation.

Scarcely a month after the election, South Carolina would become the first state to proclaim their sovereignty. In rapid secession other Southern states followed suit and by February 1, seven states would secede. All the while, Lincoln remained quiet. He feared any public remark could be construed as a threat or an apology for his election. But also, acknowledgement of secession might exasperate the issue. Even so, as representatives from seceding states vacated their seats the young Republican Party took control of both Houses were able to expel the remainders who recognized secession.

The current president James Buchanan didn't help matters either. He had four months left in his term and he hoped to see it pass quietly. He rebuked the Republicans for causing the trouble by agitating the slavery issue. To ensure the peace, he was willing to make concessions by recommending a constitutional amendment protecting slavery in the territories and annulling the personal liberty laws in Northern states. He also reintroduced a plan to purchase Cuba and allow its admission as a slave state. The Republicans would never allow such a "shameful bribe" and stated they would rather see the South secede rather than give in to their demands.

Never-the-less, a Peace Conference took place in December as the House put together a Committee of Thirty-three; one delegate from each state to discuss proposed constitutional amendments which could avert the crisis. Kentucky Senator John J. Crittenden offered a compromise which proposed the extension of the 36^0 to the west coast, prohibiting slavery in states north of that line while protecting it in those states south of the line it. A select Committee of Thirteen was formed to discuss the proposal but hardline Republican delegates following Lincoln's instructions not to accept any compromise which would allow for the expansion of slavery, were all too happy to shoot down the proposal. Crittenden suggested putting the proposal before the American people but the Republicans refused. As Senator Chandler wrote to his state's governor Austin Blair in regards to the convention "Without a little blood-letting this Union will not, in my estimation, be worth a rush," the Radicals made their intentions clear; they were ready and willing to shed the blood of the nation's youth for their cause.

Even before Lincoln would arrive in Washington to assume his role as president he had discovered that the rebellion would not be his only fight. The intrigue of the Jacobins in Washington was obvious. They had their own ideas of how to handle this matter and that was with brute force. Still stinging by Lincoln's snub regarding their suggestion for Cabinet appointments, they now detested his lenient and conciliatory attitude towards the rebellious states. There is no doubt as to the thoughts of the Radicals, who publically claimed slavery was a cancer which would destroy the morale fabric of this country and the country itself. But there were ulterior motives as well. Of the six million free Southerners only about 350,000 owned slaves. However, only about seven percent of those slaveholders owned three-quarters of the 3.5 million slaves residing in the South. This seven percent represented the top stratum of Southern society, the oligarchy. By destroying slavery, the promotion of free labor would give rise to the middle class which would then replace the aristocracy of the South. The wealthy planters would no longer dominate the political landscape in Washington which it had for the past decades.

Replacing slavery in the South with free labor would open up a capitalistic market and create an industrial revolution thus, ensuring the legitimacy and longevity of the young Republican Party. Since all classes of Southern society, slave-owners or not, accepted the practice of slavery the Radicals believed the South as a whole was in need of social reconstruction as well. To do this they intended to exploit Stowe's interpretation of Southern society.

Chapter 2

In the East

Virginia native Lieutenant-General Winfield Scott was the country's highest-ranking officer with 50 plus years of service. He had moved his headquarters to New York City to escape Washington's political intrigue which often involved him. After closely watching events unfold he returned to the capital to find it in a state of chaos. Taking charge he immediately ordered a blockade of Southern ports as Federal strongholds in Southern ports were built up, resupplied and reinforced. Scott also planned for the security of Washington and the safety of the president-elect who was due to arrive under a rumored threat of assassination in late February. Working with the recently appointed Inspector-General of the District of Columbia Militia Colonel Charles P. Stone, Scott managed to round up local militias and also recruit loyalists to provide security for Lincoln's arrival. On the 23rd, the head of the Union Intelligence Service Allan Pinkerton smuggled Lincoln into the Willard Hotel where he stayed until his inauguration.

On March 4, with about 2,600 regulars, marines and volunteer soldiers acting as security, Lincoln was inaugurated without incident. Had it not been for Scott and Stone, the safety of the president-elect may have been in doubt. After the ceremony, a friend of Lincoln offered Colonel Stone the president's gratitude on a job well done. Stone, who had the honor of being the first officer to muster into military service for the Union, replied he neither supported nor voted for Lincoln and his only interest was protecting the government. Little did Stone know that these words would come back to haunt him.

Some regarded Lincoln's inaugural address as almost brilliant. By claiming the Union was not broken the president reserved the right to hold and occupy the property of the national authorities and he would enforce the laws in all the states. But, he would neither invade nor use force unless that issue was forced upon him. His speech was meant to appease the hard-nosed Radicals of his party by taking a firm stance and yet appeased the moderates and conservatives of the Border States, Slave States which bordered northern Free States, with his conciliatory attitude. To the South, it placed the onus of a probable civil war upon them.

But the South had already taken possession of Fort Moultrie and Castle Pinckney in late December when Major Robert Anderson abandoned the forts for a more defendable Fort Sumter. The Confederate forces viewed the Stars and Stripes flying over a federal fort in the harbor of Charleston as an insult to their government. In early January, Buchanan had sent the unarmed *Star of the West* to try to reinforce Sumter with men and supplies but it was turned back when it came under fire from shore batteries on Morris Island operated by cadets from the *Citadel*, South Carolina's Military Academy in Charleston. Believing Sumter to be a threat to their own security, the secessionists wanted it surrendered.

Anderson's supplies would not last beyond mid-April. Unless resupplied he would have no choice but to capitulate. Lincoln consulted with his Cabinet. Of the seven advisors, only two, Chase and Blair, supported an attempt to resupply, the other five opposed any such action. But Lincoln had to do something. To withdraw could be construed as acknowledging the legality of secession. To take no action would certainly send the wrong message to the Confederates and certainly any foreign nation now watching the drama unfolding. If he attempted to reinforce the fort with men and ammunition, it could be construed as an aggressive act. Plus, there was no guarantee he could even keep it if it came under attack. Either move would lose him the support of the conservatives of his party and Border States.

Lincoln was under a tremendous amount of pressure at this point. He had just been sworn into office and was plagued constantly by office seekers while trying to sort out a mess left by the Buchanan administration. His own administration was a hodge-podge of radicals, conservatives, moderates and northern Democrats all divided on what action to take. In the final weeks of March, the abolitionists and the radicals turned their attention towards public opinion. The radical press increased their calls for action, inciting the northern sentiments to reclaim the government property. Incredibly, Lincoln came up with a brilliant move. By stating in his address that war was only possible if the secessionists desired it, Lincoln now intended to put that responsibility in their hands. Agents sent to Charleston notified Lincoln that any loyalists that had remained were now underground. Clearly, any action taken by the north would be viewed as a provocation of war. Aware of this Lincoln intended to make a stand at Fort Sumter.

Lincoln had made plans to reinforce Fort Pickens at Pensacola which was not considered a threat to the Confederates. By arranging the naval expedition, the Confederates had believed the convoy was headed for Charleston. Meanwhile, Lincoln intended to resupply Sumter with provisions only; no troops, arms, or ammunition would be passed along to the fort. Lincoln dispatched a message to South Carolina's governor with his intentions. The message was read to the governor by Lincoln's agent on April 8. Knowing that a naval expedition was leaving New York harbor, the Southern government was in a fix. A message sent out from Confederate authorities to Major Anderson called for his surrender. Anderson responded that he was nearly out of supplies and would surrender the fort by noon of the fifteenth. But on the morning of April 12, as the Union fleet was nearing Charleston, the rebels opened fired. No more would there be calls for peace and compromise as cries for revenge filled the air in the North.

Could it be that Lincoln had sacrificed Fort Sumter for political effect? Had Lincoln induced the Confederates to fire upon the fort thus inciting the war; a war which could then be used to destroy the institution of slavery? In any event, Lincoln was now a war-time president and would soon become commander in chief of the largest army ever amassed on American soil. But a larger army than the existing Regular Army would be needed, and raising a volunteer army would be a battle of its own.

Civilian authority's distrust of standing armies can be traced back to 17th century Britain. This practice was carried over with the independence of this nation; tight control of the military needed to be maintained. The founding fathers even placed safeguards in the Constitution in regards to their establishment of a permanent army in hopes of keeping military authority in check. This young democracy had been established on the electoral method which had so far had kept civil strife relatively in check. By the 1850s, the internal character of the military was diverse, with no single social class or specific region being represented. By keeping the military small and geographically isolated, the civil authorities were able to keep military authorities under wraps.

A class distinction existed between the military and civilian world during the first half of the 19th century although Regular Army officers recognized that their political convictions impacted their military careers. Many officers could not help but to embrace "certain" political views geared towards advancement in their military career. In the interest of national security, they kept their political conviction to themselves. Of course, that is not to say the officers could not suppress their disdain for influential politicians when they sought promotion, furloughs, or special assignment but they did not tend to flaunt their relationship.

By the 1850s however, the number of groups with special agendas were on the rise and became more disruptive as they turned to the military for their patronage. As the line separating military sector from civilian sector was quickly eroding, officers began to scrutinize these groups as divisive and self-serving. Bipartisanship among the officers' corps began to diminish also as military leaders began to blame politicians and special interests groups for the woes now afflicting the nation. The Radicals of the Republican Party especially, were being denounced for forsaking national security for their own special interests. Cadets at the military academy at West Point were instructed that national security was above all else and many of the officers who had attended the academy now gravitated towards the Democratic Party which had maintained power for the past half century. Secession had brought this all to a head. Many officers now found themselves questioning their own loyalty to a government where certain politicians, they felt, were consumed by a crusade for the Negroes.

The Regular Army had consisted of about 16,000 troops when war broke out and these troops were scattered mostly to the western frontier; leaving less than 1,000 effective troops east of the Mississippi. Of the 1105 officers, 809 would remain loyal to the Union. Proportionately, the cadets from southern states were nearly thirty per cent higher than from the north. Of the 470 who hailed from Slave and Border States, 270 would go with their state while twenty-six officers would take no part in the war. Of the 583 Union generals, only 194 were of the Regular army and another 70 were trained at West Point while the remainders were volunteers.

Another factor to consider was the South had five times as many military colleges according to the 1860 census. The most notables were the Citadel in South Caroline and the Virginia Military Institute. Nearly every southern state had a military school while the north had twice as many professional and trade schools.

Lincoln knew he needed to act, and he immediately called for a meeting of his Cabinet. Since Congress was not in session, Lincoln exerted executive authority. After setting a date for a special session of Congress to convene Lincoln ordered for a closing of all Southern ports against Seward's advice and issued a proclamation calling for 75,000 state troops to serve for three months. The response from the northern states was overwhelming and soon the War Department became so inundated that Cameron lamented that his department was ill-prepared to supply the troops. In addition, of the less than 200 clerks, secretaries, and agents, many were considered disloyal and were stealing the department blind. The pressing need for equipment had caused the department to enter hastily into contracts for "shoddy" merchandise and charges of profiteering were not uncommon.

The states had responded quickly to Lincoln's call. Many states already had militias established although they were more social in nature; drill and military instruction were secondary. But in May, when Lincoln called for an additional 42,000 three-year volunteers and authorized enlarging the regular army by 23,000 did recruitment take on a more structured regimen.   Recruitment offices were set up by prominent citizens and rallies were held. Every one hundred men enlisted were formed into a company, and every ten company was formed into a regiment. The men of the company elected its officers, one captain and two lieutenants. These officers in turn, elected their regimental officers; one colonel, one lieutenant-colonel and one major. These officers were usually commissioned by the governors of their respective states but that was not always the case. Some governors often appointed their own regimental officers, either based on prominence or reward for active recruitment efforts. This was not always conducive to unit efficiency. By July of '61, Scott instituted examinations for regimental officers to ensure a minimum standard of competence in a leadership role. The practice of electing officers was abandoned by 1863.

As General-in-Chief, Scott also made a policy of keeping Regular officers together with the regular army rather than disbursing them amongst the volunteers. One would think they would have better served as leaders for the volunteers rather than as model units.

Lincoln also received support from an unusual source. Stephen Douglas had rallied to the president's call and publically announced his support. This helped to rouse the Northern Democrats to rally with the administration in support of the war. This cooperation would not last however as the war progressed. The Radicals didn't care for Lincoln's use of his executive authority. Having ignored their suggestions for Cabinet appointments the Radicals were bent on Congress having control of the war. They would support his initial actions but they intended to limit this "backwoods" lawyer's use of executive powers. Since their party was now the majority, the Radicals intended to make the destruction of slavery as the goal of the war.

Of course, not only did those states already in rebellion officially refused Lincoln's call to arms but it also provoked other southern states not yet in rebellion to act. The thought of raising arms against their fellow countrymen had caused Virginia to secede, taking along with it Arkansas, Tennessee and North Carolina. It was now the industrious North with a population of twenty-two million pitted against the South's nine million of which three and a half million were slaves.

Lincoln faced a dilemma. With the call to arms Lincoln discovered there just weren't enough Regular officers to take the field. There were plenty in retirement who were trained in the art of war and some were called upon to serve while others quickly volunteered in hopes of finally receiving a star; a general's rank. But none of them had ever commanded more than 14,000 troops at any one time.

This meant a new appointment of generals and Lincoln was not lacking in potential officers either for there were plenty of political hopefuls who quickly realized success in the field would almost guarantee success at the polls. In an attempt to garner the popular support of the people and opposing parties, Lincoln supported the appointment of any aspiring and popular politicians, especially if had a large constituencies, regardless of their political affiliations. These politically appointed generals differed from the volunteer officers who enlisted because they saw it as their patriotic duty. They would be promoted up through the ranks based on service and merit.

But the Radicals saw their dreams of destroying slavery forever fading quickly as Lincoln reached across the table to make these appointments. The abolition movement had not yet taken hold of the country and the North believed one swift battle would end secession and the country could return back to normalcy. Lincoln, first refusing to prosecute the war for emancipation, was now appointing pro-slavery Democrats and conservatives as military commanders. To the Radicals, their cause was lost. If they were to see an end to slavery they would have to fight Lincoln for control of the military, policies, and the conduct of war.

By the end of May the blockade was having its effect on the rebels. While southern exports were still able to escape to the Gulf and the Atlantic, their total was reduced tremendously as all 189 of the harbors and coves were now under surveillance. As troops poured into Washington Lincoln would meet with Scott on a daily basis to discuss plans for subduing the rebellion. Lincoln wanted to take control of Fort Monroe and the Southern ports. This would secure Washington and allow the Union army to march right into Charleston. Scott opposed this strategy. The large army existed on paper only and secondly, the Border States; Delaware, Missouri, Kentucky, and Maryland all teetered on the brink of secession and an invasion could possibly drive them into secession and would surely drive the wedge deeper between the North and the South.

In the past, Scott had relied on tact as a first resort to diffusing situation. Now he proposed the Anaconda Plan; consisting of blockading all Confederate ports and then moving 60,000 troops accompanied by gunboats, down the Mississippi from Cairo, Illinois to the Gulf where, they could sit and wait for the Union sentiment which Scott believed still existed in the South, to take effect. The rebellion could be halted without firing a shot. Scott had chosen a young George McClellan as the commander to lead this expedition. Lincoln dismissed this plan however, believing it would take too long. The people wanted swift action and a timely resolve. The Radicals joined by Montgomery Blair, also demanded action. They saw 74 year old Scott, portly and suffering from health issues, becoming sympathetic with his native state of his Virginia and began demanding his removal.

The secession of Virginia had put Washington in danger. The only overland route to the capital was through the volatile state of Maryland. As troops passed through Baltimore they were met by a throng of pro-secessionist crowds. On April 19, as the railcars containing the 6th Massachusetts were being hauled by horses to the Washington station, the angry mob attacked the troops with bricks and rocks. Shots were fired which resulted in the death of four soldiers and nine civilians.

Scott took his old friend Robert Patterson, off the reserve list and recommissioned him as a major-general and placed him in command of the military district comprising of Delaware, Maryland, Pennsylvania and the District of Columbia. His task was to organize the three-month troops and fortify the capital with them. Patterson would not be a wise choice. Having immigrated to Pennsylvania from Ireland in 1798 at the age of 6 he had served honorably in the War of 1812 and the Mexican War. Now at 69 years of age, only Scott was his senior in military experience. Having never held an independent command, Patterson proved to be indecisive and not up to task for the role he was about to play.

To gain control of Maryland and especially Baltimore Scott ordered Patterson to open an overland route through Maryland. When Patterson failed to do, Scott restructured the district and placed another old friend, 57 year old Colonel Joseph K.F. Mansfield in command of DC and parts of northern Maryland. Meanwhile, the politically appointed Brigadier-General Benjamin F. Butler would command the tract of Maryland situated between Washington and Annapolis. This would allow Patterson to focus solely on opening a route through Maryland to the capital but again, Patterson failed to march on Baltimore.

Butler however, had secretly moved into the city by night without orders and was able to secure Baltimore, thereby keeping it under Federal control. Troops heading for Washington were now able to safely travel through Baltimore unmolested. Four months later, Lincoln having previously suspended the *writ of habeas corpus* in Maryland, arrested disloyal members of the state legislature and Maryland would remain a loyal state.

During the time Scott was trying to maintain control in Maryland, Federal forces in Harpers Ferry were at work razing the armory and destroying 15,000 stands of arms. Machine and carpentry shops were also destroyed lest they fall into enemy hands. Two days later on April 20, the shipyard and dry-dock facilities at Norfolk, Virginia were also destroyed by Federal troops.

As volunteers streamed into Washington, Mansfield began drilling them and setting them to building fortifications. To gain a foothold in Virginia, just across the Potomac, Scott set his sights on Alexandria. Since a majority of the troops in the capital were New Yorkers, Scott placed them under the command of Major-General Charles W. Sanford of the New York militia. On May 24, the New Yorkers, armed with the Enfield muskets bought from England, secretly stole into Alexandria and took control of the city without firing a shot. The only casualty was that of Colonel Elmer E. Ellsworth of the 11th New York, who was shot by the proprietor of the Marshal House when Ellsworth entered the residence to remove a confederate flag flying from the roof. On that same day, Sanford also occupied Arlington. But with the taking of Alexandria a new problem arose. Virginia was out of the jurisdiction of Mansfield's command so a new department was created, the *Department of Northeastern Virginia*. Since Sanford was not an officer of the Regular Army he was not even considered as its commander.

Following the advice of Chase and Cameron, Lincoln promoted Major Irvin McDowell to brigadier-general backdated to May 14 and ten days later, gave him command of the new department. McDowell was a West Pointer who had served on Scott's staff. An experienced staff officer and organizer, McDowell had refused the commission of major-general because he felt that promotion over officers more senior would have negative effect. Although having never led troops in combat, McDowell would be the first general to command an army of 30,000 soldiers in America's history. His tenure would be an abject lesson in modern warfare. His undersized staff lacked the experience needed to lead such a large army of green troops. Grant would later say that he got started wrong and never recovered.

Scott and Mansfield both harbored bitter feelings over the promotion of McDowell so Scott managed to have Mansfield receive his star dated the same date as McDowell. Since Mansfield, who would meet his fate at Antietam a bit over a year later, was a colonel this guaranteed his seniority over McDowell. Scott and Mansfield's lack of cooperation towards McDowell would set a trend in the military in the days to follow.

McDowell crossed the Potomac and entered Alexandria on the afternoon of May 27 and the next morning he inspected the city and his troops and was disappointed by what he saw. The lack of experience among the officers was quite obvious. The logistical problems were overwhelming. No work on fortifications had been started nor were there any means of supplying the army with food, tools, or the supplies it needed. Immediately, McDowell sent in requisitions for more Regular army officers for his staff, wagons and other supplies and services needed to effectively command the new army.

His next move would make the Radicals cringe. McDowell discovered the soldiers were occupying private homes and using fields without the owners' permission. There was still a substantial amount of Union sentiment in the area and McDowell believed that taking from the private citizens would undermine the cause for which they occupied the city. The war was with the State of Virginia and not its citizens. He immediately requested funds to compensate owners for rent, food and firewood taken from them. He even authorized the public to make application for restitution for damages incurred by his occupying forces. When Mary Custis Lee, wife of Confederate General Robert E. Lee protested the use of her home in Arlington as Federal headquarters, McDowell consoled her in a letter, informing her that he had made his camp outside the house and he also promised that when she should return, nothing would be found out of place.

McDowell also ordered that no arrests of persons solely on their pro-southern sentiments would be made and that a careful accounting should be made of all crops destroyed, buildings occupied and land used for his troops. What little faith the Radicals had in McDowell quickly vanished as it was clear his idea of the war being against the rebel army only and not the southern people was contradictive to theirs.

McDowell continued to train and drill his raw recruits. He formed his army into three brigades and appointed only Regular army officers to command them; Colonels Charles P. Stone, Samuel P Heintzelman, and David Hunter. New recruits had to be assigned by either Scott or Mansfield and they intentionally delayed sending them to McDowell. Exasperated, McDowell complained personally to Mansfield that he needed more men, more quickly. Mansfield excuse was he had no wagons. McDowell then sought out Quartermaster General Montgomery C. Meigs regarding transportation. Meigs had wagons but was informed by Mansfield that they should not be released until McDowell was ready to advance into Virginia. And so it went, McDowell was denied transportation until regiments had crossed the river and Mansfield would not release regiments until McDowell was ready to advance.

McDowell persisted however and by the end of June four more brigades were formed, totaling 30,000 troops bivouacked in and around the capitol. These were commanded by Brigadier-Generals Daniel Tyler and Robert Schenk and Colonels William F. Franklin and Orlando B. Willcox. All of McDowell's commanders were West Pointers save one, Schenk; another Democrat political appointee. Lincoln gave the former Ohio senator his star in return for his endorsement in September of 1859.

This began the personal animosity and political intrigue amongst the officers that would have a huge influence on war operations and would produce devastating results for the soldiers.

By July the Union army had swelled to 186,000 and Greeley's *New York Tribune* had issued the battle cry "Forward to Richmond." Public sentiment called for a quick and decisive blow upon the Confederacy. The Radicals, hoping to keep the Confederate congress from meeting in Richmond on July 20, also urged Lincoln to take action even though the army was still inexperience. The Radicals rationalized that a defeat on the battlefield was preferable to victory as it could only aid their cause of war upon the South.

Lincoln devised a general plan to attack the Confederates occupying the railroad junction at Manassas. After smashing their army and scattering them, McDowell could then easily march his Army of Northeastern Virginia onto Richmond and thus, end the rebellion. Lincoln, like many others in the North, believed the South would give up the fight after that. By the end of June McDowell, who had lacked any decent maps of Virginia laid his finalized version of Lincoln's plan before Scott. Believing an offensive in Virginia would only secure that one state whereas his Anaconda Plan would split the Confederacy, Scott was against it. But when his final plea for the Anaconda Plan was refused, Scott reluctantly approved McDowell's.

McDowell lamented, and rightly so, that his recruits were still too green but as Lincoln pointed out as he ordered McDowell to move, so were the Confederates. So, at 2pm on July 16, McDowell set to cross the

Bull Run just south of the Alexandria with 30,000 freshly outfitted, three-month volunteers supported by 1,600 Regulars.

The plan was sound. As Patterson's 18,000 troops neutralized Confederate Brigadier-General Joseph E. Johnston's troops of 12,000 in the Shenandoah Valley; McDowell would advance toward Manassas Junction 27 miles southwest of Washington. His goal was to drive out Confederate General Pierre Gustave Toutant Beauregard's Army of the Potomac (not to be confused with the Union Army of the Potomac which does not yet exist) consisting of 22,000 confederate soldiers who protected the vital railway there. But Confederate spies were at work in Washington and had alerted Beauregard of McDowell's intentions. The Confederate commander immediately called Johnston out of the Valley.

McDowell was correct in claiming his troops were not yet ready. It took two and a half days for his raw troops to march the 22 miles to Centreville. Along the way men broke rank to fill canteens and pick blackberries. When streams were encountered, the men would remove shoes and socks before crossing. At one point the column came upon a deep ravine; causing the men to cross via a fallen log. The officers were still too inexperienced to realize a few axes could be used to build a bridge large enough to accommodate the entire army. This early in the war there was still much to learn.

At Centreville, McDowell halted his army to allow his wagon trains to catch up and to await word on Patterson. As the men relaxed around camp rations were again passed around. The troops, not yet aware of the sacrifices needed for forced marches, had carelessly consumed their rations during the march. Cattle were slaughtered and the beef was cooked for the next few days' rations. McDowell began to notice the many civilians now wandering through camps. Congressmen, senators, businessmen, and correspondences were freely speaking with the soldiers and adding to the rumors of a large battle looming on the horizon.

On the 18, McDowell had ordered Tyler's division forward to scout out the approach at Blackburn's Ford on Bull Run. Tyler was not to engage the enemy however as McDowell did not want to alert the enemy as to his strength. Against orders, Tyler engaged with the rebels hiding in the woods opposite Bull Run. After several hours Tyler managed to disengage and fell back but not until after suffering a sharp defeat. This hotly contested engagement would pale in comparison to future battles but at this time the men were getting a taste of war. Although the men had fallen back in disorder, they were not broken.

Another two days were spent resupplying the still undisciplined troops with rations before moving on. The civilian population which included many of the Radicals now grew to several hundreds. On July 21, the two armies clashed. McDowell, intending to turn the Confederate's left flank, planned his attack from the north and his army began a tiresome march beginning at 3 AM. Without the use of proper maps his troops marched north and west and were delayed three hours in making the attack. Heavy fighting soon broke out as more troops from both sides became engaged. As the rebels began to fall back, causing a delay in action, the rebels were able to reform their lines.

As more troops are committed the Union began to lose steam. The rebels gained momentum and are able to outflank the Union and push them back. The arrival of Jackson's brigade from the Shenandoah Valley had turned the Union retreat into a rout as the volunteers ran headlong for Washington while the Regulars covered their retreat. A well-placed artillery round from a Confederate battery had rendered the bridge over Cub Run impassable as civilians and soldiers alike were caught up in the carnage as the defeated and demoralized army struggled to get away.

In Washington, Scott had been receiving encouraging dispatches throughout the day. His elation was short-lived however when McDowell sent a dispatch late in the afternoon stating "The day is lost." Scott was downcast yet he did try to console McDowell; informing him he was sending more troops. When it became obvious the Union army would not stop until they reached Alexandria, Scott stopped sending troops. While conveying confidence in McDowell, Scott was at the same time summoning McClellan to Washington.

During the week following the battle, Lincoln visited the camps around Washington. At Fort Corcoran on the Virginia side of the Potomac, Colonel William T. Sherman escorted the president as he walked through the camp speaking with the men which had a great effect upon them. Later, Lincoln met with McDowell and reviewed the troops at Arlington. A transformation seemed to come over Lincoln as he begins thinking about strategy, something his generals seem to overlook. Lincoln was beginning to grasp the overall sense of the war and an understanding in how this war should be played out if the North is to be victorious. After being briefed by McDowell, Lincoln returned to the White House and penned the "Memorandum of Military Policy Suggested by the Bull Run Defeat." In this memorandum, Lincoln proposed calling for more volunteers, strengthening the blockades and reinforcing forts already held. He later added that two military offensives should result in the capture of Manassas or the railroad near that point and a two prong attack in the West. One would be an attack on Memphis from Cairo and the other from Cincinnati into Eastern Tennessee. Lincoln knew he would need a larger man than McDowell; someone who could rebuild the defeated Army of Northeastern Virginia. The next day McDowell was relieved and replaced by Major-General George B. McClellan.

Lincoln set the date for a special session of Congress on July 4. One has to wonder why Lincoln did not call for one immediately after Sumter. Was it because there was an immediate crisis at hand or so he could send a message to Congress that he alone would make decisions regarding to the war without interference from his bipartisan administration? In his opening address read by his clerk, Lincoln avoided any mention of emancipation. By refusing to make it a purpose of the war Lincoln had hoped to keep the support of the Border States and political opposition. Lincoln did ask for 400,000 more volunteers and four hundred million dollars to prosecute the war. Congress granted these measures and retroactively approved his earlier war measures which occurred while they were out of Session.

The Confederate victory at Bull Run or as the South referred to it Manassas, had bolstered confidence in the South while in the North, their resolve to put down the rebellion stiffened. Politically, a line was drawn in the sand. The Northern Democrats were outraged at the defeat. They, along with other civic leaders, demanded that those responsible for the sacrifices of the regiments they raised be held accountable; the Radicals had wanted this battle and now they had to answer for it. Under threats of dropping their support of the war and the administration, the *Crittenden-Johnson Resolution* also known as the *War Aims Resolution* was introduced into the House and Senate where it passed by a large majority on July 25. Basically, it was a guarantee that the war was to "...defend and maintain the supremacy of the Constitution and to preserve the Union" and not a war against any southern institutions such as slavery. The Radicals had no choice but to sign it. They needed the support of the Democrats and conservatives if they were going to fulfil their own agenda. The demand for accountability had placed a bug in the ears of the Radicals and the December session would produce the results.

The Radicals were not beaten. If Lincoln would not free the slaves then Congress would confiscate them. Since many Northerners were apathetic to the slavery issue, the Radicals intended to influence popular opinion another way. The South had pressed the slaves into service at the onset of the war which allowed the whites to fight. By claiming emancipation as a military necessity rather than a moral issue was sure to produce a more desirable result. Certainly the various Unionist parties could see the wisdom in this method.

General Butler was an anti-slavery Democrat from Massachusetts and a political appointment. Reminding the president that he had campaigned against him in the recent election Lincoln responded "All the better, I hope your example will bring many of the same sort with you." While headquartered at Fortress Monroe Butler reasoning that, since Virginia was in secession the Fugitive Slave Act no longer applied to them refused to return two (some reports say three) fugitive slaves which had entered Union lines. Additionally, since the slaves were employed in aiding the enemy they were now considered contraband. By August, a thousand blacks would be put to work in Butler's camps. When many of the politicians returned from the Manassas battlefield they too shared stories of how slaves were employed on the field building fortifications and breastworks thus leaving the Southern men to fight. The Radicals decided to act upon the "contraband of war" principle and were able to pass the *First Confiscation Act* which allowed for the confiscation of confederate property used in rebellion such as weapons picked off the battlefield and weapons taken away from citizens with intent to rebel. Since the South had considered their slaves as property the bill also applied to them as well. The bill passed by a slim majority in both Houses and was signed into law by Lincoln on August 6, 1861.

Congress had entered a gray area here. Lincoln had contended that secession was illegal so technically those states in rebellion were still protected by their state rights. But, under international law, the blockade of Southern ports was a weapon of war thereby the Confederacy was recognized as a sovereign nation, contrary to Lincoln's belief.

Chapter 3

To Appease the Radicals

Control of the West, especially Missouri, was crucial and the responsibility fell to the belligerent Brigadier-General William S. Harney, commander of the Department of the West. Missouri was split into four factions at the onset of secession; pro-Union moderates, sympathetic southern moderates, militant Unionists and militant secessionists. Although Missouri had voted to remain neutral their newly-elected governor Claiborne Jackson was pro-secession and, refusing Lincoln's call for troops now planned to take the state by military coup.

Harney had been run out of St. Louis, the state's capitol, by a mob twenty-six years prior for the murder of a young slave girl. He had allegedly whipped her to death for misplacing his keys. Harney now returned and made the city his headquarters. Known as a safe haven for Unionists in the state, St. Louis was home to Jefferson Barracks, a large arsenal commanded by Captain Nathanial Lyon. Upon secession Lyon had immediately shipped out all surplus weapons at the armory to Illinois lest they fell into the hands of the belligerent militias now being formed around the state. Frank Blair Jr., powerhead of the Republican Party in Missouri, recruited Lieutenant John Schofield to enlist volunteers from among the many St. Louis Germans and the *Wide-Awakes* to form the *Unionist Home Guard*. The Wide-Awakes was a political club which sprang up across the country to combat political opposition to the Republican Party by marching at rallies and conventions. They readily enlisted at Lincoln's call but General Harney, whose loyalty was questionable, refused to arm them. When Harney was recalled to Washington however Captain Lyon officially accepted the volunteer regiments of Colonels Blair, Franz Sigel and Henry Boernstein.

On May 2, a special session of the Missouri legislature convened at Jackson's request and authorized a state militia to be organized at Lindell Grove in St. Louis. Fearing a takeover of the arsenal, Captain Lyon informed his officers on May 7 that the camp, renamed Camp Jackson, must be taken. Without authorization from Harney, Lyon led his Unionist Home Guard against the camp and captured the recruits in training. As they paraded their captives through St. Louis on their way to the arsenal a bloody riot occurred and dozens of locals were killed. Lyon, after forcing Jackson out of Jefferson City, then installed a pro-Union government. The state legislature responded by reorganizing the rebel militia into the *Missouri Home Guard*, tasked with resisting Federal forces invading Missouri.

The *"Camp Jackson Affair"* horrified General Harney. Having returned from Washington, he entered into negotiations with Sterling Price, commander of the Missouri Home Guard. On May 21, the *Price-Harney Truce* which basically stated the Home Guard would control all of Missouri while federals forces would restrict their movements to St. Louis, was signed. This truce did not allow a safeguard against recruitment of Confederate forces nor did it guarantee safety to the Unionists throughout the state.

Shocked by the terms Blair immediately notified Lincoln who authorized him to relieve Harney and appoint Lyon to temporary command the Department of the West. The first thing Lyon did was to call for another meeting with Price, Jackson and his secretary Thomas Snead, and Blair. After several hours of useless discussion an impatient Lyon finally jumped to his feet. "Rather than to concede to the state of Missouri for one single instant the right to dictate to my government in any manner however unimportant," he began before approaching each person and stabbing them in the chest with his finger he continued, "I will see you, and you, and you, and you, and every man, woman, and child in the state dead and buried! This means war!" The meeting was thus concluded as he stormed out the door.

On July 3, Lincoln officially appointed John C. Fremont to replace Harney. Lincoln believed this appointment had its advantages. As the first presidential candidate for the Republican Party in 1856, Fremont still possessed a large following and strong political influences which could keep a handle on Missouri. Fremont also enjoyed the sponsorship of the politically powerful Blair family. Frank Sr., father of Montgomery and Frank Jr. was an unofficial advisor to the president. Lastly, by appointing Fremont, an avid abolitionist, Lincoln had appeased the Radicals. This would not make up for his ignoring their cabinet suggestions but to the Radicals, the appointment of Fremont meant they had one of their own in a position of command.

On a military level, Fremont was a poor choice. His claim to fame was the crossing of the Rockies as an explorer for the Army Corps of Topographical Engineers, thus earning the moniker Pathfinder. But, Fremont was no soldier and many of the West Point officers resented the appointment of the arrogant appointee.

It took Fremont three weeks to finally leave for St. Louis. His mission was clear; recruit, train and equip an army of volunteers. Once Missouri was secured he would then head down the Mississippi to Memphis. But, upon his arrival to St. Louis, the unprepared Fremont became overwhelmed by the enormous task at hand. Guerilla activity, rebel sympathizers, lack of gunboats, raw troops and want of competent administrative officers plagued Fremont's command. His constant requests to Washington for more troops and supplies had gone unanswered while paying outrages prices to greedy contractors for the building up of defenses around St. Louis. Had he not surrounded himself by a staff that isolated him from men and officers with important business he may have fared better but access to the Pathfinder by competent subordinate officers was found to be nearly impossible.

While Fremont was frantically building up defenses in St. Louis, Lyons was heading towards Springfield with a force of 6,000, many of whom ninety-day enlistment was about to expire to prevent a junction of Confederate forces. His plea to Fremont for support went unheeded. Just outside of Springfield on August 10, Lyon's troops engaged a superior force. The Battle of Wilson's Creek was a Confederate victory but a greater loss for that of the North was the death of General Lyons who had maintained a prominent position on the line. Bolstered by their victory, the Confederates were now able to move north to the Missouri River and lay siege to a small Union force at Lexington.

Aroused sentiments and recruitment for secession after the Union defeat at Wilson's Creek had triggered a nervous Fremont to establish martial law in Missouri on August 30. This law decreed confiscation of all property including the slaves of those bearing arms against the government and also approved capital punishment. The Radicals vigorously applauded the order but Frank Blair Jr. who had been critical of Fremont's business dealings, now viewed the Pathfinder as a political rival, and he too vehemently opposed the proclamation. Fremont in turn, had twice placed Blair under military arrest and jailed him for insubordination. Lincoln of course was mortified when he heard of the proclamation. He knew the edict would alienate Northern and Border State conservatives who supported a war for restoring the Union only, but not for emancipation. When Fremont refused to modify the order, Lincoln had no choice but to rescind it thus, receiving the wrath of the Radicals.

Rather than reinforce Lyons Fremont, who had limited manpower decided to send Brigadier-General Grant to reinforce Cairo, Illinois. Although neighboring Kentucky had declared neutrality, Union forces began openly recruiting within its borders. Confederate forces, fearing the buildup of Union troops, immediately occupied the high grounds at Columbus, Kentucky overlooking the Mississippi River. Both armies had now violated the state's neutrality. Grant countered the move by occupying Paducah. Knowing he couldn't take Columbus by force, Grant instead sent a 3,100 man expeditionary force south to Belmont, Missouri just opposite Columbus where a rebel outpost was situated. A sharp engagement against a force of 5,000 Confederates ensued and the rebels were sent fleeing. But the victorious Union soldiers were still inexperienced. Rather than march back to their transports with their prisoners in tow, they took to plundering the rebel camp, allowing the confederates reinforcements from Columbus to arrive and give chase. Grant's action ultimately ensured Kentucky would remain in the Union while denying confederates easy access into Missouri. The battle at Belmont had also caught the eye of the president.

Under his command Fremont had given up nearly half of Missouri, and Lincoln was coming under increasing pressure from the Blair family and others to relieve the Pathfinder. Against radical opposition, Lincoln sent General David Hunter to 'advise' Fremont in the second week of September. Hunter's actual task was to covertly look into the affairs of Fremont's department and report the true state of affairs there. Fremont ignored Hunter completely however, so a couple days later Lincoln sent Meigs and Montgomery Blair to advise and investigate. Meanwhile, Fremont's overbearing wife Jesse, suspicious of her husband's possible dismissal, immediately headed to Washington to meet with Lincoln regarding her husband's case. Her meeting with the president did not go well for her husband in fact, she made it worse.

A week later Lincoln sent Secretary of War Cameron to St. Louis to 'inspect' the fortifications there. Cameron also carried orders relieving Fremont of command. But he was too late. Fremont was on the move with 38,000 troops and heading towards Lexington to rescue approximately 3,500 Union troops surrounded there. After a small engagement known as the Battle of the Hemp Bales, the Union force had surrendered. When Cameron had caught up to Fremont, the Pathfinder, hoping to trap the rebels against the river begged Cameron not to deliver the order. The secretary returned to Washington; never delivering the order while the rebels made good their escape out of Missouri and into Arkansas.

By mid-October Fremont received another visit from Cameron to investigate the building of fortifications around St. Louis but this time he was accompanied by the radical Senator Chandler and Adjutant-General Lorenzo Thomas, to once again investigate Fremont's contract and business dealings. Even the House Committee on Government Contracts had arrived to investigate the contracts for building forts in that city and the purchase of 5,000 Hall carbines which had recently been scrapped by the Ordinance Department.

The report stated Fremont was "...incompetent and unfit for extensive and important command." At Cameron's request, General Lorenzo Thomas's scathing report on Fremont was mysteriously leaked to the press and this time even the Radicals could not save him. On October 24, Lincoln sent orders via General Lorenzo Thomas to General Samuel Curtis, commander at St. Louis, relieving Fremont of command and appointing General Hunter.

Fremont knew what was coming so he tightened security around his headquarters; banning anyone access to him. Curtis gave the order to Iowa Captain J.C. McKenny, who then dressed as a farmer and was able to get into Fremont's camp. When he finally gained access to the Pathfinder he delivered the order. Fremont was gracious about it but most likely he was probably more relieved that the ordeal was over.

The Union military command in the West was then reorganized into three separate departments. Hunter, who had led a division at Bull Run until he was severely wounded and had to turn his command over to

Burnside, now commanded the Department of Kansas. The Department of Missouri went to Maj. Gen. Henry W. Halleck, and the Department of the Ohio was given to Brigadier-General Don Carlos Buell.

By January 1862, Lincoln wanted the situation in the West under control. With three rivers, the Cumberland, the Tennessee, and the Mississippi to move men and materials Lincoln was dismayed that the western armies were at a standstill. Buell and Halleck were not communicating with one another and McClellan, who had by now succeeded Scott, was on his sick bed with possible typhoid fever. He was not issuing orders to anybody. But, McClellan soon made a miraculous recovery and met with Lincoln and his advisors on January 13 in regards to the Western situation among other items. The little general now insisted Buell and Halleck make a move.

After Kentucky had been secured Lincoln set his sights on eastern Tennessee since Union sentiment was strong there. Buell made plans for General George Thomas of Virginia to go through Kentucky and enter into eastern Tennessee through the Cumberland Gap. But Buell, worried of Confederates entering central Kentucky, called off the expedition before it even got started, citing the approach of winter as the reason. Now, with renewed pressure Buell reluctantly ordered Thomas to resume his movement. By now, the weather had made the roads impassable and Thomas was slow in making any headway. Eighty miles shy of the Cumberland Gap, Thomas had won a tactical victory at Logan's Run. By then the expedition had to be called off.

Meanwhile Halleck, under pressure from Lincoln to advance finally gave in to repeated requests by Grant and Flag Officer Andrew Foote to move on Fort Henry on the Tennessee. February 1 saw a joint venture by the Army and Navy. As Grant moved his land forces down from Paducah, Foote's Union gunboats had forced the confederates to retire from Fort Henry on the Tennessee to their stronghold at Fort Donelson on the Cumberland. Two weeks later Grant's troop had marched towards Fort Donelson which was under the command of General John B. Floyd, the former Secretary of War in the Buchanan administration. Floyd was nervous and had good reason to be. Plagued by scandal the Virginia native was an inept secretary of war. After Buchanan requested his resignation Floyd began sending arms to Federal arsenals in

Southern states in preparation for the split which was inevitable. To be captured now would be his head.

As Grant began to surround the fort Foote moved his flotilla up the Tennessee and down the Cumberland to challenge the heavy guns of the fort. After sustaining heavy damage from a brutal bombardment, Foote orders his ironclads back to a safe distance. Embolden by their victory, the Confederates attempted a breakout on February 15 to escape the tightening noose by Grant. Caught by surprise the Union troops began to break but as they attempted to reform their lines, the Union troops are astounded to see the rebels suddenly break off the engagement and began to retreat back towards the fort.

Grant hurried to the scene and ordered a counter-attack. Then, surmising the Confederate right was weak, Grant ordered an assault along that line as well. General Charles Smith's division made the assault and a large portion of that ground was recaptured. Nightfall halted their advance. All hope was lost now for the Confederates and during the night, Floyd along with General Gideon J. Pillow and cavalry commander Nathanial Bedford Forrest made good their escape, leaving General Simon Buckner to surrender the fort on February 16.

With the center of the confederate line in Kentucky cracked, the rebels had no choice but to pull out of Kentucky completely and falling back through Tennessee, evacuating Nashville and heading to northeastern Mississippi. On February 25, Nashville became the first state capital to be taken by Union troops under Buell. Western Tennessee would be denied to the Confederate armies foraging within its borders and the fall of Donelson would be hailed as the first great Union victory of the war and the news would resonate in the South and the East.

Grant, a West Pointer had turned in his commission after the Mexican War and returned to civilian life. When the new war broke out, he volunteered his services and began recruiting volunteers for an Illinois company. Grant's connections with Illinois Congressman Elihu Washburne, a close friend of the president who had helped Grant obtain a colonelcy and would later sway the officer's political convictions.

When Lincoln heard of the forts' surrenders he ordered his own, secret investigation. Grant, who had earned the moniker 'Unconditional Surrender,' was an officer Lincoln would continue to watch.

Although Halleck gave Grant little credit for the fall of the forts he did nominate him for promotion to major-general of volunteers. Of course, promotions went to Buell and John Pope whose successes paled in comparison. The relationship between the cautious Halleck and the aggressive Grant had been strained since the fall of Fort Donelson. Grant had gone to Nashville to consult with Buell after the fall of the forts but when Halleck did not receive any reports from Grant, Halleck suggested to McClellan that Grant had gone back to his old ways, meaning drink and was neglecting his duty. Rather than arrest Grant as McClellan suggested, Halleck instead relieved Grant of command. But when Grant explained that the telegraph operator who he had sent all his dispatches through had deserted Halleck had no choice but to reinstate him to command on March 13.

Grant was then ordered to travel up the Tennessee to disrupt communications. He disembarks at Pittsburg Landing and on April 6, the confederates launched a surprise attack, pushing the Union's right dangerously back against the river. Only darkness saved the Union of a disastrous defeat. The next day Grant would counter attack and manage to eke out a victory.

News of the battle reached Washington, along with rumors and allegations that Grant was incompetent, derelict and drunk. With calls for Grant's removal Lincoln himself ordered an inquiry into the accusations. Halleck arrived at Pittsford Landing on April 11 but could not find evidence to substantiate the rumors. Privately, Halleck wrote to the chairman of the *Army Board* Colonel Ethan Allen Hitchcock that Grant was unable to organize and regulate his forces nor could he properly conduct a campaign.

The Radicals who saw Grant as a potential Democratic candidate also sent investigators to gather evidence against him for future use should the need arise. Washburne and Ohio Senator John Sherman, the brother of Colonel Sherman, were the only two to defend Grant. Lincoln, under increasing pressure to fire Grant, paid close attention. In the end, Lincoln decided to keep Grant in command stating "I can't spare this man; he fights."

The horrific losses at Pittsburg Landing had caused the cautious Halleck to move more slowly after the Confederates who were now headed south to Corinth which contained a vital railroad junction. By entrenching after every advance Halleck had allowed the rebels to fortify their defenses in the city. As the Union settled in for a siege the Confederates, knowing they could not hold the city made other plans.

Near the end of May, Grant had realized that trains heading into Corinth were not bringing Confederate reinforcements in but rather taking them out. The Confederates were evacuating the city. On May 30, Union forces occupied Corinth.

Chapter 4

A New War

When the war started Major-General McClellan was given command of the Department of the Ohio made up of federal troops from Ohio, Indiana, and Illinois. His early successes consisted of clearing out western Virginia of the small pockets of Confederate forces who were trying to gain a foothold there. The northern press however hailed McClellan as a hero and dubbed him the Young Napoléon. Not a real test for a general but they were victories which led to the formation of the new state, West Virginia. And victories were what Lincoln had sought.

McClellan was a West Point Democrat who served as an engineer officer on Scott's staff during the Mexican War. In 1855, McClellan was one of three officers sent to Europe by the War Department. There they studied the organization and methods of the continental armies. As letters of support flooded his headquarters, McClellan's ego swelled; his confidence reached the point of cockiness, and his contempt for Lincoln also grew. The Radicals didn't like McClellan for several reasons but one in particular was when, while in western Virginia, the general informed the people that they were not there to interfere with slavery.

One lesson learned from Bull Run was that an army of disciplined soldiers would be needed for a long war and McClellan proved to be the general needed to drill and train this demoralized army. Energetic and active, McClellan had relieved unfit officers and a strenuous training program was put into place. By merging several departments the Army of the Potomac was formed and grew from 52,000 in July to 120,000. McClellan had managed to mold the Army of the Potomac into a first-rate fighting force and a mutual friendliness had grown between McClellan and his men as he spent time in their camps. But the young general appeared to be unwilling to harm his newly restored army.

During the pleasant autumn weather the Radicals began to pressure McClellan through Lincoln to attack. McClellan resisted, begging Lincoln not to let them hurry him as his army was not yet ready for a full-scale campaign. On October 25, Senators Wade, Chandler and Trumbull, again believing that defeat was preferable to victory, grew weary of the inactivity of the armies. They called upon McClellan to press him into action. For three hours they implored him to make a move but McClellan resisted, offering various excuses; General Scott being one of them. Frustrated, the trio called upon Lincoln the following night but their attempts were in vain; Lincoln would not interfere with McClellan's planning.

Fortified by Lincoln's support, McClellan could now set his sights on the position held by General Scott. Once teacher and student, they were now adversaries as McClellan had complained bitterly that General Scott was overly cautious and holding him back. Rather than getting himself involved in the intrigue General Scott resigned his position on November 1; McClellan was now the supreme commander.

McClellan's victory over Scott would eventually lead to his own downfall however. He could no longer blame Scott for his lack of action. He would now be held personally responsible for any movements or lack thereof, of the armies. He alone would secure the wrath of the Jacobins if he could not produce results.

As in most cases with the appointment of new military commanders, a restructuring of the army usually takes place and McClellan was no different. Considering his overall task McClellan decided to reorganize the Western armies which he felt was poorly equipped and disorganized, by adding western Kentucky to the Department of the Mississippi. He then appoints General Halleck as its commander with orders to restore order out of the chaos caused by Fremont. His army would be positioned on the Mississippi and Halleck would prepare for interior operations. General Buell would command the Department of the Ohio which now included the remainder of Kentucky and Tennessee. His orders were to hold Kentucky and also move into eastern Tennessee, occupy Knoxville and to protect the Unionist there. Both Lincoln and McClellan reiterated that preservation of the Union was the main goal; the commanders were to assure the population that they were fighting to restore the Union. There would be no talk of emancipation.

By autumn of '61 the Radicals were getting discouraged. They resented Lincoln's all-party administration strategy. Congressman George W. Julian of Indiana had estimated that five of the department heads which regulated supplies, munitions, pay, and arms and four fifths of the general officers were Democrats. With Halleck and Buell in the West and McClellan in the East, also Democrats and openly defiant of emancipation, the Radicals' hope of bringing the support of the growing army into the fold of the radical policies began to fade.

Some commanders had welcomed the tens of thousands of former slaves who had sought refuge inside their lines although they were technically not free. But other commanders, especially in the Border States were returning the fugitive slaves to their owners. Even in Missouri Halleck had gone as far as issuing an order in November, evicting all fugitive slaves from camp, believing they were acting as spies. To the Radicals, this meant that, unless these generals were replaced by officers who adopted the radical program, the armies could not be victorious and their cause would be lost. The armies needed to be conditioned. They would need to learn to hate the South and all it stood for and declare total war.

Total war upon the South the Radicals claimed, was the only option; cause and effect. To do so meant unrestricted warfare against the enemy; their military and the infrastructure with acceptance of collateral damage. Nothing would be spared. It should be total war with complete victory as opposed to peace by truce and compromise.

But the Democrats viewed the war differently. To them, the war was caused by a handful of wealthy slave owners thus, they advocated for a limited war ran by professionals. Any conciliatory tactics could certainly bring the average Southerner back into the fold of the Union. To the Radicals, these tactics were paramount to protecting the interests of disloyal slaveholders. Since the influence the slave powers held over the social order in the South was immense, the only way to halt the rebellion was to crush those powers and restructure the entire Southern hierarchy.

Since slavery was the cause of the war, confiscation, emancipation and enlisting Negroes were the answer. These harsh conditions they believed were needed to defeat the South. Going against Lincoln's plan of a coalition, the Radicals now worked to unravel the alliance Lincoln had carefully tried to nurture. They would need to rid the armies of those unwilling to stomp out slavery. They needed more generals like Butler and Fremont. So, during the summer of 1861 the Radicals held secret meetings to conspire and strategize.

Their chance came during the second session of the 37th Congress in December. The Radicals gritted their teeth as Lincoln's message was read to Congress. Preservation of the Union was the goal of the war, nothing more. There was no mention of freeing slaves but merely the suggestion of colonization in another country for all slaves freed by confiscation. The Radicals were furious. Lincoln still refused to use the military to abolish slavery or make emancipation an objective of the war. It was time to take matters into their own hands. The Radicals planned to strip away the stumbling blocks that were preventing their program from being realized. One of the first things they did was refuse to readopt the *Crittenden-Johnson Resolution* contrary to the substance of Lincoln's speech.

The next block to be removed was McClellan who they believed had control over Lincoln. The outspoken, pro-slavery, West Point narcissist was purposely delaying the war until the Democrats could regain power. Should that happen, McClellan could surely secure the nomination and the chance for destroying slavery would be lost. If the administration would not address the issue of slavery then it was up to the Radicals to bring the issue out into the open. This meant making the military advance and fight. Every inch of Southern land to fall under Union control meant more fugitive slaves seeking asylum. The administration would have no choice but to face the issue. But, first they had to take down McClellan and his gang and now they had their chance.

McClellan's army had not been entirely idle during the fall of 1861. To assure Lincoln that Washington was safe McClellan shifted troops about; countering the movements of the enemy so near the Capitol. On October 20, McClellan ordered the recently promoted General Charles Stone, who had organized Washington's defenses six months prior, to send a scouting party across the Potomac to investigate elements of the Confederate army stationed around Leesburg, the hub of communication between Centreville and the Shenandoah Valley. That night an expedition crossed the Potomac and, mistaking a row of trees for Confederate tents, reported back the discovery an unguarded Confederate camp.

Colonel Charles Devens had effected a crossing the next day and immediately ran into a company of Mississippi infantry. Hearing the fight, former Oregon senator turned officer Colonel Edward D. Baker decided to reinforce Devens, even though he possessed only four boats to ferry his troops across. While the troops trickled across the river, the Confederate forces were able to organize their defenses and began pushing Union troops back to the steep cliffs of Ball's Bluff at their backs. The fighting was hot while Baker, with sword held high tried to rally his troops. Encouraging his men forward Baker never saw the lanky, hatless rebel approaching. When he was within five paces of the former senator he began firing, hitting the officer five times; one round smashing into his skull, killing him instantly. Immediately, all musket fire was upon the rebel and his life was taken nearly as quickly. The battle should never have taken place.

Colonel Baker who had been a close friend of Lincoln's and many others in Washington was eulogized in Congress that December. His untimely death would play right into the hands of the Radicals.

Not only was Ball's Bluff the only battle in which a sitting member of Congress was killed it also set into motion a new strategy to be used by the Radicals. Civilian investigative committees were not a new concept to this country. Article I, Section 8 of the Constitution specifically granted Congress a broad range of power regarding the military. In 1791, Congress had authorized such a committee to investigate General Arthur St. Clair, whose defeat by Native Americans in the Northwest Territory was this country's worst in history. St. Clair was exonerated and no official reports were filed. A second committee was proposed in 1813 by Representative Stephen R. Bradley of Vermont to inquire into the malfunctions of arms. Neither committee was very large or influential but they did set a precedent.

So on December 2, when New York's Republican Congressman Roscoe Conkling proposed a resolution requesting Cameron to inform the House what, if any, steps were being taken to find who was responsible for the disaster at Ball's Bluff, the resolution was adopted without debate. Three days later, Chandler proposed in the Senate the appointment of a three member committee to investigate the disaster of Bull Run and Ball's Bluff. And so it began, amendments adding other areas to be investigated were debated back and forth until it was finally decided to vote on Senator Sherman's proposal to include every aspect of the war, its military departments, and its personnel. A red flag should have been raised when the Senate promptly turned down Kansas Senator James Lane's proposed resolution calling for an investigation into the defeat at Wilson Creek, the authorities' failure to relieve the troops at Lexington and the truth about Fremont's administration.

The formation of the *Joint Committee on the Conduct of the War* (CCW) on December 9 would pit the legislative body against the executive body with emphasis on the fact that Congress alone controlled the military. The prescribed responsibility of the seven-member committee was not only to expose mistakes made but to determine future war policies as they saw fit. It mattered little that none of the committee members had military experience, and the distain they held for the military was obvious. They did not believe the art of war was a military science where commanders needed to be schooled in specialized techniques. They would impose their own military strategies upon the commander which was always the same, attack, attack, attack. Their creed was "In military movements delay is generally bad-indecision is almost always fateful." This would produce an adverse effect on commanders who would recall the words of Senator Henry Wilson, "We should teach men in civil and military authority that the people expect that they will not make mistakes, and we shall not be easy with their errors."

Although Congress had power bestowed upon them under Article I, Section 8, the intent of the intent of the newly-formed CCW was unprecedented. Members of Congress intended to wrest control from the executive branch in their attempt to making war policies in the guise of full prosecution of war. They also intended on using this power to remove and replace leading officers who were not willing to accept these policies. By reasoning that since public money was being used to prosecute the war then it was clearly their duty to investigate all military affairs, and most especially Union losses on the battlefield, and to make recommendations. To do this, the committee would be split into two sub-committees, the investigative which traveled to contested areas, usually in the Eastern theatre, and identify problems; and the advisory or recommending committee which would offer their remedies to administration to correct the failures in the prosecuting the war. They could not dictate policy but they could however, subpoena witnesses and recommend legislation. Of course, all testimony at the hearings would remain confidential but some information would be conveniently leaked when it served their own agenda.

This new committee had caused mixed feelings in Washington. Senator Lafayette Foster of Connecticut opposed the idea believing the committee would produce more harm than good by tampering with the war effort. The military, he believed, was the only department fitting to investigate its own. But he was checked by Fessenden who insisted that, since Congress controlled the purse strings in conducting the war, they had every right to a voice in the operations of the military. Many conservatives voted for this bill without fully realizing it's potential.

The CCW was chaired by Senator Wade, chosen for his extensive legal experience. Other members included Senators Chandler and Andrew Johnson (D) of Tennessee. When Johnson was appointed military governor of Tennessee in March 1862, he was replaced by Joseph Wright, the former governor of Indiana. House members included Republicans Julian of Indiana, John Covode of Pennsylvania, and Daniel Gooch of Massachusetts. Moses Fowler Odell from Brooklyn, New York, was the sole Democratic House member. All members were lawyers except Chandler, who was a successful merchant in Detroit.

It soon became clear the committee's underlying goal was to expose McClellan's alleged intentions of restoring the Union back to its old self through procrastination. During their initial meeting on December 20, the committee discussed their course of action. The McClellan issue needed to be addressed immediately. As supreme commander, he openly fraternized with and allegedly discussed peace negotiations advantageous to the South with prominent Peace Democrats. He also refused any newspapers with Republican slant in camps. McClellan's failure to advance was evidence enough to warrant an investigation. But since McClellan still enjoyed the support of the president the committee knew they would be wasting their time taking the general on directly. So, if they could not investigate McClellan, the committee could at least begin building a case file on the arrogant Little Napoleon.

But first, since the Radicals had plans for him, McDowell would need to be vindicated for the Bull Run disaster. To do this a scapegoat was needed and General Patterson, a long-time Jacksonian Democrat, would serve nicely. As one of the largest mill-owners in the United States and heavily involved in sugar refineries and cotton plantations, Patterson had business connections with the South. After Fort Sumter, Philadelphia residents, knowing of Patterson's pacifying, conservative views on slavery and advocacy of Southern rights, demonstrated at his residence and pelted his home with rocks. Only when he announced that he would lead them into battle did the crowd disperse. He aroused suspicion however when he addressed his troops the first week of June, telling them their job was to put down sedition, protect the loyal, and suppress servile insurrection only.

During the Bull Run campaign Patterson was to lead his troops across the Potomac at Williamsport, Maryland and advance south to Martinsburg, Virginia. By continuing southward to Bunker Hill, he could force Johnston to retreat to Winchester. Scott had ordered Patterson to attack only if certain of victory otherwise, he was merely to make a demonstration. Patterson, believing he was outnumbered and knowing the three-month enlistment his 15,000 man army was about up ruled out an attack.

On July 16, Patterson received word from Scott that McDowell was ready to move. Patterson had sent out a small force towards Winchester where it encountered obstacles blocking the road. Believing McDowell would be in battle shortly and confident of his own demonstration, Patterson retreated to Charlestown the following day, allowing Johnston to withdraw from Winchester. When Patterson discovered Johnston's withdrawal, he notified the War Department on July 20; a full day before the battle of Bull Run.

Because he was unable to contain Johnston in the Shenandoah, Patterson's name was libeled in the Northern press. Patterson in turn, began publishing his own version, placing the blame on Scott. In November, Patterson was defended by his chief of staff and assistant adjutant-general Fitz-John Porter, who spoke to Senator Sherman about petitioning the War Department for a Court of Inquiry. It was refused on the grounds that Scott was in Europe. Patterson convinced Senator Sherman to introduce a resolution into the Senate asking the War Department to publish all correspondence relating to the events between Scott and Patterson. This idea was shot down by none other than McClellan who felt it was not in the public's best interest. So when Patterson learned of the new committee being formed he was excited at the chance to clear his name. Patterson's joy was short-lived however. The Bull Run investigation would set the tone for subsequent hearings.

Witnesses had been ordered before the board and a variety of very viable explanations were given for the Bull Run disaster. Inexperience, confusion of the troops, miscommunications, committing troops into battle piecemeal, and the loss of two Union batteries were all mentioned, and they did affect the outcome. Even fighting on a Sunday was blamed. But these were not the answers the CCW had hoped for so they switched tactics and began asking leading questions. This produced the desired results. The Radicals could now claim that McDowell would have achieved a great victory had it not been for Johnston's arrival.

Patterson was then called before the board and the first thing Wade did was to deny him access to the damaging testimony. With Gooch leading the assault the old general was grilled ruthlessly. Previous questions were reworded in an attempt to draw out contradictory statements. When asked why he had neglected to follow Scott's orders or notify him of Johnston's movements Patterson assured them that he had. But since the correspondence was suppressed by McClellan the CCW would not accept Patterson's answer.

Finally, Patterson was allowed to give a general summation of his actions. He had ninety-day volunteers whose terms were set to expire, something Scott was aware of. Patterson's outline of all proposed movements had been sanctioned by Scott; he was also informed by Scott that McDowell would attack on July 17, the day Patterson headed for Charleston. And finally, Scott was informed of Johnston's movement on July 20.

The cross examination, again led by Gooch was designed to dissect the orders and offer different interpretations. It was obvious that Gooch lack of military experience now worked in his favor; to the professionally trained soldier the orders were clear. But Gooch hammered on. By the middle of February someone finally stood up for Patterson. Frank Blair Jr., enemy of the Radicals and now the CCW, spoke on the House floor stating that, even though he did not feel Patterson's actions were prudent, he did follow Scott's orders and informed him of Johnston's departure from Winchester.

Never-the-less, Patterson, who had pushed Johnston to Winchester, was blamed for allowing Johnston to escape Winchester and support Beauregard at Bull Run. He was also blamed for not communicating this information with Scott. Evidence which had been withheld by the CCW would also be omitted from the published records in January of 1863.

The ordeal was over. Although his service during the present war was not glorious Patterson, who had been allowed to muster out of the service with his men on July 27, '61, had performed his duty. He now returned home with his reputation tarnished.

Bolstered by their success with the aged, fragile general, the committee couldn't wait to build their case against McClellan. Bedridden with possible typhoid fever however, McClellan was unable to appear before the board. This was of no concern to the committee for they had already decided on which tactic to employ. They would subpoena his subordinates for questioning.

As each officer appeared before the committee, they were informed that the purpose for the inquiry which was to answer the question as to why the Army of the Potomac was not advancing. They quickly discovered however that officers, especially West Pointers were reluctant to answer to a civilian board when questioned about their commander. Due to military code of honor many subordinate officers would not critique their superior's action on and off the battlefield. This would soon change however, when they discovered the committee controlled promotions.

As the investigation played out it was soon discovered that some subordinates were irritated by McClellan's refusal to hold Councils of War but instead shared his thoughts with only a select few of his least senior corps commanders. With the promise of a command as incentive General Heintzelman, one of the five division commanders under McClellan's command who accepted the radical program and refused to return fugitive slaves, spoke freely against McClellan in his testimony. The opinion was forming that McClellan was exaggerating enemy numbers and deceiving the president.

Generals Fitz-John Porter and William B. Franklin evaded answering any questions directly but that didn't matter. When the inquiry was over seeds of dissention had been firmly planted amongst the upper echelons of the Army of the Potomac. Although the committee did not have enough to hang McClellan they were convinced that he was stalling for time. So, if they could not pin anything on McClellan just yet they could target his subordinates and the Ball's Bluff incident gave them the perfect opportunity.

General Stone, a close friend and fellow West Pointer of McClellan, commanded the right flank division on the Potomac and it was his jurisdiction under which Ball's Bluff fell. Stone's loyalty, already in question after statements made at Lincoln's inauguration, was doubted even more when rumors spread that he ordered fugitive slaves returned. This was true. In late September members of one of his regiments had caught and returned two runaway slaves who they had discovered coming into their lines. This set off a firestorm of letters between Massachusetts's radical governor John A. Andrew and Stone. When Andrews learned the soldiers in question were from his state he wrote one of the officers involved denouncing Stone and forbidding Massachusetts men to act as slave-catchers. Stone protested this civilian interference bitterly and soon, radical Massachusetts senator, Charles Sumner was informed of the incident. Stone was making dangerous enemies.

It was also reported that Stone had allowed packages and communications with rebels to cross lines in his sector and that he had allowed the enemy to erect fortifications near their lines. The committee accepted any gossip or rumors regarding Stone, whose wife had relatives in the South, as fact.

The committee began building their case against Stone by secretly examining select witnesses from the Army of the Potomac. Many of the volunteer officers selected to testify either opposed the strict military discipline imposed upon them by the West Point officer or they harbored a grudge against him. They were asked misleading questions designed to paint Stone as a disloyal, southern sympathizer. Badgering and intimidation produced the desired effect if correct answers were not given.

Stone was finally subpoenaed to appear before the board. On January 5, in a routine interview, Stone answered every question and added that Baker had been responsible for his own his demise. Yes, he did return fugitive slaves but only when asked to do so by the proper civilian authorities. He neglected to tell the board however, that McClellan had directed him not to answer questions nor reveal McClellan's plans regarding military matters. When Stone left the interview he believed the matter closed. He was mistaken.

The investigation continued as the committee now began to question a long list of civilian residents from within Stone's military district. On January 11, with evidence now in hand, the inquisitors paid a visit to the War Department to present their case against Stone to Secretary of War Cameron. To their surprise however, Cameron who had finally been forced to resign amidst allegations of inefficiencies and corruption, was busy packing his bags to assume his new role as Minister to Russia.

Former Democrat Edwin Stanton had been the Attorney General under the Buchanan administration and was instrumental in changing that administration's position away from tolerating secession to denouncing it as unconstitutional and illegal. After Lincoln was elected president, Stanton agreed to work as a legal adviser to the inefficient Secretary of War, a position Stanton had coveted and was now awarded.

The members of the committee immediately met with Stanton to see which way his loyalties lie. Delighted to hear his views the Radicals pledged their full support to his office, individually and as a group. In return, they each received a card giving them full access to the new secretary day or night. Stanton would be an invaluable ally. His control over the military and access to all decisions by Cabinet members would benefit the committee. Believing they now had a free pass to rid the army of any conservative generals, they hoped Stanton would be the man who could "break the traditionalism of West Point" and make the army fight.

They presented Stanton with their case against Stone. The summary of allegations were as follows: ordering Baker's men across the river with no adequate means of transportation, failure to reinforce Baker, allowing correspondence between the lines and allowing rebels to build forts beneath his guns. On January 28, Stanton notified McClellan that a warrant was issued for Stone's arrest. A military hearing at McClellan's request was denied by Stanton but he did grant a temporary stay. Stone would be allowed to state his case before the CCW on January 31.

Although Stone had trusted McClellan to save him he had appeared before the board a desperate and dejected officer. Just as Wade had done with Patterson, the CCW refused to allow Stone to read testimony against him. He answered every charge brought up by the board which painted him a traitor. By the line of questioning being used Stone knew he was doomed.

McClellan was in a fix. He had figured out that he was the actual target of the investigation. To stand by his friend Stone would certainly lead to his own demise but, by a stroke of luck, McClellan was informed that a fugitive slave had come into his lines claiming knowledge of Stone's cordial relationship with the Confederates in his area. Notifying Stanton of this information, McClellan had absolved himself of any responsibility for what was about to happen to Stone. He could now, with clear conscience, order Stone's arrest. On February 8, Stone was arrested and imprisoned at Fort Lafayette in New York Harbor. Democrats were outraged by the news and many of them denounced Stanton for cozying up to the Radicals but to no avail. For the next fifty days, Stone sat in solitary confinement until, under his doctor's protests that his health was failing; he was transferred to Fort Hamilton in Brooklyn. Stone would be held for 189 days with no charges ever leveled against him nor answers to his repeated request for a Court of Inquiry or military trial. Under the articles of war, Stone was entitled to a prompt trial and Stanton willfully and knowingly violated this right. On August 16, Stanton would finally bow to continued protests and ordered Stone's release from Fort Hamilton.

The disaster at Ball's Bluff could not be tied directly to McClellan but it did uncover evidence that certain corps commanders were possibly guilty of disloyalty, at least by committee members' definition. Members of the CCW would make note of this for future use.

While the investigation of Stone and Patterson was being conducted, the committee also worked towards vindicating Fremont who had been relieved of command amidst rumors of incompetence, fraud and corruption. But, rather than investigate him, the committee decided to investigate the actions of the administration which had brought the charges against him. Not only did they hope to have Fremont reinstated but they actually believed he could replace McClellan. But the report of Lincoln's agents on Fremont had been incriminating. Even the zealot Chandler wrote to his wife admitting that Fremont was a failure. The Blairs of course, not only supported Fremont's removal, they advocated it; their close friendship shattered by Fremont's ego, corrupt contracts, and military strategy. Of course, the Radicals and the press friendly to their cause also blamed Lincoln for snatching a victory out of Fremont's hands. Lincoln had anticipated this beforehand and therefore, had ordered Fremont to be relieved only if he was not in battle or prepared to make an assault.

Requests to the War Department for all paperwork on Fremont were fruitless as Secretary of War Cameron replied his office possessed no such reports. The committee then decided to investigate the case itself.

Fremont's first appearance before the committee was on January 10. Rather than submit him to the grueling session as Stone and Patterson had to endure, Chairman Wade merely requested Fremont prepare a written statement and return at a later date.

An offensive by the committee was about to begin. As Fremont and his wife Jesse thrilled the social circles of Washington, Julian took to the floor of Congress to denounce the administration for removing Fremont. He gave a scathing speech defending the Pathfinder, stating that Fremont's removal was a victory for slavery. He continued that it was his emancipation order and not his spending which caused his dismissal. Even Greeley came to his support writing that critics should not focus on Fremont's spending habits but rather on all his accomplishments while in the West.

A few days later, Fremont reappeared before the committee with a detailed statement prepared in which to refute every charge against him. He wrote he had no specific orders from Lincoln or the War Department when he assumed command of an army which lacked supplies, arms and men. Montgomery Blair, who had sponsored his assignment, had told him to take whatever precaution necessary to defend and protect the people within his department. Fremont believed he was given free rein to command as he saw fit.

As for Wilson Creek, he stated that Cairo and St. Louis needed to be secured before Missouri could be cleared of the enemy. Lyon's demise was of his own making. Since the government failed to provide support and supplies Fremont was forced to make rash decisions. The several ordnance purchases made without the necessary paperwork was approved Quartermaster General Meigs due to urgency. He blamed the Contracts Committee for encouraging insubordination, discrediting and weakening the authority of a commanding general while absent in the field. As for his confiscation order, Fremont felt it was a military necessity due to the turbulent nature within the vicinity. Satisfied with his testimony, Fremont was released, and Gooch took his written statement to his office for review.

Wade had put down on paper the committee's official opinion thus far, writing that Fremont's administration was characterized by earnestness, ability and loyalty. Conveniently, Wade gave these secret writings to Charles Dana, his ally at the *Tribune*, with instructions to write a glowing report on Fremont in an attempt to sway public opinion.

Fremont returned before the board on January 30. Gooch led the inquiry in an attempt to reinforce Fremont's testimony and to dispel rumors and allegations. The hearing was very cordial as they discussed certain points in his statement. The committee was either oblivious or just indifferent to the contradicting statements made by Fremont. When asked why he did not stop construction of the five forts surrounding St. Louis, Fremont responded that the rebels wanted the city and the forts were a military necessity. This was an odd statement considering a short time later Fremont had released a full regiment to Lincoln's close friend Ward Hill Lamon who was recruiting troops to complete a Virginia Union Brigade. Fremont had remarked releasing these troops were not detrimental to the safeguard of the city. To any neutral party this contradictive line of reasoning alone would have raised a red flag.

The committee felt Fremont was the hapless victim of a sinister plot at the hands of the administration, and they continued their investigation. They began by questioning subordinates but few officers from the Western command would defend Fremont, while there were others who wanted to see him ousted. Frank Jr. and Montgomery Blair came to testify. The committee allowed Montgomery to read a prepared statement but his brother Frank was not as fortunate for they scrutinized him at length. The contractor who built the costly forts around St. Louis also testified and blamed Fremont for his lack of oversight. The contractor received condemnation from the board for his testimony. When St. Louis attorney Samuel Glover came forward with information critical of Fremont he was completely ignored by the committee.

General Hunter also appeared before the committee to testify against Fremont and he too received a cold reception and condemnation. This would no doubt have influence on his future command. Hunter would soon command the Department of the South, consisting of Georgia, Florida and South Carolina. Realizing the power the CCW wielded, on May 9, 1862 Hunter had ordered that all slaves within his command were forever free. Immediately, an alarmed Lincoln rescinded the order which obviously did not set well with the committee.

The committee was confident that they had performed their job well and armed with overwhelming evidence, they now set out to have Fremont reinstated. But Lincoln could not be swayed. The members were prepared for this so, although their committee was bound by an oath of secrecy, Fremont's testimony managed to be printed in the *Tribune* on March 1. When this became public, Lincoln could no longer ignore the cries for Fremont's reinstatement.

Lincoln was now at a crossroads. Does he cave to the pressure of the Radicals and reinstate a less than capable officer or, in an attempt to preserve bipartisanship does he ignore their demands? On March 11, Lincoln decided to give Fremont a minor assignment as commander of the new Mountain Department. His realm would consist of West Virginia and parts of Kentucky and Tennessee. Not a very prominent command but Lincoln figured Fremont could do no harm here. The Radicals, joyful with the victory of having Lincoln fold to their demands, were even more elated when the troops needed to fill up its ranks of the new department would come from McClellan's command.

Chapter 5

Sabotage

Before the committee set to work removing what they considered the undesirables, they had met with Lincoln and his Cabinet in the first week of January in hopes of convincing the president to find a replacement for McClellan who claimed to be very ill. They condemned the general's lack of action and his unwillingness to divulge his intentions. No one, not even McClellan's subordinate commanders knew where the army stood. The Radicals insisted upon a commander who was in good health and willing to conduct the war on radical principles. McClellan, they said had also bred dissention within the ranks. When Lincoln asked who he should replace him with, Wade responded, "anybody." But Lincoln responded saying "Anybody will do for you, but not for me. I must have *somebody!*" All the Cabinet members except for Secretary of the Treasury Chase rejected the committee's proposal.

But Lincoln was becoming worried. Should anything happen to McClellan what would become of the army? On Meigs suggestion, Lincoln consulted with McDowell and Franklin. The former suggested a move on Manassas and the latter opted for a water route east of Richmond. After the meeting Stanton, needing the support of both McClellan and the Lincoln's advisors to secure the appointment as Secretary of War, notified the bedridden McClellan that Lincoln was consulting with other generals and warned "They are counting on your death..." A very grateful McClellan experienced a miraculous recovery. By giving McClellan a heads up, Stanton gave the general the impression that he would have a friend in the War Department. McClellan would have been wise to steer clear of Stanton had he known of his ulterior motives.

On January 13, McClellan was well enough to attend a conference with Lincoln and his advisors to discuss the overall affairs of the military. When McClellan entered the room it was obvious by the look on his face that he was not happy to see McDowell. McClellan now began to distrust his predecessor. When the discussion turned to the Eastern Theatre, Lincoln asked what advances were to be made. McDowell again suggested taking Richmond from the north. McClellan remained silent until Chase demanded the general disclose his plans. It would not be prudent, McClellan replied, to reveal his plans to such a large group stating that he had no doubt it would end up in the newspapers the next day. However, he would disclose his plans to Lincoln and Stanton only if ordered to do so. McClellan did share however, that he had a kick off date and revealed a general plan but would not go into details. Satisfied, Lincoln would not prod the general any further.

So, it was rather incredible when, two days later with Stanton making the arrangement, that McClellan granted an interview with his largest supporter of the press, the *New York Herald*. Although they didn't print the details, they did print an outline of his plan in their paper.

Over the next several weeks the newly appointed Secretary of War Stanton, who vowed that once the machinery of his office was cleared out he would push to see McClellan fight, met with committee members to pore over the testimony they had gathered against McClellan. The public wanted action and Washington officials were now voicing concerns and disappointment over the Lincoln/McClellan team. Wade and Stanton, armed with evidence of the testimony again stated their case to Lincoln and insisting action was needed.

Lincoln finally gave in and on January 27, he issued General Order No. 1, calling for a general movement of all naval and land forces to begin by Washington's Birthday. McClellan was to first provide for the safety of Washington and then move southward to attack the railroads supplying Confederate forces under Johnston at Manassas.

McClellan was floored. Not only did Lincoln's directive put the Confederates on notice but he also felt it was impractical. McClellan protested and insisted on his Urbana Plan which he had just now revealed. The plan consisted of loading his army on transports, steam down the Potomac River to the Rappahannock River and up to Urbana; his two alternate sites were Mob Jack Bay and Fortress Monroe. Here he could disembark on the southern bank, 50 miles from Richmond and in the rear of the Confederates along the Manassas line. McClellan had claimed that his plan was so complex that he could not possibly meet the February 22 deadline but would have to wait until spring to move.

Still not convinced Lincoln said he would approve the plan only if Washington would be secured and if the general could answer three questions. Would McClellan's plan save time and money? Would victory be assured? And, could the army rely on a safe route of retreat in case of disaster? McClellan presented his case in a lengthy letter, explaining that an advance on Manassas meant frontal attacks upon an entrenched enemy, lengthening supply lines and no promise of decisively defeating the rebel army. His plan however, offered the shortest route to Richmond over "favorable" terrain, his flanks would be protected by the fleet on either side, and with Richmond being threatened rebel troops would have to fall back from Washington to protect their own capitol.

This early in the war the president was still unwilling to step on the toes of his commander so he consented to the Urbana Plan. Lincoln would not rescind his general order of January 27 but he would not force McClellan to abide by it. Again the Radicals were up in arms. Lincoln had once again sided with the McClellan.

But Stanton would not be denied. Success in the West had put Richmond in deep despair. Six days after the fall of Fort Donelson, Jefferson Davis was inaugurated as president of the Confederacy. In his address, Davis admitted they had been met with serious disasters in the West. Six days later he would proclaim martial law in a ten miles radius surrounding the Confederate capitol. While the rebels were recovering from Fort Donelson, the people of the North intuitively cried for action. Even they knew the time to strike was now.

A very shrewd Stanton was not about to let this opportunity pass and he began to put pressure on McClellan. On February 19, the secretary sent a letter to the *Tribune* praising the efforts of Grant and his victories in the West and offering him the Nation's gratitude. A master propagandist, Stanton's letter was full of innuendos; designed to contrast Grant's aggressive campaign to McClellan's lack of initiative. The fighting in the West had reaped a bountiful harvest while all remained quiet along the Potomac. With the fall of Fort Donelson and the South in despair McClellan had allowed his opportunity to strike a mortal blow slip by. McClellan had refused to yield to the cries of the Country.

When the committee finally got to interview McClellan they questioned him at length and demanded his reason for inactivity. McClellan's response was that communications with Washington was not yet perfected nor were there enough bridges across the Potomac. In response to their innuendos of cowardice, McClellan responded a good commander always secured his retreat. At that point Wade exploded. With the size of his army, the senator retorted, the army did not need an avenue of retreat, they only needed a chance to fight. Let him march his army over the Potomac and keep them there, Wade continued, until either a victory was had or "let them come back in their coffins." This ended the interview.

McClellan was the one fired up now and he did one more thing to rile the members of the committee. He defied the policy of keeping all testimonies and interviews secret (which the committee had already broken.) Thanks to Stanton for again making the arrangements, McClellan not only granted the *New York Herald* an interview but he twisted the whole story around. The *Herald* reported that the committee was using the general's recent illness as an excuse to "...supersede him in favor of Fremont or Senator Ben Wade, who represents the radical sentiment." A later article in the same paper claimed McClellan had proven the ignorance of the committee in regards to military matters and had convinced them of the folly of a direct assault on Manassas.

McClellan did give the impression of preparing for action when he sent two dispatches to Halleck on February 20. The first stated that, if Western forces could take Nashville or at least hold its own, then he hoped to have Richmond and Norfolk in three to four weeks. The second dispatch stated the rebels were holding Manassas and in less than two weeks he would move his Army of the Potomac and hoped to be in Richmond soon after Nashville was taken. Union forces occupied Nashville on February 24 and still McClellan was not even prepared to move.

The committee had had enough. Since they failed to move McClellan, the Radicals tried a new tactic. Since the battle of Bull Run, the enemy had occupied fortifications on the Virginia side of the Potomac around Manassas and Centreville. Their artillery had the ability to contest any movement by Union forces on the lower Potomac. To foreign nations it appeared the Capitol was under siege. Having the enemy so near, flaunting their "rattlesnake" flag was as humiliating to the administration as the Stars and Stripes flying in the Charleston Harbor had been to the residents there. Knowing Lincoln constantly fretted over the security of Washington, the Radicals would now use this to their advantage. They told Lincoln that the people and party members were all demanding the removal of this humiliation which even foreign nations had noticed and unless he acted, Congress and public opinion would turn against him.

Lincoln also had enough. Fearing a split in his administration, he sent for McClellan. The president needed reassurance that Washington was safe from attack and he ordered McClellan to march on Manassas directly from the Capitol but again McClellan insists on his Urbana Plan. On March 8 Lincoln, mustering up all the tact he could, decided to place both plans before the division commanders and let them chose the better of the two; Lincoln lost.

Politics in the Army of the Potomac split the twelve divisions into two hostile factions and the previous sessions with the CCW did not help. McDowell, Samuel P. Heintzelman, Edwin V. Sumner, John G. Barnard and Erasmus D. Keyes were experienced senior officers. All were Republicans who adopted the radical program of an aggressive war with emancipation as a military necessity. They resented McClellan's rapid rise to power and they scorned the officers who backed him. McClellan's pets, as referred to by Stanton, were Fitz-John Porter, Andrew Porter, William B. Franklin, William F. Smith, James F. Negley, Louis Blenker and George McCall.

These young officers all shared the same views as their commander, and it was these men from whom McClellan sought advice. The outcome of the vote had been obvious. In an eight-to-four vote, the decision was for McClellan's Urbana Plan. Oddly, Keyes voted for McClellan. Of course, the Radicals were outraged by the decision. McClellan's plan meant maneuvers and strategies; tactics taught by West Point. To the Radicals, the way to win this war and end the humiliation was an all-out assault upon the enemy. By choosing McClellan's Urbana Plan, the eight commanders who voted for it, in their estimation, were refusing to fight.

Lincoln however, was not surprised by the decision but he remained true to his word. He would allow McClellan to go through with his plan but, before his departure, Lincoln reiterated that Washington must be secure. The commander would not be allowed to move more than half his force until the rebel batteries across the Potomac were no longer a threat.

With an increase in activity in Washington the Confederates who employed an excellent spy network, knew something was afoot. They quickly abandoned the fortifications which had for so long threatened and humiliated Washington and moved toward the Rappahannock River. This movement now rendered McClellan's Urbana Plan impractical. Since McClellan had no back-up plan in place, it would take time to develop a new one. In the meantime, McClellan decided to have his troops investigates the abandoned fortifications which had for so long restricted his movements on the Potomac. When Union troops, accompanied by journalists marched into the rebel fortifications only to discover that the fortifications had been manned by a very small force.

With great embarrassment, Lincoln could no longer defend McClellan against the assault of the Radicals. McClellan immediately drafted the Peninsula Plan, but it was too late to appease Lincoln. The onslaught of ridicule by the radical press was merciless and the pressure of the Radicals was relentless; they could not afford to have McClellan lead a successful campaign and they would see to it that that would not happen. At the insistence of the CCW, Lincoln now ordered the reorganization of McClellan's army. The twelve divisions of the Army of the Potomac would be restructured into five corps based on the European model *corps d'armee*. No longer would McClellan's senior officers be ignored for they would each command a corps. McClellan would now have to plan his campaign with five commanders who would scrutinize his every move and would surely report back to Washington.

The next blow came on March 11 when Lincoln relieved McClellan as general-in-chief. From that point on all department commanders, would report directly to Stanton at the War Department. Lincoln eased the blow by explaining to McClellan that this order was not meant as punishment. Aware of the monumental endeavor of which McClellan was proposing Lincoln wanted to ensure McClellan gave the new plan his full attention. McClellan could have accepted the last order without complaint had it not been for his reading of his demotion in the newspaper. Lincoln, in a rare move, had sent copies of the order to be published in the newspapers. Finally, Lincoln gave McClellan a step off date of March 18 but, only after McClellan ensured a large enough force left behind to secure Washington.

McClellan, who had already lost Blenker's division 10,000 men to the newly established *Mountain Department* commanded by Fremont, had 20,000 troops in and around the capitol under the command of General James S. Wadsworth. With an additional 35,000 soldiers under General Nathanial Banks occupying the Shenandoah Valley and securing the approaches to the capital, McClellan believed he had followed Lincoln's orders. On April 1, the general departed Washington to join his gathering army at Fortress Monroe. But the Radicals were not through yet.

General Wadsworth was no friend of McClellan's and he immediately reported to Stanton that 20,000 green and undisciplined troops were too few and totally inadequate for defense of the city. McClellan's negligence had left Washington unprotected. Immediately, Stanton notified the CCW and Hitchcock that Lincoln's orders were not followed; the capital was in danger. They in turn, notified Lincoln. Since Stanton had ordered a halt to recruitment in early April due to recent victories in the West, McClellan would have to be relieved of somewhat experienced troops to guard Washington. Lincoln, not realizing the 35,000 in the Valley protected the approaches of the capital and Stanton never dispelling that thought, had no choice but to allow Stanton to detain either McDowell or Sumner's corps to be detained for defense of the city.

Stanton's choice of McDowell over Sumner was a calculated move for he knew McDowell could be easily manipulated now. Having been vindicated for the Bull Run disaster, he would be a useful tool for the Radicals. If McClellan's campaign proved successful, an early victory would mean a cessation of hostilities with slavery intact but more important still, a victory would also almost certainly guarantee a victory for the Democrats at the polls especially if McClellan decided to enter the presidential race. So, while McClellan was slugging it out on the peninsula, McDowell could easily advance upon Richmond, capture it and end the war; but only after all the pieces were in place. A victory for McDowell would mean certain victory for the Republicans at the polls. So, McDowell's corps of 30,000 would be used to bolster the ranks protecting the capital and its commander McDowell would answer directly to the Secretary of War. McDowell later admitted in confidence to Franklin that this move was intended to harm McClellan.

The political intrigue of Stanton and the Radicals did not go unnoticed however. Democrats and Conservatives were shocked that the Radicals would conspire to ensure for the defeat of an army rather than give a military commander the support needed for a successful campaign. The Radicals were once again putting "party before people." And in their attempt to destroy any chance of McClellan's successful Peninsula

Campaign, they had cost Lincoln the unified coalition of support he desperately tried to maintain. Lincoln was rapidly losing the trust of his political allies and this latest move by the Radicals would certainly have repercussions at the fall elections.

Amidst all the commotion and rumors of sabotage a thoroughly disgusted McClellan, who had lost nearly 1/3 of his army, began the Peninsula Campaign.

As McClellan kicked off his Peninsula Campaign with 70,000 soldiers (an additional 30,000 would soon join him) the radical press, not wanting the public forget the abandoned fort fiasco, began sniping at McClellan from the rear; chiding him for his slow, sluggish movements. They were constantly finding fault with his use of West Point tactics, to dig in rather than fight, allowing the rebels to safely retreat into their fortifications. Constantly over-estimating the enemy strength based on information from the head of the Union Intelligence Service Allan Pinkerton, McClellan confronted 17,000 rebels at the old Revolutionary battlefield at Yorktown. Rather than attack, the general decided to settle for a siege. When his huge siege guns were finally in place, the rebels fell back to a new position. Thus, the tone was set for the remainder of the campaign.

As McClellan bore the diatribe from those in Washington, the Army of the Potomac struggled through the marshes of the peninsula, fighting muddy roads as disease plagued his army. His faulty intelligence had convinced him he was outnumbered and his constant calls for reinforcements were ignored. As the pressure increased, so did McClellan's contempt for the *corps d'armee* order. He simply ignored his senior officers while resorting to confiding only with his favorites. Fed up with Heintzelman constant complaints, McClellan finally gave Lincoln an ultimatum, either let him fire the corps commanders he felt incompetent and replace them with new ones or to allow him to go back to the division structure. Lincoln allowed McClellan to return to the division structure as long as he promised to fight. McClellan's minor victory of course infuriated the Radicals.

For the next two months McClellan slowly and methodically, made his way up the peninsula. At each obstacle he would settle in for a siege and wait for the heavy artillery to be moved up into place only to have the enemy fall back after a brief engagement to another fortified position. By the end of May, the Army of the Potomac was stalled mere miles from Richmond when misfortune fell upon him. On June 1, General Robert E. Lee assumed command of the army defending Richmond when Johnston is wounded at the battle of Seven Pines. Lee wasted no time going on the offensive. Calling for General Jackson who was playing cat and mouse with the armies of Fremont and Shields in the Shenandoah Valley, Lee planned to attack McClellan's army.

On June 26, the enemy attacked and for the next seven days, McClellan's division commanders managed a skillful fighting withdrawal; fending off and inflicting heavy casualties upon the enemy as they fell back to Harrison's Landing on the north bank of the James River. Battered but not beaten, the Army of the Potomac could finally breathe. McClellan took stock of the situation. As if his eyes were suddenly opened to all that had transpired since he had arrived at Washington, McClellan now took this opportunity to wire to Stanton: "If I save this army now, I tell you plainly that I owe no thanks to you or any other person in Washington. You have done your best to sacrifice this army." Obviously, the telegram did not sit well with Lincoln who had caught wind of it.

McClellan was proud of his movement to the landing and he dispatched a courier to Washington to say as much while asking again for reinforcements. And again, Lincoln found himself caught in the middle of the struggle between the general and the Radicals. For the past couple months the president had been contemplating a drastic piece of legislation and he needed to see first-hand how the army was holding up. Lincoln paid a visit to McClellan at his new base in the second week of July. Surprised and relieved at the fine spirit of the army, Lincoln met with McClellan to discuss the option of staying or returning to Washington. Of course, McClellan again insisted more men would be needed before Richmond could be taken. Lincoln said he would do what he could for him. The next day, the president met with the five previous Corps commanders and asked each if the army was safe in its present position and could it be safely removed to Washington. All five responded the army was secure at present while three answered removing it now would be ruinous to the cause.

At the end of his visit McClellan handed Lincoln a letter. The now infamous *Harrison's Letter* stated McClellan's own views on policies. "Neither confiscation of property...or forcible abolition of slavery should be contemplated for a moment." "A declaration of radical views, especially upon slavery, will rapidly disintegrate our present armies." If Lincoln agreed to these terms, McClellan would be willing to remain in command. Lincoln may have dismissed the content of the letter but his Cabinet members did not. Chase and Stanton viewed it as a denunciation of the administration and Secretary of the Navy Gideon Welles believed it would be the downfall of McClellan.

Although the letter was meant for Lincoln's eyes only, the Radicals viewed it as another attempt for McClellan to garner Democratic support. By advocating a conservative policy, he was dictating to Lincoln views contradictory to their own. But their fears were unfounded; McClellan had not been a successful general of late so it is doubtful that Lincoln at this point would have even considered his opinion as valid. Although the West Point clique tended to shy away from political intrigue, this early in the war it was not unusual for professional military officers as well as the many volunteers to publically announce their political views. Fremont was a good example of this when he dictated political policy as a military measure in Missouri. But McClellan had crossed the line. No general should be dictating policy to the president.

To be sure, there are pros and cons to every campaign. McClellan had made Richmond the objective and not the rebel army. This scenario would play itself out time and again until the right commander was found. But, in McClellan's defense, as complicated an undertaking as the Peninsula Campaign was, it could have been a success...under a different commander. The mere fact that he was able to mobilize 70,000 troops by water so early in the war was a feat in itself. McClellan could not afford to risk a battle which could end in defeat. That was what the Radicals wanted. Nor would he sacrifice his army needlessly. The sniping from the rear and the lack of support from those in positions of power was certainly unwarranted and had obviously weighed on his mind. The fearful bloodshed at Seven Pines had a tremendous demoralizing effect on the young general as well. McClellan loved the men under him and he was now aware that politicians were willing to sacrifice them just to take him down.

The wasted expenditure of time, money and lives was certainly not for a positive but, the Radicals made it clear; they were willing to accept defeat as long as slavery existed for the end justified the means.

It was an untested army that landed on the peninsula, much like the one that had fought on the field of Manassas. But no longer, for these men had fought valiantly as they fell back to Harrison's Landing. And when they emerged from the peninsula, they were veterans. Their morale was higher as a result of their experience and, they were learning to hate the rebel soldier.

Chapter 6

Transformation

While McClellan trudged through the mud of Virginia and Halleck slowly inched his way towards Corinth, Farragut had taken New Orleans and the Radicals grew bolder in their demands. If Lincoln was still unwilling to make emancipation as one of the war goals, then the Radicals would continue to find other ways of doing it. One way was to prevent the military from acting as slave catchers. Since slaves could now be confiscated as contraband the Radicals began to assail military commanders who returned fugitive slaves to their masters. The government, they believed should be protecting and employing any escaped slaves who made it to Union lines.

To force the issue, they continued to whittle away at the institution by passing a string of laws. On March 13, they put through as an article of war the *Act Prohibiting the Return of Slaves*, which prohibited the employment of the military for the purpose of returning fugitive slaves; basically a repeal of the *Fugitive Slave Act*. They were enraged however, to learn from General Sickles one month later that the law was never officially communicated to the army. Then, on April 16, Lincoln signed into law the *DC Compensated Emancipation Act* which paid slave owners residing in the District of Columbia $300 to free each of the nearly 3,100 slaves in that district. Two months later, on June 19, another bill was signed into law abolishing slavery in the National Territories.

One bill introduced and heavily debated was the *Second Confiscation Act,* a law which would punish the South for causing an unjust war over slavery. Lincoln had remained silent throughout the debates until the bill was ready to be voted on. At this point, Lincoln finally spoke up stating he would veto the bill should it pass. He had no intentions of allowing congressional overreach to dictate the conduct of neither the war nor its policies. With no time for a second vote Fessenden had called on Lincoln to ask about his objection to the bill. Lincoln said he would sign it if two provisions were pulled out. The first, which would confiscate slave property of persons committed before the Act and the second, the clause which would work a forfeiture of his real estate of the offender beyond his natural life. To the Radicals these two clauses were the heart of the bill. With time running out there would be no second vote. Reluctantly, the Radicals attached the amendments and the Act was passed on July 17. The law now read in part, that anyone in rebellion in Confederate Territory occupied by Union forces had 60 days of within the Act's passage to surrender. If they did not, then their slaves would be freed by criminal proceedings.

One glimmer of hope was buried in Section 11 of the latest law; a clause authorizing the president to employ as laborers people of African descents as he saw fit. By this time, as the number of Union volunteers increased so did the number of fugitive slaves. However, the growing need of the army due to attrition had caused the government into considering the option. The idea of using freed slaves to dig ditches and build fortifications in the sweltering heat of the South would free up white soldiers to continue the fight. If pressed, the Radicals believed public opinion would shift toward accepting these measures and emancipation. Surely, no one would consider returning to bondage any person who assisted in putting down the rebellion. This was the *Militia Act of 1862*.

The Radicals didn't know it yet but Lincoln had already moved towards the radical program. One of the only constant philosophies Lincoln believed in other than to fight to preserve the Union was to have no policy. He preferred the flexibility of not being tied down by anything he said. But, by signing these bills into law Lincoln had put himself in a precarious position. He risked losing the dwindling support of the Democrats and conservatives. Although his views on slavery were always clear, Lincoln was reluctant to alienate the Border States or force emancipation by compensation. The progress of the war so far had been disappointing, and yet, Lincoln allowed the Radicals to introduce extreme measures in the form of the confiscation acts. To many government officials, Lincoln was being coerced into accepting the radical program. But, by allowing the Radicals to push for these measures, Lincoln's hands remained relatively clean. Also, these acts may have been a prelude to something bigger which Lincoln had in mind.

On July 12, Lincoln approached representatives of the Border States for a third time, hoping to convince them accept emancipation through compensation; explaining that they risked losing all should the South lose the war. His first attempt was in March when a resolution was voted on in Congress. Passed unanimously by the Republicans, 85 per cent of the Democrats opposed it, citing the resolution reeked of federal coercion. They also disputed the amount to be paid, the right to appropriate such funds, and possible economic ruins. But their biggest fear was it would result in a race war. Many feared that freed blacks would migrate north to settle in white neighborhoods and take away jobs. Lincoln second attempt was in May; again with the same result. This last time, Lincoln's request was more of an ultimatum. The Republicans could see the writing on the wall. Although the Union armies had not achieved any major victories as of late, the rebels were wearing down. Again, the agents of the Border States turned him down. With no other option, Lincoln decided now was the time to issue his greatest piece of legislation.

Action in the Shenandoah Valley in the spring of 1862 had opened Lincoln's eyes. With Scott's resignation and McClellan's downgrading, Lincoln was now acting general-in-chief. He watched as Union forces meant to defend Washington and secure the Shenandoah Valley were being manhandled by Confederate General Jackson. The lack of a concerted effort between McDowell's Department of the Rappahannock, Fremont's Mountain Department, and Banks' Department of Shenandoah allowed Jackson to shuffle about and keep each of these forces occupied, thus preventing them from threatening Richmond or assisting McClellan.

Ever since Sumter, Lincoln had been studying the art of war. Armed with a greater understanding of the military tactics and strategy he decided that by consolidating the smaller departments, along with Sturgis' brigade from the Military District of Washington and placed under one commander, a more effective fighting force would be the result. He therefore ordered these forces surrounding Washington to be combined into one army and on June 26, the *Army of Virginia* was created. General John Pope was called in from the West and appointed its commander. Exiting on a quiet note was Fremont who had outranked Pope. The thought of transferring his command to a subordinate was a humiliation Fremont refused to bear. His resignation was eagerly accepted.

A great self-promoter Pope often embellished reports, giving himself more glory than he probably deserved. Although he had known Lincoln before the war Pope kept up a steady correspondence with old Senator Trumbull with whom he eagerly shared his radical views, knowing they would be passed on to the Radicals. Pope was also very critical of McClellan which thrilled the Radicals more and they lauded his military exploits to Lincoln every chance they could.

On July 14, Pope's addressed his newly assembled army with a speech drafted by Stanton. The address was rife with rhetoric and indirect assaults on McClellan's idea of policy and how to conduct the war. But Pope also alienated the soldiers when he told them that he came from the West where they always saw the backs of their enemies. This was basically a slap in the face to the men who had faced Stonewall in the Shenandoah Valley. When Pope declared that his headquarters would be in the saddle the men couldn't help but quip that the general didn't know his headquarters from his hindquarters. But Pope was energetic and began issuing a barrage of orders to his new command. Bring back the Army of the Potomac to Aquia Creek to join his, he said, and together they could advance. The Radicals cheered Pope, believing he alone could force the administration to adopt the policy of total war.

Lincoln now had to deal with McClellan. The crisis between the general and the Radicals had now spilled out onto the Senate floor. As usual Chandler led the assault. After denouncing the charges of sabotage by the Democratic press Chandler assailed McClellan and his Peninsula Campaign and demanded a full report from the War Department. Radical members of the senate demanded of the CCW an official account of the failed campaign but one thing stood in their way, the committee's policy of secrecy. This was an odd excuse considering the committee had already broken its own policy. But to rectify this, a special meeting was called by committee members on July 15 and a motion was made by Chandler to abolish the secrecy rule. Conveniently, Johnson's successor and fellow Democrat Senator Wright was not notified of the meeting. The motion was approved unanimously by all members present.

The next day Chandler once again took his place on the floor and read the entire account of McClellan failed leadership since taking command. Even Lincoln was not spared from the onslaught as Chandler took swipes at him; claiming the president had known of all of the general's shortcomings. Yet, he had sustained him throughout. Radical newspapers reported the tirade and even painted the pro-slavery officers which had supported McClellan as traitors.

The Radicals began to pressure Lincoln into giving McClellan's precious Army of the Potomac to Pope. Even Jay Cooke, who handled the government's war loans and attributed the dramatic drop in subscription to McClellan's inactivity and blunders, advised Lincoln to replace McClellan. Lincoln's patience with McClellan had also expired but he believed the coalition he so carefully tried to maintain would certainly collapse if McClellan were to be dismissed now. Lincoln would keep the general on until after the mid-term elections.

The best way to deal with the situation Lincoln decided was to call in a permanent military advisor and on July 11, Lincoln ordered Halleck to Washington and appointed him general-in-chief of the armies. Halleck lacked the looks, manners and demeanor of a military great but he was studious and intelligent in military strategies. His was to be a thankless job for when there were victories the credit went to the generals. For defeats, the blame went to Halleck. The reluctant general would hold this position until the end of the war.

The choice of Halleck had many of the Radicals believing that Lincoln was again catering to the Democrats but Halleck had reversed his thoughts on policies and now accepted the radical program. The previous year he and Buell had turned out fugitive slaves from their camps but now Halleck began advocating the employment of slaves as laborers for the war effort. But still, the Radicals didn't fully trust Halleck due to his friendship with McClellan. When Halleck arrived in Washington, he was immediately pressed by Stanton and Chase to transfer McClellan's Army of the Potomac to Pope. This was probably not a wise choice. As long as McClellan remained at Harrison's Landing the threat to Richmond remained real; it would be unwise for the rebels to move.

Yielding to the pressures of the Radicals, Halleck paid a visit to McClellan at his camp on the James on July 25 and gave him an ultimatum; begin another offensive immediately or withdraw and join Pope. McClellan of course, requested more men before another advance could be made. Lincoln could not provide them. Lee however makes a drastic decision and begins to move toward Washington. When word was received in Washington that Lee was on the move, Halleck ordered the removal of all sick and wounded men. Then on August 3, he ordered McClellan to move his army with the utmost secrecy to rendezvous with Pope at Aquia Creek. Pope was thrilled with this turn of events and now promised to "bag the whole crowd" in one fell swoop. The outspoken Fitz-John Porter, who felt the Army of the Potomac should stay put, was very critical of this move however and wrote to a leading Democratic editor that the government's management of affairs in Virginia deserved to result in defeat. Statements like these were dangerous and not to be taken lightly.

True to form, McClellan would not be hurried and he took his time in executing the order to withdraw and transfer troops. With McClellan no longer a threat to Richmond, Lee decides to attack Pope. Halleck continued to pressure McClellan because Pope, who had moved his army south of the Rappahannock, was now facing elements of Jackson's army with Lee following closely behind. Pope was in dire need of McClellan's support. McClellan, seeing a chance to be restored as supreme commander now sent a barrage of dispatches to Halleck, asking who would have authority of his detachments as they arrived to Pope. He also confounded Halleck by stating perhaps he should now advance upon Richmond. Poor Halleck, doubting Pope's ability to command a large army, now promised McClellan command of all armies in Virginia if he could just join Pope in time. McClellan, aware of Pope's criticizing and now leery of Halleck, still refused to be hurried. Even Burnside, stationed at Fortress Monroe, assured McClellan that Halleck was serious. And still, McClellan would not be rushed.

By August 24, the Confederates had now moved to the rear of Pope and cut off his communications with Washington. With no word from Pope, Halleck anxiously ordered McClellan to Alexandria where he could seek the general's counsel. As the situation worsened, Halleck relied more heavily on McClellan. By the end of August the situation was as such that Halleck who outranked both McClellan and Pope refused to command either. Each commander was on their own as both Pope and Lee's armies maneuvered around Manassas.

Until now, Lincoln had wanted to stay out the fray between the generals. He had brought Halleck to Washington for the purpose of conducting the war without his interference. But now, an anxious Lincoln was frantic for information regarding Pope. In a telegraph to McClellan,

Lincoln now asked for an update on Pope. McClellan had avoided contact with Lincoln but, seeing an opportunity, McClellan replied with advice; either open lines of communication for all forces under Pope or "let him get out of his own scrape."

Lincoln was astounded by McClellan's statement. Did McClellan actually wish defeat upon Pope? Correctly sensing that McClellan was seeking overall control, Lincoln responded that the first advice was probably best and he left the matter to Halleck.

The next day, August 30, Halleck finally received word from Pope; the enemy had been driven from the field after a terrific battle. The joy was short-lived however, when Halleck received a second telegraph informing him of the crushing defeat of Pope's Army of Virginia.

With the defeat of Pope's army, the Radicals again saw danger on the horizon. Pope would probably be removed and their old nemesis McClellan would be restored to command. Their control of the Eastern army would again be lost. The Radicals had to move fast to convince Lincoln that it was McClellan and not Pope who was at fault for the disaster. Even as Pope's defeated soldiers were slowly making their way into Washington the Radicals were busy thinking of ways to repair the damage done by this latest defeat.

Upon hearing rumors that McClellan had intentionally held troops from Pope, Stanton ordered Halleck to substantiate the stories officially. McClellan's lack of alacrity might not be enough to prevent his restoration to command but the Radicals could still use it to build their case against him. Meanwhile, they needed to find someone to pass the blame onto and this time the unfortunate Fitz-John Porter, the most outspoken of McClellan's pets, would be the scapegoat.

A humiliated Pope now had to own up to his actions. There was no one to blame but himself. It wasn't until he arrived in Washington and met up with Chandler that Pope had a glimmer of hope. Chandler stroked the defeated commander's ego by praising him for his brilliant campaign which, Chandler continued, would have been successful had it not been for Porter. His only fault, Chandler told Pope, was allowing Porter to leave the battlefield alive. Pope had never questioned Porter's performance at Manassas, nor did he have a reason to. But after his meeting with Chandler, Pope began to see things differently.

Seeing a way out, Pope now intended to prefer charges against Porter for not supporting him. At the not so unexpected news of this, the

CCW had their golden opportunity before them. If they could prove McClellan and Porter were in cahoots, Lincoln would have no choice but to leave Pope where he was. But alas, there was no time for the CCW to take action for Lee was again on the move. Knowing the army had lost confidence in Pope, Lincoln needed a commander who could rebuild and lead the army. On September 12, having no other generals to choose from, Lincoln ordered the Army of Virginia merged into the Army of the Potomac and decided he had no other choice but to reinstate McClellan as its commander.

Chapter 7

The Prayers of Twenty Million

With Union forces no longer a threat to Richmond, Lee sought to take advantage of his recent victories by foregoing the South's policy of a defensive war and taking the fight to the North. Upon entering Maryland he discovered that Union troops at Harper's Ferry could threaten his supply line, so he dispatched Jackson to capture the garrison as Lee continued north.

McClellan gave chase and when Union soldiers discovered a copy of Lee's orders wrapped around three cigars in a house occupied by enemy forces, McClellan learned that Lee had split his army. Here was the perfect opportunity for McClellan to crush one and then the other of Lee's outnumbered forces. After ordering Franklin to try to relieve the troops at Harpers Ferry, a sharp battle with Lee's rearguard at South Mountain led McClellan to believe he had achieved a great victory when the belligerents fell back. McClellan telegraphed Lincoln of his success; telling the president that Lee was on the run. All McClellan had to do was to move quickly and overtake Lee before he could set up a defense. But, it was the same McClellan and his pursuit was slow and deliberate.

McClellan had stayed to the east side of the Blue Ridge Mountain as he headed north, parallel to Lee's main body. When he finally arrived at Sharpsburg, McClellan discovered Lee positioned behind defensive positions on the crest of a hill with both his flanks anchored on the Potomac situated behind him. To Lee's front was Antietam Creek which ran somewhat parallel to his line. The position was not a strong one but McClellan had allowed Lee time to dig in.

On September 17, McClellan launched his offensive, assaulting first the right flank, then the center, and then the left of the enemy line. The confederates gave some ground on their left but still manage to hold.

Their right flank was in danger however and had McClellan committed his reserves he could have possibly carried the day. But he didn't and the arrival of the remainder of Jackson's men ended the fighting. The next day both armies recovered from the bloody fighting and neither side was willing to make a move. That night, Lee's army slipped away and taking with it any chance of complete victory by McClellan. Technically, Antietam was not a victory but, by remaining on the field, McClellan was able to claim it as such.

The Battle of Antietam had been fought and in one bold stroke of the pen, Lincoln took a giant yet indirect step towards emancipation. Only Lincoln's advisors had known of his intentions. Earlier in July, Lincoln had shared a rough draft of his preliminary Emancipation Proclamation to Seward and Welles in which the former suggested tearing it up. But, nine days later, on July 22 Lincoln read the draft to his Cabinet, explaining that preservation of the Union was still and would remain the primary purpose of the war. The proclamation however was based on military necessity. Lincoln also hoped that it would motivate loyal slave states into accepting a gradual emancipation. For months he had been trying to convince them to accept emancipation through compensation. Now, they would know Lincoln intended to free all slaves if given the chance. Cabinet members accepted the move but Seward suggested Lincoln wait for a military victory before issuing the edict. Antietam was as close as Lincoln could hope for and on September 22, he issued the Emancipation Proclamation.

Lincoln had a great knack for timing. He had never let on he was contemplating such a radical move. Even Horace Greeley, the staunch anti-slavery editor of the *New York Tribune* and perpetual thorn in Lincoln's side was unaware of the president's intentions. When Greeley printed his article *The Prayers of Twenty Millions* on August 20, Lincoln saw his chance to work the crowd in the North as well as the South.

Greeley had published his concerns of the Northern populace in the form of an open letter to the president in which he collectively listed their grievances in regards to his failure to fully prosecute and enforce the confiscation acts recently signed into law. This is where Lincoln once again, showed his brilliance. In his public response to Greeley's letter, Lincoln refused to reveal his plan. Rather than say a proclamation sat on his desk waiting to be announced Lincoln instead informed Greeley that he would use any means necessary to save the Union. If that meant freeing some, all or none of the slaves in order to do so, so be it. This response recused Lincoln of openly attacking upon the institution of slavery.

Even with recent military disasters in the Eastern theatre, public opinion appeared to be changing. Lincoln presented the edict as one of military necessity. By including possible colonization of freed blacks he had hoped to make the proclamation more palatable to the opposition. After the failed Peninsula Campaign however Lincoln had wanted to test the waters before issuing the decree. He was reluctant to call for additional troops, thinking people would see it as a desperate act but after Northern war governors had pledged to support Lincoln, the president issued a call for 300,000 three-year term enlistments in early July. The response was not encouraging.

A month later, Lincoln issued another call for an additional 300,000 more nine month volunteers. For states unable to fulfil their quotas a draft would be instituted. This resulted in several riots breaking out across the north. Lincoln decided to make the proclamation tentative; it would not go into effect until January 1, '63.

The general view of the administration was that the Northern soldiers had accepted the proclamation; not so much from the humanitarian standpoint. Many had wanted to exact a sort of revenge on the rebels. The Union soldier had had enough. If emancipation would weaken the rebel army and help to achieve a decisive victory, then many were willing to accept the proclamation. A study of letters written over the course of the war revealed that only about ten per cent of Union soldiers had fought to preserve the Union and halt the expansion of slavery but not for emancipation. By spring of 1863, these feeling changed as more soldiers now understood the potential of freeing and even arming the Negroes as a military necessity.

Also, Lincoln needed to appease the Republican conservatives who were now joining the ranks of the Radicals. Lincoln knew their support was needed to avoid disruption in the administration. Lincoln had also suggested colonization to calm the fears of the Democrats. Congress had already authorized $600,000 for such a plan to ensure passage of their confiscation acts.

All across the North, church bells pealed and public meetings were held passing resolutions of thanksgiving but the Radicals viewed the proclamation with mixed emotions. It was a paradox. Technically, the edict would free the slaves only in rebellious states which were not yet under Union control as a means of military necessity. Although, any slaves which made it to Union lines would now be considered free. The purpose of the war was still for saving of the Union, leaving military emancipation a secondary measure. According to the proclamation, if the rebels laid down their arms tomorrow they would be able to keep their slaves. The proclamation could not be legally applied to loyal states either since the Federal government had no power over state rights.

Not all were happy with the proclamation, however, and they were sure to inform Lincoln about it. One strange case was when military governor of North Carolina Edward Stanly protested to Lincoln personally just days after the announcement. Lincoln responded that it was a military necessity for he believed the Radicals would withhold funding for the war if the he didn't do something for them. Oddly, Lincoln said that he had prayed to the Almighty to spare him of this deed saying, "If it be possible, let this cup pass from me," but the prayer went unanswered. It is strange that Lincoln would deny ownership of this act unless it was again, to place the onus on the Radicals if reaction to the edict was against him. Lincoln also lamented to vice-president Hannibal Hamlin that "The North responds to the proclamations sufficiently in breath; but breath alone kills no rebels." Lincoln claimed that, after just six days stocks had declined. There were now fewer men in the field due to attrition, and new volunteers were reluctant now to answer the call.

The Emancipation Proclamation had infuriated the Peace Democrats. Dubbed *Copperheads* by an Ohio Republican newspaper in the fall of '61, their reaction to the proclamation was one of outrage. Initially, the Copperheads had supported the war for the Union but they opposed the total war concept. They preferred peace through negotiation and compromise. This did not make them southern sympathizers but they were, by definition, white supremacists. Many viewed the edict as an overreach of presidential powers with intent to make blacks equal to whites.

McClellan and Fitz-John Porter were just as harsh in their criticism of the edict as most Democrats. Porter announced that "The Proclamation was ridiculed in the army – causing disgust, discontent, and expressions of disloyalty to the views of the administration, amounting I have heard to insubordination, All such bulletins tend only to prolong the war by rousing the bitter feelings of the South – and causing unity of action among them – while the reverse with us." Of course, this may have been a wrong assumption for it only spoke of the views of the Army of the Potomac however the utterance of these feelings would have disastrous repercussions for Porter.

The timing of the proclamation was also for the benefit of the foreign nations closely watching the struggle. By intending to free a portion of the slave population, Lincoln now made a moral issue of the war. As Confederate envoys pointed out to British officials, Lincoln's response to Greeley was proof that the war was not about slavery but about Northern dominion over the South. Heavy debates were taking place in Britain but eventually the anti-slavery sentiment won out.

Lincoln's timing even upset the plans of the *Loyal War Governors' Conference* in Altoona, Pennsylvania. The thirteen governors had planned to meet on September 24 to protest the war policies of the administration and to discuss ways to assist the Radicals in their quest for a full prosecution of the war. When word of the edict was out, the governors were elated and sent to the president the resolution "We hail with heartfelt gratitude and encouraged hope the proclamation." But the governors, firmly committed to the belief that McClellan was a failure, decided that a committee led by Massachusetts Governor John Andrew, should travel to Washington to demand of Lincoln in person that McClellan be removed. Having read of the meeting in the papers, Lincoln was ready for them. After the initial salutations, Lincoln monopolized the entire conversation and before they could even air their grievances, their allotted time was up and Lincoln was ushering them out the door.

The congressional election of 1862 may have been a telling sign as to the state of affairs in the country. After the fall of Fort Sumter, a wave of patriotism; a strong sense of love and devotion to one's country, had swept over the Union as political parties united for a common cause; to put down the rebellion. But now partisanship had re-emerged. Military failures, the suspension of the writ of *Habeas Corpus,* the Conscription Acts, and the draft had conservatives and Democrats believing Lincoln was caving to the Radicals. States in the Midwest, hit particularly hard economically by the closing of the Mississippi River felt their economic interests were being sacrificed to New England anti-slavery fanaticism. But it was the Emancipation Proclamation that the Democratic newspaper looked to exploit. With their slogan "To maintain the

Constitution as it is, and to restore the Union as it was" coined by Ohio Representative and leader of the Copperheads Clement Vallandigham, they worked on the fears of northern whites. The war for the Union had been replaced by a war for emancipation and Democrats across the North denounced the decree, believing the influx of freed slaves would further tax them economically and on the job front. Fears that former slaves would migrate north and settle into their neighborhoods neared reality. The result was open opposition to the policies of the administration and Democratic victories at the polls.

The Democrats had gained 32 seats, the governorship of New York and New Jersey and legislatures in Illinois, Indiana, and Pennsylvania. The election was a setback but not a defeat. Even though Republicans still controlled both House and Senate the Democratic victory could not be ignored. As talks of peace grew louder it was obvious that Democrats were willing to fight for preservation of the Union but nothing more. The Radicals could not be too despondent though. They had managed to retain power and pass the Homestead Act, the Land-grant College Act or Morrill Act, and the Pacific Railroad Act, the Legal Tender Act, the Internal Revenue Act, and several confiscation acts; all geared toward the modernization of northern capitalism. But, the Radicals still had their work cut out for them.

While Halleck was scrambling between McClellan and Pope in the East, Lincoln had also wanted him to focus on the armies in the West. In August, the Radicals had complained to Lincoln that Buell had cost the Republicans the elections in Ohio and Indiana. State leaders in Tennessee, Indiana and Illinois were joined by Buell's own officers in calling for his removal.

Lincoln was also unhappy with Buell for his slow progress and failure to liberate eastern Tennessee on his way to Chattanooga. The general's excuse was he needed to maintain a long supply train. This was true. Confederate cavalry and guerillas were constantly attacking his supply lines. Lincoln posed the same question to Buell as he had to McClellan, "...why can't you travel as the confederates travel?" In September, the rebel army at Chattanooga suddenly invaded Kentucky causing Buell to backtrack from Nashville to protect his base at Louisville.

On September 24, the president dispatched a courier to Buell directing him to relinquish his command to General George Thomas of

Virginia. The message would be delivered *only* if Buell was not preparing for an advance or had just won a victory. When Halleck caught wind of the order he intervened on Buell's behalf. Lincoln agreed to give Buell a chance to redeem himself but the courier had already delivered the order. Buell promptly turned over the command to Thomas who wrote Halleck that he was refusing command, stating Buell was ready to move.

Once the miscommunication was straightened out Lincoln sent Buell a message saying his army must enter eastern Tennessee by autumn while the roads were passible. Halleck reiterated what Lincoln had said; neither the country nor the government would tolerate any more delays. Buell missed his opportunity however when he failed to defeat Confederate General Braxton Bragg's small force at Perryville on October 8. Bragg was forced to withdraw from Kentucky with Buell half-heartedly in pursuit. The high command in Washington would finally force Lincoln's hand and on October 24, Major-General Rosecrans replaced Buell as commander of the renamed Department of the Cumberland. The Radicals applauded the promotion of Rosecrans since he shared the same political views as them.

Rosecrans had stalked Bragg through Tennessee and in the first days of January, 1863 fought him to a standoff at Stone's River. For the next six months following Stone's River, Rosecrans remained at Stone's River until the patience of Lincoln had worn out. With the warning to either move his army or have them sent elsewhere, Rosecrans had pushed Bragg to the extreme southeast corner of Tennessee toward Chattanooga, a vital and strategic location for the South. As the gateway between east and west, railroads from Vicksburg and Mobile pass through Chattanooga to towns in northern Mississippi, Tennessee and Kentucky.

In his attempt to capture Chattanooga, Rosecrans had moved his army up and down the river banks of the Tennessee. Bragg evacuated the city and moved into Georgia, giving the impression he was retreating. In effect, Bragg had wanted to draw Rosecrans in. The two armies met on the banks of Chickamauga Creek and on September 18, Bragg struck first and the battle of Chickamauga was fought. Bragg missed his chance to destroy Rosecrans army but he did place Chattanooga under siege. Rosecrans was relieved of command at Chattanooga and replaced by Virginia native Major-General George H. Thomas.

When Halleck was called to Washington in July, he had reinstated Grant as field commander of the Army of the Tennessee. Stanton then met with Grant in Louisville and gave him full charge of all Union forces between the Alleghenies and the Mississippi. Next, Washington ordered Sherman's forces to Vicksburg while Hooker and Howard's division were detached from the Army of the Potomac and sent to Tennessee. Their job was to open a new supply route to relieve the starving forces at Chattanooga and on October 28 the "cracker line" was opened. In mid-November the three-day Battle of Chattanooga was fought resulting in a huge victory for Grant!

Chapter 8

Valley Forge

McClellan had remained idle after Antietam but Lincoln would not or could not relieve him until after the election. The Democrats were blasting Lincoln for not sustaining McClellan while the Radicals blamed the president for keeping him on for so long. But, when the polls closed Lincoln sought McClellan's replacement. For continuity or because of Pope, the president wanted an officer from the Eastern command but his choices were limited. Of the senior officers, Sumner was old and his health failing, Franklin was dominated by McClellan and Hooker was junior to Burnside and hostile towards McClellan. Possibly in an attempt of retaining even a shred of Democratic support Lincoln decided on Burnside, another West Point Democrat to succeed McClellan as commander of the Army of the Potomac.

Burnside owed his rise in the army to McClellan. Before the war, McClellan had provided Burnside with a position with the Illinois Central Railroad. Although McClellan blamed Burnside for his slow movement at South Mountain and failure to carry the Confederate right at Antietam, Burnside did lead a small army on a successful campaign on the coast of North Carolina in early 1862.

On November 5, an order was sent from the War Department to McClellan's camp appointing Burnside as the new commander. Burnside initially refused the order but accepted the command upon hearing that Hooker was next in line for the appointment. The Radicals, at first jubilant to finally rid themselves of McClellan now found themselves frustrated at the choice of his friend as his replacement. With his appointment it was obvious Lincoln still clung to the notion of an all-parties coalition.

Burnside was a good divisional commander when someone else made the decisions but he lacked the confidence and competence as an overall commander. His new appointment made him a nervous wreck. The people of the North, having grown weary from the long, drawn-out war, were again demanding action. Fully aware of this Burnside began working long hours; his lack of sleep bringing him to the point of physical illness. But he did come up with a plan. Rather than operate along a line east of the Blue Ridge Mountains which Lincoln had suggested, Burnside chose to depart from his base in Warrenton, Virginia and shift eastward along the north bank of the Rappahannock to Falmouth and ford the river at Fredericksburg. Burnside had surprised everyone by making the 40 mile march in just two days. From there, his army could march on to Richmond. Halleck and Lincoln did not agree with the plan but reluctantly, they give their consent.

The appointment of Burnside meant the continuance of McClellan's dominance over the Eastern army and the Radicals resented the McClellan's influence on the opinion and attitude of the army regarding policies. The committee now saw their chance to finally expose and destroy McClellan and his cronies for good. In December, Michigan Senator Jacob Howard introduced a resolution for the CCW to officially report their findings thus far to Congress. But recent developments would delay any action.

Just as quickly as the CCW resumed their investigations into McClellan's Peninsula Campaign, Second Bull Run and Antietam it was halted as news of Fredericksburg reached Washington. Burnside's plan to take Richmond had a slim chance of succeeding even if executed with haste but, miscommunication between Halleck and Burnside had led to a costly and damaging delay. When Halleck had ordered that pontoons, small flat-bottom boats secured end to end to support bridging, to be waiting at Falmouth for Burnside, he never followed up to see that the order was carried out. Burnside arrived at Falmouth on November 17, only to discover he had no pontoons in which to affect a crossing. The eight days Burnside waited for their arrival gave Lee plenty of time to occupy Fredericksburg and prepare for the assault.

Anticipating Burnside's movement, Lee decided to dig in and allow the Union army to cross. On December 13, Burnside made the crossing and hurled his army against Lee's defenses. It is possible that Burnside could have broken their lines had he attacked one point of Lee's lines with overwhelming force but instead, Burnside made the oft-repeated mistake made by other commanders of sending in his army piecemeal. By the end of the day, the Union army had suffered over 12,000 casualties.

After the battle, Burnside had broken down completely. Riddled with guilt, he planned to personally lead one final charge the next morning but was stopped only by the protest of Franklin and others. By now, Burnside had lost the respect and confidence of his command. Many of his commanders, especially Hooker were criticizing his generalship, and he became convinced that his officers were against him. Burnside had no options left and with tears in his eyes, he ordered a withdrawal.

Days later, Burnside heard that Lincoln was being blamed for pressing him into action. To his credit Burnside offered Lincoln to publish a letter absolving the president of any blame. Lincoln was moved by this selfless act and was very grateful for it.

The North was horrified when news of Fredericksburg reached them. The terrible loss of life caused morale to plummet and many Democrats and Conservatives felt that Fredericksburg would vindicate McClellan. Fearing the Democrats would use the defeat as reason for a peace movement or, worse yet a call for McClellan's return, the Radicals needed to act fast. Acting on rumors that McClellan's pets had actively tried to undermine Burnside in retaliation for McClellan's removal, the Radicals again used the powers of the CCW to go and identify a scapegoat.

On December 19, with the investigation of McClellan on hold the CCW immediately sent their investigative committee to Burnside's camp in Falmouth to take testimony. Again, Burnside took full responsibility for disaster, stating the lack of pontoons as the apparent reason for the defeat but the committee of course, could not accept that answer. Other witnesses including Meade, Sumner, Franklin, and Hooker also pointed to the lack of pontoons as the apparent reason for the disaster. Hooker however, always angling for promotion, had more to add and eagerly pointed a finger at Franklin. Had he committed all his troops, Hooker said, the rebels would have surely been swept from the field. Of course, Hooker shared with the committee his own heroic deeds on that fateful day. When the committee asked Burnside why Franklin failed to carry the left wing in the assault, the commander's reply was the position and the strength of the enemy was too strong. Except for Hooker's testimony the interview had not gone as planned.

Upon their return to Washington, the committee interviewed Quartermaster Meigs and Colonel Daniel Woodbury, commander of the engineer brigade in charge of the pontoons. Woodbury was unaware of the urgency for pontoons and blamed red tape for the delays. Had he known of their importance he would have seized teams, teamsters and wagon masters to deliver them to Falmouth. Meigs only knew that Burnside needed supplies for his men but knew nothing of the pontoons.

In their initial report to Congress on December 23, the CCW absolved Burnside of blame. Halleck and the high command were responsible for the defeat due to the lack of pontoons. Rather than find a scapegoat the committee found fault with communications in the upper echelon; a fact which had disparaging effect on the public. But rather than attach an official report or comment in his address to the Senate, Wade decided it was best to let the results of their investigation die quietly. The CCW appeared to have failed in their mission but on the bright side, Burnside would remain in command.

The results of the mid-term elections compounded by the Fredericksburg disaster led to a growing demand by the Copperheads for a peace compromise. The Radicals feared any compromise now would ultimately leave slavery intact. To show that the administration was a unified body insisting on full prosecution of the war the Radicals attempted a coup on Lincoln's Cabinet. For months Secretary Chase, jealous of Seward's close relationship to the president, had been feeding the Radicals rumors of a dysfunctional Cabinet. In private letters he complained that Lincoln refused to consult his entire Cabinet regarding the country's state of affairs.

Seward was the president's most trusted advisor and Chase led the Radicals to believe that it was Seward who had been responsible for Lincoln's retention of McClellan, his refusal to accept full emancipation as a war goal, and for the party's recent loss at the mid-term elections. To neutralize Seward's influence on the president, the thirty-one Republican Senators caucused for two days in mid-December resulting in a proposed resolution calling for Seward's removal from the Cabinet. Fearing a feud between Congress and the president which would hinder their cause the senators reworded their resolution to read a "reconstruction of the Cabinet." This was again amended due to fears that Chase would then be removed. A final resolution for a "partial reconstruction of the Cabinet" was finally passed with only one dissenting vote. A nine member committee was selected to act as representatives of the people and they planned to call on Lincoln with their demands. The Radicals had no idea that Lincoln would be ready for them. Although the caucus was to remain secret, Senator Preston King had informed Seward of the conspiracy. Seward in turn immediately wrote out his resignation and had King deliver it to Lincoln when he went to apprise the president of the situation.

Lincoln met with the committee at the White House on the evening of December 18. Over the course of three hours, Lincoln allowed the committee members to air their grievances. They were concerned that the Cabinet did not jointly endorse the principles and policies regarding the current state of affairs in regards to the national strife. They also criticized Lincoln's choices of military leaders, specifically McClellan, Buell, and Halleck, who had not conducted the war as efficiently as generals like Fremont and Hunter would have. The members continued, telling Lincoln that, while he had the full support and confidence of the Senate, they felt that Seward was detrimental to the war efforts. They believed Lincoln, acting on bad advice from Seward, had failed to pursue the war in a vigorous manner. The Senators continued that the army was led by pro-slavery men who were sympathetic to the South and it was unfortunate that officers such as Fremont and Hunter had to experience the disgrace of being relieved. The conversation remained free and casual as Lincoln politely listened. At the close of the meeting, Lincoln promised to give careful consideration to their concerns.

The next morning Lincoln called for a secret meeting of his Cabinet to inform them of Seward's resignation letter and what had transpired the night before. Chase was obviously shaken as Lincoln informed each of his advisors that he needed them. After assurance from each member that they would support him, Lincoln proposed a joint meeting with the Committee of Nine that evening.

That night the senators called upon Lincoln at the White House and were surprised to find the entire Cabinet except Seward waiting for them. Lincoln opened the meeting defending each member of his Cabinet and, while acknowledging that time restraint kept Cabinet members from attending every meeting, they never-the-less were unified in the full prosecution of the war. One by one, Cabinet members spoke up in support of Lincoln's assertions that the Cabinet stood in unison once a decision was made. Even a nervous Chase had gotten up in support of Seward. Lincoln then put the senators on the spot, asking each of them to list the merits or demerits of each of the Cabinet members. Fessenden objected, stating this should not be done in their presence. After nearly five hours, five of the nine had reversed their position regarding Seward's removal. Lincoln's victory was nearly complete.

The next morning Lincoln sent for Chase. They had both been deeply affected by the meeting the night before so when Chase arrived it was no surprise that he offered Lincoln his resignation. Lincoln's eyes lit up. He took the envelope, opened it and read it quickly. Stanton, who was also present, offered to submit his as well. Lincoln, knowing he now had the upper hand, declined it. If the Radicals insisted on Lincoln accepting Seward's resignation then, Lincoln rationalized, he would also have to accept Chase's as well, much to the displeasure of the Radicals. Lincoln decided that, since both these men were very good at their jobs, he would keep them both. The Cabinet Crises had passed.

Although discouraged, the Radicals tried one more, last-ditch effort to take control of the war. This time, Stanton took the lead and enlisted head of transportation General Herman Haupt, to try and convince Lincoln of a plan to form a military council consisting of Stanton, Halleck, McClellan, and McDowell. Together, they would share responsibility for military planning and shaping war policies. Lincoln listened politely as Haupt pitched his proposal, explaining that, while the nation still had faith in him, recruitment would suffer and the army would lose its effectiveness in the field unless Lincoln adopted a more radical stance. Like many others, this scheme had failed as well. Lincoln saw through the ruse and the proposed military council was not to be.

The Radicals' attempt at usurping Lincoln's powers again illustrated that their priorities were not in the best interest of the country. The time wasted in conspiring for control of the war and its policies could have been better spent in a full prosecution of the war itself.

As 1862 drew to a close, the Radicals were depressed. By outfoxing them on their latest scheme to control the Cabinet, Lincoln had retained executive power to conduct the war. He also balked at embracing full emancipation. His Emancipation Proclamation was too soft a policy. To the Conservatives, it was a foolhardy plan and the Democrats well they just plain didn't like it. Lincoln had risked his all-party administration on this edict and no one was happy with it. The Radicals did finally rid themselves of McClellan, only to be disappointed by Pope and Burnside. They had lost their favorite son Fremont to a West Pointer while the radical Butler was relieved of the Gulf Department in December and replaced by General Banks. The war in the East was a dismal failure while in the West Grant was meeting up with his own setbacks trying to take Vicksburg. Sherman had suffered a defeat at Chickasaw Bluff and the only thing to halt the plummeting morale was Rosecrans costly victory at Stones River. All at an alarming cost.

The Radicals did experience some victories however. In early 1862, they had stopped the enforcement of the Fugitive Slave Act, passed three confiscation acts with a militia act, and were able to rid the District of Columbia of slavery through compensation. They were also able to establish a joint committee to rid the army of pro-slavery officers. The Republicans managed to retain the majority after the election but the lack of a sweeping victory was disappointing. On December 1, in his latest message Congress, Lincoln proposed a compensated emancipation in every state where slavery existed if done by January 1 and Lincoln even proposed colonization. But the Radicals still did not trust Lincoln and they threatened to block spending on the war effort should he try to renege on the proclamation come January 1.

But the defeat at Fredericksburg had demoralized the soldiers of the Army of the Potomac even further. With warehouses bursting with supplies, the men suffered from poor rations, sickness and lack of medical care. Desertion rate had soared to 200 a day. They felt betrayed by their government and generals and lost all confidence in them. There was an intense lack of discipline and as one officer described it, "It was the Valley Forge of the war." Depression permeated the army camped at Falmouth as severe bitterness now existed towards Burnside. Radicals feared that Lincoln would again call upon McClellan to resume command of the once-mighty Army of the Potomac.

The Radicals' hope for the full destruction of slavery before the war's end rested in part upon the eradication of conservative generals. And the removal of West Point influence upon the army was the key. They believed the academy was only good for making engineers and drill sergeants. The notion that war should be fought by strategy, with precious time spent on preparation and drilling was preposterous. Fortifications and defensive strategy was a sign of cowardice, they proclaimed, and would not win this war. The previous December, the Radicals had opposed the appropriation bill for the academy, claiming it to be a southern institution and breeding ground for disloyalty, but the bill passed 29-10. But now the Radicals were about to embark on a savage operation in which smear campaigns, court-martials, and congressional denunciations. The great purge of West Point generals was on.

Chapter 9

The Purge

In order to eliminate their reliance on foreign instructors in the art of engineering and artillery, President Thomas Jefferson established a military academy on West Point on the Hudson River in 1802. In its infancy, there was no age limit or determined length of study required in its crude curriculum. When Sylvanus Thayer became the superintendent in 1817, he introduced a new curriculum which stabilized and brought structure to the teachings at the institution. Cadets were now held to a higher standard and followed a strict regimen of study and discipline. As a result, only the serious applied. Administrators stressed a system of order and obedience; and instilled in the cadets loyalty, pride, and prestige. By isolating cadets from civilian politics, the national image of the institution and its cadets were elevated to a higher standard.

Officers and cadets shunned politicians who they perceived as shifty and compromising; and promoting only their special interests and policies over national security. For the academy the principle responsibility of the military was to the nation and not a political party. However, the Democratic Party had dominated the political scene for a majority of the young country's existence so it was only natural that the products of the academy gravitated toward this party and resisted the emergence of secular factions promoting anti-slavery views which the Republican Party was now engaged in.

In January, Radicals in the Senate launched a great assault against the institution claiming the art of building fortifications and the use defensive strategies was not the way to win wars. Even Senator Trumbull denounced the professionally-trained soldier and declared that the war would be won by the citizen soldier. He demanded that every man who knew how to build a fortification should be dismissed and replaced with men who possessed indomitable spirit. Wade estimated that one half of the Regular officers were inept and disloyal; not all traitors, he claimed, had joined the confederacy in 1861. The German-born Radical General Carl Schurz even blamed the results of the last election on West Point Democratic generals.

As long as this institution continued filling the ranks of the higher echelon of the military then victory could never be had. According to the Radicals who conveniently forgot that Lincoln had just set established a national cemetery in July that year for the growing number of Union dead, the army was full of volunteer soldiers who just wanted a chance to fight. But, since the Radicals were unable to take down the military institution by defunding it then they would unleash the powers of the CCW upon the products of that evil institution. They were resolved to send a message to all high-ranking West Point officers; conform or else!

The investigation of Fitz-John Porter, who had been arrested in November of 1862 for his part in the Second Bull Run defeat, was immediately reopened and a court martial ensued. Suspicions had been raised when he vocalized criticism of Lincoln and Pope; the latter of whom he made indiscreet comments about in official correspondences. To ensure the outcome, Stanton had hand-selected the court officers. General David Hunter was appointed president while Generals Rufus King, Benjamin Prentiss and James Ricketts, all of whom had suffered battlefield humiliations, served on the prosecution. Representative General James Garfield, and Generals Ethan Hitchcock, Silas Casey, and Napoleon B. Buford all nursing grudges against the McClellan clique, were also on the board. The Judge Advocate General Joseph Holt, who would later indict Mary Surratt, was the prosecutor.

The court-martial became a very public affair and resembled more of a circus than an official military proceeding. Even though he had been very vocal in his opposition to political policies, it was plain to see that Porter was being railroaded. Both political parties were represented by their respective press which wrote biased articles in an effort to taint public opinion of the proceedings. In the end Porter was convicted of disobedience to orders and misconduct in front of the enemy. He was dismissed from service and would never be allowed a retrial as long as Senator Chandler remained in office.

Buell was next. Wanting to be cleared of the charges of inefficiency, he had requested a Court of Inquiry regarding his dismissal. This was denied by Stanton but the secretary did however grant the general a "military commission," a polite term for a court-martial. The Radicals' baseless fear of Buell's influence in the Western army was unwarranted but they wanted to prevent any chance for his return to command. Although there were no official charges, prosecutor Don Piatt saw to it that, by his line of questioning, witnesses and reports, Buell's military record had been effectively tarnished. With his loyalty was now in question, any chance of Buell receiving another command was highly doubtful. For a year and a half his career was spent in limbo. When he declined Grant's offer of a command serving under Sherman or Edward Canby, both of whom he outranked, Grant called this "...the worst excuse a soldier can make for declining service." Buell left the military service on May 23, 1864.

Even McDowell, a former radical favorite, had lost favor with the Radicals. In June the previous summer, the *Tribune* had published a letter written by a soldier accusing the commander of ordering the protection of homes and property of secessionists. The letter also claimed that Confederate prisoners enjoyed much better food and lodging than what the Union soldiers were receiving. McDowell was also being scrutinized for his poor performance at the first battle of Bull Run. General Abner Doubleday was a damaging witness but what saved McDowell was his willingness to testify against Porter. After a two year hiatus, McDowell was transferred to the Department of California where he served as its commander.

Perhaps bolstered by their success, the committee decided that McClellan, who was now unofficially on the campaign trail, could somehow be found directly responsible for the Ball's Bluff disaster. Stone was called before the committee one last time on February 27, 1863. To his surprise, Stone discovered that since their last meeting, the inquisitors appeared to have developed something of a conscience for they were very civil and the interview was almost cordial. This time they allowed Stone to see a copy of the charges and he was able to answer each one specifically. Stone was officially acquitted but there would be neither public vindication nor promise of command. The government would not publically admit to any wrongdoing. His quiet release would have to suffice. After months of badgering, Stone was finally assigned as Banks' chief of staff in the Gulf Department in May of 1863.

Reacting to new developments regarding Burnside's command, the committee decided to reopen its investigation into Fredericksburg. After the defeat, Burnside had wavered between either resigning his command or plan another advance. Ignoring the open criticism of his soldiers and officers, Burnside opted for the latter, proposing to cross the river once again and smashing headlong into Lee's army. Holding a council of war his three Grand Division commanders Franklin, Sumner, and Hooker, had raised serious objections fearing a repeat of Fredericksburg. Undaunted, Burnside continued planning out his strategy. In a serious breach of military etiquette on December 20, Generals Franklin and W.F. Smith secretly notified Lincoln by telegram of the proposed movement; attached to the message was a counter plan of their own. Lincoln orders Halleck to travel to Falmouth and scout out prospective crossings for the army. Halleck, resenting tone of the order and the idea that he should take to the field to do the jobs of his subordinates, grudgingly obeyed.

Then, on December 30, two officers under Franklin's command, Generals John Newton and John Cochrane, had stolen away to Washington to inform the members of the CCW that the army and officers had lost confidence in Burnside and he should be removed. When no committee members could be found the two decided to search out Lincoln. Convinced that these officers had no ulterior motives for their mission (intrigue amongst his officers was now the norm) Lincoln immediately telegraphed Burnside with instructions not to make a move until it was approved by him. On January 1 Burnside cancelled the movement and met with Lincoln to explain his plan.

Still skeptical, Lincoln sent for Halleck and Stanton to join the conference. While they waited Burnside, aware of the secret visitors but not their identities offered to be relieved based on the fact that he had lost the confidence of his senior commanders. He also informed Lincoln that Halleck and Stanton had also lost the confidence of the army and they too should be removed. Lincoln said he would take it under advisement.

The two day conference bore no results and Burnside returned to Falmouth still intending to cross the Rappahannock. But now, he wanted a direct order from Washington to do so. On January 5, Burnside wrote to Halleck seeking general direction in which to make his advance. Halleck, still seething from Lincoln's order responded by accusing Burnside of evading responsibility. He then ordered that Burnside should affect a crossing at some place, at some time, with part or all of his army and should do so only if on favorable terms. Incredibly Lincoln, who had come into his own militarily, endorsed the letter but he also added that Burnside should understand that the government was not pushing him.

Word of Cochrane and Newton's visit had been leaked to the press and the public was now aware of the army's lack of trust in Burnside's. Accounts of dissention within the ranks of the Army of the Potomac were now being published in the press. Hooker, seeing his chance to capitalize on the situation, seized the opportunity by telling the press that a new regime was needed and would prevail if he were in command.

Incensed at all that was happening, Burnside was determined more than ever to redeem himself by making another advance against the advice of his subordinates. The plan was simple; cross the Rappahannock and assault Lee's left flank in an attempt to draw the confederates out into the open. Franklin had so opposed the movement that he complained loud enough that General Charles Wainwright recorded in his diary that Franklin "...talked so much and so loudly that he has completely demoralized his whole command and so rendered failure doubly sure." After several days were wasted due to delays the army moved out on January 20. That night the rains began to fall. For two days the men fought to advance their wagons and artillery pulled by triple-teamed horses only to be mired in the deepening mud. On the other side of the river the rebels heckled and taunted their adversaries' slow, painful movements and held up signs saying "This way to Richmond."

After two days a humiliated Burnside called off the march. Furious with Franklin, Hooker and several others officers for their open criticism of him and his plans during the march, Burnside drew up orders dismissing Hooker, W.T.H. Brooks, Newton, and Cochrane from service. He also relieved Franklin and W. S. Smith of command. Lincoln intervened however, stating Burnside did not have the authority for such action.

Burnside had had enough and on January 24 he once again turned in his resignation. The ever gracious Lincoln, not wanting Burnside to give up his commission, would not accept it. We need you, he told the general. A conference was held the next day between Lincoln, Halleck, Stanton, and Burnside and it was decided that the commander would be relieved of his own volition and reassigned. Hooker would finally be rewarded for his efforts; command of the Army of the Potomac.

When the CCW had heard that Franklin had dispatched subordinates to Washington to undermine Burnside's plans, they saw their chance. They believed the conspiracy was meant to have McClellan reinstated and the Radicals could not take the chance of this happening. Immediately, the investigation of Fredericksburg was reopened. No time was wasted as all those who had testified previously were recalled and fully scrutinized with the exception of Hooker, of course.

When Burnside reappeared before the committee on February 7, he was a new man with radical ideas. He was now an outspoken opponent of the South and slavery; he even suggested to Senator Julian that the Northern soldiers and the people must be taught to hate the people of the South and their institutions. As for the battle, his story also changed drastically. He withdrew his earlier statement that Franklin failed to carry the left due to superior enemy strength and now blamed Franklin for not acting with alacrity. He delayed, Burnside claimed, until the chance for victory had passed. After Burnside told the committee of Franklin's intrigue before and during the mud march, Cochrane and Newton were interviewed next. It was obvious what the conclusion would be. Franklin, who was behind their covert mission to Washington, had wanted Burnside to fail. Cochrane had defended Franklin with a flurry of letters written to the committee. That evening after his session with the committee, the members hailed Burnside as a conquering hero and escorted him to the homes of members of Congress where he was affectionately received.

On March 16, Meade, whose division was the smallest under Franklin's command and had attacked the Confederate right, was called before the committee. He testified that he could have carried the right if properly supported. Franklin testified next, telling the committee his orders were to attack with one division and prepare to pursue the enemy to Richmond. (His actual orders were to attack with no less than one division.) In regards to Burnside's order to attack with an entire command if possible on the afternoon of December 13, Franklin stated that it was more of a request. Since the attack had already begun he sent word back to Burnside that it was not possible.

In their initial report on Fredericksburg, the CCW reserved any comments but now a drastic revision was published. The CCW now censured Franklin and charged that he willfully disobeyed orders for failing to support Meade's division in the attack and that he attacked with the smallest division available. Franklin, who had graduated first in his class, was relieved of command and transferred to an obscure post in the West.

Burnside, whose transformation was complete, was now of course, absolved of any wrongdoing for Fredericksburg. He would be appointed commander of the Department of Ohio and his headquarters would be in Cincinnati. In response to rising Copperhead activities in that part of the country, Burnside issued General Order No. 38 which stated treason would not be tolerated. The order was supported by Lincoln's previous suspension of writ of habeas corpus of September 1862. On May 5, 1863, his soldiers arrested the Copperhead Vallandigham for a treasonous speech he had made. The arrest resulted in his banishment to the confederacy.

The committee had perfected their trade and the purge produced the desired results. Commanders quickly realized that, regardless of military success or not, they either adopt the radical platform or incur the wrath of the CCW. Any commander who practiced or condoned behavior which could be construed as sympathetic to the South would suffer the consequences. Many commanders bent to the pressure and now fell into line with the Radicals' way of thinking.

But the optimism of the Radicals was a bit premature. After Fredericksburg the Copperheads became more vocal in their call for a truce and peace on terms sympathetic to the South. The Democratic press demanded the return of McClellan while hometown editors received and published letters denouncing emancipation and the government from angry officers and soldiers. Newspapers even instructed the soldiers not to fight for emancipation. Democratic peace clubs sprouted up in the North and especially in the Northwest. The lower house of the Illinois legislature even passed a resolution calling for an end to hostilities and a truce. Rumors were circulating that the soldiers would not fight for anyone else but McClellan. Indiana had tried this but Governor Morton convinced Republicans not to sit in during legislation thus denying its state senate a quorum to vote on whether to withdraw troops from the war.

All the while, the Democrats had sent McClellan off on the campaign trail throughout the New England states where he was received as a hero. He met with Democratic leaders at receptions and events of the major cities, to which many of the local, high-ranking leaders of the radical factions were excluded. His speeches were flavored with marked partisanship. McClellan's popularity grew as he flaunted himself a high-minded general and a genius whose carefully laid plans were sabotaged by the radical faction. The New York legislature even passed a resolution commending his military record as commander of the Army of the Potomac.

With McClellan's growing popularity on the campaign trail, the Radicals were once again nervous. They needed to undermine his campaign; to exploit his military failures and his sympathetic, conciliatory attitude towards the secessionists. Now was the time to resume their case against McClellan. Although, not all who testified at McClellan's previous hearing were against him, many of his commanders were. Generals Heintzelman, Sumner, John G. Barnard, Hooker and Silas Casey, all critical of McClellan were all willing to point out the general's shortcomings.

McClellan had been called once again before the committee on February 28. The meeting was cordial yet the questioning was thorough. He brought with him the requested written testimony which would later be compared with the testimony of the other witnesses. Of course, nearly every material detail was contradictory to McClellan's twenty-page report. While waiting for his next session with the CCW, McClellan took the time to write his wife, telling her that he had many bitter enemies who were preparing to mount their last grand attack. On March 2, McClellan was recalled for a second hearing and this time he was met with hostility. Gooch's line of questioning was more like accusations being hurled in McClellan's direction.

The investigation continued into March as more hostile witnesses testified; Hooker of course, did not disappoint the committee. In answer to why the Peninsula Campaign was a failure, Hooker responded it was due to want of generalship on the part of the commander. Hooker even proclaimed that, rather than stage a siege at Yorktown, he would have marched his army through the redoubts and into Richmond in two days.

Heintzelman criticized McClellan for laying siege at Yorktown and not pursuing the enemy at Williamsburg. He cited McClellan's failure to counterattack after the battle of Seven Pines on May 31. He also noted the general's absence from the field of battle during the heavy fighting; leaving subordinates to make critical decisions. Heintzelman failed to mention McClellan was bedridden with malaria at the time of the battle. Other reports cited McClellan was back of the lines with the engineers strengthening fall back positions. Haupt contended troops landed at Alexandria had plenty of time to make the march to Pope but instead, waited on transportation via the railroad. Sumner criticized McClellan's leadership at Antietam stating he committed his troops in piecemeal fashion. Burnside also blasted McClellan for refusing him troops at Antietam even though Fitz-John Porter had 15-20,000 troops who had not yet seen action.

As the secret hearing continued rumors were being conveniently leaked to the press and making headlines in an attempt to stir public interests. Near the end of the investigation Wade, knowing the strength of good propaganda, increased the leaks to the press as he announced that the committee would issue its report in a matter of days. The radical press proclaimed McClellan and others were set to be taken down while rumors asserted Lincoln or possibly Seward was taking action to suppress parts of the report. All the while, the Copperheads were accusing Wade of whetting the appetite of the public in an effort to taint their opinion of McClellan.

As April 1 quickly approached, workers in the government printing office toiled day and night, preparing the first of the three-volume report to be ready for publication. Three days later the *Washington Chronicles* printed the report and bales of the papers were sent to Hooker's army stationed at Falmouth. Wade made sure copies of the first volume were sent to the *Associated Press* and metropolitan papers.

Almost the entire 60-page report covered the history of the Army of the Potomac from its inception until Antietam. The opening lines of the report took a stab at Lincoln; claiming he alone was responsible for the failures of the Army of the Potomac thus, absolving Congress of any wrongdoing in conducting the war. They also blamed the Army of the Potomac itself for not crushing the rebellion and claimed that it neutralized, if not entirely destroyed all that was won by the victorious armies in the West.

The report, subtle with hints of disloyalty throughout, then settled into McClellan's botched handling of the Army of the Potomac during his tenure as its commander. It highlighted his refusal to advance in the fall of 1861, his opposition to the reorganization of his command into corps, his covert planning, his plans of the Peninsula Campaign, leaving Washington unsecure, sabotaging Pope and his failure to apprehend Lee after Antietam. Not every instance was a fault of McClellan but the CCW conveniently omitted these facts from their report. The report also took a stab at West Point and its theory of winning wars by strategy.

One small section absolved Burnside for Fredericksburg and placed the blame on Franklin who refused to attack with his full force. The committee also took another stab at Lincoln for hosting the informers and meddling into Burnside's planning.

The Radicals, believing their attack would rejuvenate public opinion that the war must be seen to the end, now promised 1863 would be a year of victory. They expressed a new hope to the people that Hooker would be the general to lead the faltering Army of the Potomac to victory and a successful conclusion of the war. Their satisfaction with the results of their attack on McClellan, West Point, and the administration would be short-lived however. Weeks later the committee released its massive testimony from which the report was written and the Democrats immediately saw their chance to undermine the work of the CCW.

After studying the testimony, the Democrats recognize the biased report complete with inconsistencies and errors, for what it was; merely a piece of propaganda. Not only did it attack McClellan but its attack upon Lincoln and the administration was now their excuse as to why Lincoln and his party should not be considered to lead the country after the 1864 election. If Lincoln did interfere with military planning and was at fault for the state of demoralization of the army as the testimony stated then surely, he should not expect to be reelected.

On April 9, the remaining two volumes which focused on Fremont, Stone and First Bull Run were released. These reports were somewhat anticlimactic and did not provoke public reaction as the first report had. What did provoke public reaction was the War Department's General Order No. 143. On May 22, the Bureau of Colored Troops was created. This was nothing new to this country, for blacks had served in the Revolutionary War and the War of 1812. But recruitment, in response to

Lincoln's Emancipation Proclamation had been slow. Enlistment soon picked up thanks to the effort of Frederick Douglass. Thousands of blacks now rushed to enlist into the Federal ranks known as United States Colored Troops (USCT) and state militias. They served mostly under white officers and were given substandard supplies and rations for less pay. At first, many of their duties were restricted to noncombat roles such as carpenters, chaplains, guards, laborers, nurses, scouts, spies, cooks, teamsters, laundry, and sappers; all important functions needed to sustain an army. But soon they were serving in infantry and artillery units. Reviews in the North differed but many believed that, due to recent losses, the Union was in dire need of more troops and the inclusion of black soldiers could supplement the ranks.

Chapter 10

Propaganda

Lincoln didn't like Hooker who was a schemer, self-promoter, and highly critical of his superiors. Hooker's continued intrigue had finally paid off in the form of gaining the command of the Army of the Potomac and the conniving commander boldly stated that nothing would be right until a dictatorship was set up. Lincoln was not appreciative of the challenge and quickly informed the cocky officer that only victorious generals could set up dictatorships and he was willing to risk it. The Radicals however were overjoyed and fully endorsed Hooker as the general who would finally be the one to oust the disloyal generals and carry the fight to the enemy. "May God have mercy on General Lee," he announced, "for I will have none."

In a matter of weeks a transformation of the Army of the Potomac had taken place. Improvements in rations, camp cooks, sanitary conditions, the quartermaster system, hospital reforms, and the furlough system helped to increase the morale within the ranks. This led to a drop in the desertion rate. Of course, an increase in court-martials also curtailed the desertion rate but not as much as Lincoln's March 10 amnesty proclamation to all deserters who returned to duty. Hooker did away with Burnside's Grand Division system and brought back the corps structure. To aid in morale and *esprit de corps* he also introduced insignia corps badges. The scattered cavalry, which the War Department had shunned since the beginning of the war, was now organized into one corps and placed under Brigadier General George Stoneman. Artillery battalions now fell under control of the infantry division commanders. Reminded of the recurring slip-up of previous commanders Lincoln offers Hooker prophetic advice, "In your next fight, put in all your men." Unfortunately, these words will go unheeded.

Hooker had talked rather boldly regarding Lee and now it was time to live up to his words. About to lose 23,000 volunteers whose nine month and two year terms were about to expire, Hooker devised a plan that had an excellent chance of success. Outnumbering Lee 130,000 to 60,000, Hooker took his army across the Rappahannock above Fredericksburg to meet Lee head on. But Hooker reportedly had a fondness for the bottle which the Radicals conveniently overlooked. At the start of the campaign however he had sworn off the booze which was probably not a good idea for, after making a successful river crossing, Hooker suddenly lost his nerve. Paralyzed by indecision, Hooker abruptly fell back to a defensive position at Chancellorsville. Lee made another of his daring moves, splitting his forces again and sending Jackson around the Union right. Every sign of Jackson's flanking movement was ignored until the rebels smashed into General O.O. Howard's division, rolling up his flank while Lee attacked Hooker's front. As his large army was being pushed back by the two smaller forces, an enemy artillery round struck the pillar of the house Hooker used as his headquarters. Struck on the head by a part of the column, Hooker gave the order to retreat before passing out.

On May 3, the battle of Chancellorsville was fought and lost and Fighting Joe Hooker blamed his defeat on Halleck and the McClellan clique as the Democrats again clamor for McClellan. Oddly, the Radicals remain silent; there was no cry for an investigation into the disaster as when a conservative general had lost a battle.

Although the committee refused to conduct an official investigation, possibly afraid of what they would learn, Wade and Chandler did travel to Falmouth to visit with Hooker and his corps commanders. When some of the corps commanders began denouncing Hooker, Wade and Chandler ignored them. When the visit was over, the two returned to Washington loudly boasting of the fine condition of the army which was waiting to be led to victory by Hooker. But Lincoln wasn't convinced. Hearing of the discontent of Hooker's subordinates the president decided to interview them personally. After assessing the situation Lincoln wrote to Hooker, warning the general that he had lost the confidence of his senior commanders which, Lincoln continued, could be ruinous to him.

Meanwhile, Lee decided another invasion of the North was needed. He reasoned he could take pressure off of Richmond and the garrison at Vicksburg which Grant had under siege, while at the same time threatening Washington, Baltimore and other vital cities in the North. By bringing the fighting north it was possible that a faction of the North would continue to push for peace negotiations.

Simultaneously Confederate cavalry commander General John Morgan, against the wishes of Lee, would lead a 2,500 confederate cavalry into Indiana and Ohio in an attempt to relieve pressure off of Lee invasion and to demoralize the North. But they soon discovered that the North was not as demoralized as they had hoped. Although heralded as somewhat successful, the *Great Raid* produced high casualties and the capture of Morgan and his remaining handful of cavalrymen.

Lee had planned to forage off the lush Pennsylvania countryside and the generosity of the locals but he was hit with a drastic realization when he crossed the border. His invasion had caused the North to band together. As Lee moved throughout the state his army demanded tributes from local communities and availed themselves to their foods and livestock. Northerners became furious as the rebels "recaptured" blacks and sent them south. Lee's invasion had instilled in the northern population a renewed hatred for the South.

Hooker became anxious. Chancellorsville had unnerved the braggart and rather than meet Lee head on Hooker proposed to cross the Rappahannock, attack the rear of Lee's column and then take Richmond. It would appear Hooker would forsake the head of the snake and instead attack the tail.

Lincoln and Halleck both saw the folly in this. As Lincoln puts it, he does not want Hooker's army half across the river "like an ox jumped half over a fence, and liable to be torn by dogs, front and rear, without the ability to gore one way or kick the other." Lincoln tells Hooker he must stay between Lee and Washington. When Hooker protested Lincoln again explained it was Lee's army and not Richmond that was the goal.

Hooker begrudgingly kept between Lee and Washington but as he as neared the capital he began to believe he was outnumbered and called for more troops from Washington. Animosity had existed between the Halleck and Hooker from back in their California days so when Halleck informed no troops could be spared Hooker complained to Lincoln that he had lost the confidence of Halleck. When Halleck refused Hooker's request to withdraw the troops at Harpers Ferry, Hooker saw his chance to get out of facing Lee again and asked to be relieved.

On June 28, orders were prepared. A staff officer quickly travelled to Frederick where he found Meade half-dressed and asleep on his cot. When Meade was awakened, the officer informed the general he had bad news, that he has been relieved as corps commander. Strangely, Meade said he was not surprised and was half expecting it. Quickly, the staff officer told Meade of his promotion to commander of the Army of the Potomac. Meade expressed no jubilation.

The first thing Meade did was withdraw the garrison at Harper's Ferry which Halleck denied Hooker and called them to Frederick where he was consolidating his forces.

Meade was a West Point Democrat with no political ambitions. Prior to the war he had served as an Engineer and had never commanded troops until he was 46. He was stern, disciplined and possessed a solid reputation for handling troops. And now the Army of the Potomac was dropped into his lap. Lincoln gave Meade great latitude to move his army as he saw fit as long as he was clear that his army was a covering force for Washington and a striking force against the enemy. He was to maneuver his army in such a way as to achieve both.

But Lincoln was troubled by Meade's decision for a defensive strategy while Lee's army extended far and wide across Pennsylvania. Meade decision was sound however, correctly reasoning that Lee was not on friendly ground and with the North to his back, Lee had no choice but to try and break Meade's lines and return to safer grounds. Meade had first thought of entrenching at Pipe Creek just south of the Pennsylvania border but General John F. Reynolds alerted him to the fact that the grounds around Gettysburg was a more desirable piece of real estate to defend. Unlike his predecessors Meade listened to the advice of his subordinates and ordered his army forward.

Lee was also aware of Gettysburg's strategic location and immediately decided to occupy it. What would follow many will say later, was the turning point of the war. As a former Engineer, Meade could well read the topography of the surrounding countryside. His use of the grounds and West Point tactic of defense which the Radicals had so openly detested was textbook perfect. Knowing his enemy, Meade held the high ground and waited for the impending attack.

For the next three days 150,000 Union and Confederate soldiers would do bloody battle in and around that little town. The first day, July

1, saw heavy fighting as Lee's armies pushed the Union army through town to the high ground. He then probed the Union lines looking for weaknesses. The next day he attempted to break the Union left and failed. On the third day, Lee ordered a massive assault on the Union center in a futile attempt to break their lines but was repulsed and forced to fall back. On July 4, both armies were spent and as they rested the storm clouds gathered.

Meade was hailed a hero after Gettysburg, but it was short-lived however when Lee managed to slip back into Virginia. To be fair, Meade did follow Lee until July 11 when he came to within striking distance of the rebel army. The anxiety of the previous two weeks had taken its toll. Meade decided to hold a Council of War regarding an attack on July 13. Five out six corps commanders advised against the attack. The next day, Meade discovered that Lee had managed to cross the swollen Potomac.

The Radicals refused Meade accolades for the victory. To do so would only undermine their point that West Point officers could not make successful commanders. By allowing Lee to escape, Meade had unknowingly handed the Radicals the excuse they needed to build their case against him. Rumors were now beginning to circulate that the battle had been won by his Republican corps commanders.

Meanwhile in the West, another general continued to make a name for himself. By the spring of '63, Grant had changed his views on the war. He now believed that the rebellion could only be put down by the full subjugation of the South. With that in mind, he made plans to take Vicksburg and Port Hudson; the last two holdouts on the Mississippi. After several failed attempts, Grant set off on a campaign to take the high ground behind Vicksburg. In less than two weeks Grant had crossed the Mississippi, marched one hundred and eighty miles while inflicting heavy casualties upon the rebels. His forces captured artillery pieces along the way while destroying arsenals and military factories. Finally, Grant was in a position to where he decided to settle in for a siege and on July 4, Vicksburg was surrendered, which allowed Banks to take Port Hudson. With the fall of these two strongholds, Union forces now controlled the Mississippi River, effectively dividing the confederate armies in the east from those in the west. Except for one port in North Carolina, the Anaconda Plan which Scott had advocated two years previously was now in effect.

The fall of Vicksburg and the victory at Gettysburg had a tremendous impact on the morale in the North but the Radicals are despondent; they were not ready for a cessation in hostilities as long as slavery still existed. If the South were to quit the fight then surely they believed, Lincoln would allow slave owners to retain their slaves not yet freed. Charles Sumner wrote victories are more dangerous now than defeats and asserted more delay and suffering would be needed to assure the prospect of full emancipation. As some of the Radicals believed that the war behind the lines in Washington must continue other Radicals were becoming a bit more optimistic. They saw a slight transformation in Lincoln and are beginning to believe that the president will hold firm his stance on emancipation.

In late August, Lincoln reinforced that opinion when he declined an invitation to a meeting held in his hometown of Springfield hosted by men opposed to emancipation. In an open letter published in the papers, Lincoln rebuked those opposed to emancipation; writing that men who supported the cause for reunification must also support emancipation, for it was the only way to crush the rebellion. Lincoln promised never to revoke any part of his proclamation.

In September of '63 Lincoln went one step further by suspending the writ *habeas corpus* in certain Northern States. He was applauded for doing so by the Radicals and other abolitionists such as Henry Ward Beecher, for they knew that this act would mean trouble for the Copperheads in the upcoming election. But now, the Conservatives think Lincoln was becoming too radical in his ideas while many of the Radicals are still apprehensive of the notable change coming over the president. They know however, that they have gained a strong foothold on the administration as they plan for the upcoming election and reconstruction.

Enfranchising the soldier was not a new idea. During the American Revolution, New York's Committee on Safety permitted soldiers to vote in the gubernatorial election of 1777 but no provision had ever been entered into the state's law books so it could not be enforced for the 1863 mid-term elections. During the War of 1812, Pennsylvania and New Jersey had passed acts to enfranchise their soldiers but in 1820 New Jersey repealed the act, leaving Pennsylvania to be the only state to allow soldier suffrage. In October of 1861, the soldiers from the Keystone state cast their votes from the fields of Virginia but fraud in the election proved to be high when 900 votes from one regiment were casted for a Republican in Philadelphia when less than 70 soldiers of that regiment were from that city. After several contests were challenged, state legislature in Pennsylvania reversed its ruling on soldier suffrage and in May of '62, the soldiers were stripped of the right to absentee voting.

As the fall election approached the Radicals were cautiously confident. In the first year of the war Lincoln had enjoyed bipartisan support and neither party had considered the worth of the soldier's vote. By the second year of the war however, bipartisanship had fallen apart and the Democrats wanted to extend the vote to the soldiers but the Republicans resisted. They claimed that as long as the army was being led by conservative generals the soldiers could not make informed decisions. But an encouraging transformation had been taking place since the beginning of the struggle. The army was steadily coming under radical control and military success throughout the summer had restored the confidence of the people in the Republican Party. Since the Democrats, who enjoyed a limited success at the polls previously, now planned on placing three Copperheads on the ballots in Ohio, Pennsylvania, and Connecticut, the Republicans now reconsidered army suffrage.

After scanning the results of the 1862 election, Republicans had noticed that closely contested races could have been offset by the votes of the soldiers. On July 1, 1862, there were 186,751 soldiers in the army. By the end of that year the number had reached 527,204 and that number steadily grew. In January of 1863, in a closed-door session, the Republicans debated the idea of enfranchising the soldier through state rather than Federal legislation. Missouri, Iowa, Wisconsin, and Minnesota had already passed legislation allowing their soldiers to vote from the field. Ohio Democrats' attempted to enfranchise their soldiers a year earlier but the Republicans, fearing McClellan's influence had blocked it now they heavily endorsed and passed it. But many still resisted the notion because they believed that McClellan's influence, coupled with his allowance of such newspapers as the *New York Herald* and the *New York World* to circulate freely within the Army of the Potomac while excluding pro-administration newspapers, had turned the army into an anti-Republican machine. To allow the soldier the vote now would mean they might vote for the wrong party. But all that had changed.

In the end, the Republicans supported soldier suffrage and the vote from the field, claiming that it was the republican soldiers who had enlisted to fight the war while the Democrats remained at home and voted. But now the Democrats opposed the soldiers voting from the field, arguing that "...the purity and sanctity of the ballot box" would be threatened due to fraud while collecting the vote from the field. Some Democrats even argued that soldiers gave up their citizenship when they enlisted and had therefore given up their right to vote. But the Republicans insisted however, that it was the soldier, above all others, who deserved the right to vote. And to strip the soldiers of this right would reduce them to the level of Negroes in regards to their civil and political rights. In an attempt to salvage what support they could, the Democrats countered by stating that, since the soldiers were uninformed on the issues and the candidates, then the soldiers should only be allowed to vote at home. So, while the state legislatures battled over the rights to extend suffrage to the soldiers in the field, the Radicals set their eyes on the military. Before any soldier cast their ballot, they would first need to be conditioned and the Radicals resorted to their tried and true tactics of patronage, coercion, and intimidation.

Morale was at an all-time low during the winter of '62-'63. The Fredericksburg disaster, the Mud March, and the Emancipation Proclamation all affected the attitude of the soldiers, making them vulnerable to the anti-war sentiment now sweeping the country. The Copperhead newspapers and letters received from home encouraged soldiers to desert. After January 1, 1863, many regiments were so broken up or decimated by, what the Radicals viewed as disloyalty that they no longer existed. Rosecrans in fact, reported to Halleck that his Army of the Cumberland experienced 40,000 absentees from the roll as of February, 1863. It seemed that Lincoln's emancipation edict was dividing the Union, militarily and on the home front. Soldiers were willing to fight for preservation of the Union but not for emancipation. Soon, officers were resigning while the enlisted soldier chose to desert, feign illness, or produce self-inflicted wound. As one Illinois sergeant put it, "Abe Lincoln has broken his oath and I have a right to break mine."

Just as the CCW was overhauling the higher echelon, the lower ranks would need adjusted as well. Officers were no longer allowed to simply resign but were now summarily tried with or without a court-martial and dismissed from service and it was the same for enlisted men as well. Even Sherman, who opposed emancipation and enlistment of Negroes, knew the army could not afford dissention within its rank. He preferred public punishment rather than simply allowing officers to resign. From October, 1862 until February of 1863 saw the highest desertion rate of the war. Court-martials for desertion had peaked between January and March of '63 and punishment included fine, public reprimand, imprisonment, being drummed out of service, and even execution.

The "right of free discussion" no longer applied as Articles of War prohibited soldiers from criticizing the president or the policies of the administration, speaking out against the enlistment of the Negro soldier, uttering pro-Southern sentiments or anything which could be construed as inciting mutiny. Stanton had sent General Lorenzo Thomas to address soldiers in Kentucky that the policies of the administration must be carried out and that an officer's rank could protect him if he opposed it. In February of '63 Grant, now embracing the radical platform even set up a board of examiners near Vicksburg to rid the Army of the Tennessee of disloyal officers. Head of the board, Colonel Thomas W. Bennet boasted, "We will give the army a good purge and a healthy puke of all Copperheads." Even McClellan early in the war had believed that the role of the soldier was to obey orders and not question policy. In General Order No. 163 he urged his soldiers to obey the policies but oppose them at the ballot box.

Bullying was another tactic used. In the interest of self-preservation, regimental officers on orders from the higher echelon began issuing political resolutions, condemning anti-war sentiments while pledging acceptance of governmental policies. Either by a show of hands or yea/nay vote, commanders could identify those opposed to emancipation. Those who did not raise their hand in support of these resolutions could face intimidation, arrest for disloyalty, or threats of being placed in the front lines for the next battle. As one Ohio soldier wrote "they would make the service too hot to hold them." It was the officer's goal to proudly proclaim to their hometown papers their command was loyal to the cause.

Republicans also looked to the home front. Early in February, the Radicals in Congress proposed to adopt articles of war which would censor any newspapers which contained objectionable articles to be distributed to the army. Not waiting for congressional consent they halted the circulation of newspapers which could be construed as creating dissent within the ranks. Furthermore, proprietors who violated these articles of war were punished and made to sell their presses. This type of censorship was meant to keep soldiers from becoming aware of the growing discontent among their comrades. Officers and soldiers alike were also encouraged to write their local paper in support of emancipation and the administration while denouncing democratic legislators for claiming the war effort a failure. The term Democrat was now synonymous with Copperhead, traitor, and Southern sympathizer.

There was also the influx of new recruits to consider. One reason for new regiments being raised rather than to supplement existing regiments depleted by attrition was that governors could again dispense patronage by appointing new officers thus garnering more political support. Another reason was that many existing regiments did not want to lose their identity. Most regiments which usually consisted of a thousand soldiers were raised in one locality of a state and had its own character or distinction. As a result, many regiments throughout the war would end up understrength, fielding a few as two hundred men by the end of the war. Sometimes conscriptions would supplement these depleted ranks but new volunteers preferred their own regiment.

Another fact to consider was the battle of Fort Wagner in South Carolina. On July 18, a colored regiment, the 54th Massachusetts fought a brave but futile battle near Charleston Harbor. Although they were defeated many of the white soldiers now looked at the new soldiers with a different view. By this time, thousands of Union soldiers were seeing for the first time the horrors of slavery. They saw first-hand the auction blocs, whipping posts, and the sufferings of the slaves. Now, to hear of blacks fighting and dying for their own caused had changed the mind of many whites. Even if not considered equal, white soldiers appreciated that blacks were now sharing the terrific burden of battle. The scenes they witnessed, coupled with the victories of the summer's campaigns had resolved many a soldier to the fact that full prosecution of the war must continue until victory and with that victory the destruction of slavery.

The Peace Democrats had vehemently opposed the recruitment of blacks. In February, forty-three Democratic Representatives had signed a round robin petition where signatures are in the design of a circle as to hide the leader, condemning the idea. To combat the Copperheads on the home front, Republicans began establishing political clubs. The Republicans had the *National Union League* and the War Democrats established the *Loyal League.*

Stanton also took his turn at swaying public opinion. He knew how to manipulate the public mind as seen by his February of '62 letter praising Grant while slamming McClellan. He had even evoked the Almighty to gain support from the clergy for their Holy Crusade in the letter. Since the Democrats controlled the Associated Press, Stanton had to rely on private organizations and smaller newspapers which he supported financially and sent them official dispatches conveniently edited for content, and to get their message out.

Stanton also turned to the United States Sanitary Commission for assistance. The organization was set up in June of 1861, after First Bull Run, and tasked with seeing to the needs of the hospitals in their care of the wounded. Their responsibilities grew as the war progressed and now Stanton ordered the Sanitary Commission to investigate and write lurid reports of atrocities committed by confederates upon Union prisoners. Employees at the War Department were also encouraged to write letters on behalf of their boss and his party.

The *Loyal Publication Society of New York and the Boston-based New England Loyal Publication Society* supported by the Union Leagues, published material emphasizing Northern stability, Copperhead treachery and morale issues. They also slowly developed an anti-slavery theme.

By suppressing the voices of the opposition among the lower-ranking officers and soldiers within the ranks, the composition of the army appeared to be transforming. Even if they would not accept emancipation the soldiers detested the peace advocates who claimed the war was a failure. And for those who did not accept the policies of the administration, they learned to suppress their views deemed contradictive to the new war goals lest he be labeled a Copperhead; a disgraceful stigma which could lead to court-martial or dismissal. Rather than being driven out of the army, many Democrat and conservative soldiers learned to remain silent; for their resolve to restore the Union remained stronger than their loyalty to party.

As the election neared, Stanton also ensured that enough soldiers voting Republican were furloughed; providing transportation to the states where their legislation had not yet extended the army suffrage to the field. So, while Wade, Chandler and Julian headed to the Northwest to stump for candidates of their party, Stanton informed Fessenden, Hannibal Hamlin and other party leaders that he would furlough enough men to vote in the hotly contested election for governor. Stanton made sure enough Ohio troops were sent home to oust the notorious Copperhead Vallandigham, who Lincoln had banished earlier and was now running his campaign from Canada. Stanton's plan had worked and the soldiers' vote insured pro-Union War Democrat John Brough victory over Vallandigham by a vote of 288,374 to 187,492. Although only thirty per cent of the Ohio soldiers had voted, ninety-five per cent of those votes went to Brough.

Hordes of Pennsylvania troops were also furloughed to help to re-elect Governor Andrew Curtin, the organizer of the Loyal War Governors Conference, over his challenger Democrat George Woodward. The contest was close, 269,506 to 254,171. But there was no doubt the soldiers vote helped to eke out this narrow victory. In Wisconsin Republicans won 14/15 of the soldiers' vote while in Connecticut, Governor William Buckley won reelection over Copperhead Thomas Seymour thanks to furloughed soldiers and an aggressive letter-writing campaign. The election was close but again the soldiers' vote had maintained a Republican victory for that state.

To offset opposition by New York governor Horatio Seymour who vetoed suffrage legislation, Stanton made sure nearly 18,000 troops from western and central New York were furloughed home to vote. Other states which had not passed legislation allowing soldiers to vote from the field; New Jersey, Illinois and Indiana, also saw many of their boys returned home to vote. So many soldiers were sent home in fact that regiments were being depleted. And with these furloughs came acts of violence. Reports were made that Copperheads were attacked and Democratic newspaper offices were wrecked by the furloughed soldiers.

The economy also influenced the election. Although some industries suffered during the first year of the war they had rebounded quickly. In fact, by the summer of 1863 the economy was booming. The export of crops and livestock had doubled due to crop failures in Western Europe. Even with a large portion of their farm labor away in the military the advancement in agricultural technology had allowed women and children to replace those fighting the war. Hundreds of thousands of immigrants were now employed in factories which massed produced necessary items needed to ensure soldiers could continue the fight. The need to improve the infra-structure led to jobs as the now government-controlled railroads carved up the landscape which needed bridges and roads. Shipping routes through canals and rivers also increased the transportation of goods across the North.

The Radicals were jubilant. The soldiers' votes had made the difference! Every state except New Jersey was taken. Even in Pennsylvania where Governor Curtain nearly suffered a defeat, the soldiers had rescued him. It was estimated that ninety-two per cent of the soldiers' vote was for the Republican ticket which made it appear that soldiers and civilians alike were now accepting and endorsing the policies of the administration; even emancipation. With the election safely behind them, the Radicals no longer feared confrontation with Democrats or conservatives; for the public had spoken. The Radicals could now set their sights on conditions for readmission of the conquered states, reconstruction and...Negro suffrage.

Lincoln also viewed the election results as a mandate that the public had accepted the policies of the administration. In his address to Congress in December, he again calmed the fears of the Radicals by reiterating that he would not attempt to retract or modify the Emancipation Proclamation. The relief of the Radicals was short-lived however when they learned Lincoln would not yield his executive powers regarding reconstruction to the growing number of Radicals in his administration. The announcement of his *Ten Per Cent Plan* showed he stood firmly by his plan of reconstruction by executive action.

Although accepted by most conservatives, the Radicals were appalled by the leniency of the plan which basically offered a presidential pardon and amnesty to any rebel, excluding Confederate government officials or leading military officers, who vowed loyalty to the United States. Additionally, when any state in rebellion had ten percent of their registered electorates as of 1860 swear allegiance to the United States; a new state government could be formed and recognized by the Union. Finally, states that returned to pro-Union rule would be encouraged to create policies in dealing with free blacks so long as they were not returned to slavery.

Lincoln rationalized that, since secession was illegal then Southern state governments had been seized by rebels. Since the states were technically not apart from the Union, he maintained executive responsibility of reconstruction. By reestablishing pro-Union governments, white Southerners could technically return to the Union which, in turn would ultimately hasten the conclusion of the war. And Lincoln looked to Louisiana as a proving ground.

General Nathaniel P. Banks was a Massachusetts Democrat before the war but, as an abolitionist, he broke with party ties over the slavery issue. Now a Moderate Republican, Banks enjoyed powerful political connections and an eye on a presidential bid. As a politically appointed general, his military career thus fair had been mediocre at best and the Radicals viewed him with suspicion. Banks' course of action in Louisiana led them to believe he was merely a tool of Lincoln.

Louisiana was one of the first states influenced by the result of the Emancipation Proclamation since a majority of the state was not under Union occupation. But in New Orleans and surrounding parishes a large portion of the middle class including the 10,000 free blacks were loyal to the Union as hordes of former slaves left their farms and plantations in unoccupied Louisiana and came to New Orleans in search of relief in the army camps. Not only was it a drain on military resources but the lack of the former slaves to work the fields meant no crops to be harvested thus creating an economic as well as agricultural drain on the local economy.

To remedy the situation, Banks installed a new labor system for the state in January of 1863 which called for all abled-bodied Negroes to enter into contracts with masters of their choosing and work the plantations for a wage, food and support. He also issued orders forbidding army recruiters from enlisting former slaves into service. The Radicals were furious but, with the spring elections approaching, they decided to bide their time rather than begin another feud.

That fall Lincoln decided Louisiana was ready for a civil government to be set up. But the radical *Free State General Committee* made up of radical anti-slavery advocates failed to hold a constitutional convention so Banks, under the authority of Lincoln took charge. Rather than hold the convention first, Banks issued a proclamation calling for a general election for state officers to be followed by an election to select delegates for a constitutional convention. Opposition quickly arose amongst the Radicals, insisting that the constitutional convention should be held first to ensure emancipation. But Banks, wanting to give the impression that loyal residents of the state would be allowed to choose their governor and other state leaders as long as slavery remained null and void, ignored the objections and continued on with his work.

Washington interjected however, and the timing could not have been worse. Halleck wanted Banks to attempt a second expedition up the Red River and into Texas, his previous attempt in September of '63 having failed. There were several reasons Washington had for endorsing the *Red River Expedition*. By taking Shreveport, the path lay open for a potential invasion into eastern Texas and southern Arkansas, thus freeing up a large supply of cotton and other raw materials in that area. Also by occupying Texas, Lincoln hoped to deny the French government any chance of establishing a puppet monarchy in Mexico in defiance of the Monroe Doctrine. Union forces could also prevent the rebels in that trans-Mississippi region from supporting their comrades in operations east of the Mississippi.

For two months Banks, preoccupied with the election process, communicated back and forth with Halleck who refused to give Banks any direct orders or specific instructions in regards to the propose expedition, thus leaving the onus on Banks. The timing of the expedition meant the elections of delegates would have to take place in military camps at Grand Encore and Alexandria along the way. As a result, Banks' man Michael Hahn, a moderate Unionist, won the governorship over the more radical candidates of the Free State General Committee. The Radicals were furious believing Banks had used military coercion to force the outcome of the election. Lincoln tried to appease the Radicals by suggesting to Hahn that their convention should consider extending the vote at least to "the very intelligent" blacks and those who served in uniform. The closest they came was to add into their constitution the possibility of Negro suffrage at a future date.

The Red River Campaign was a bungled affair from the beginning. Three separate commands, working with the navy would attempt a junction in Alexandria. Franklin would lead a force up from New Orleans while General AJ Smith, who borrowed 10,000 troops from Sherman to supplement his forces, would drop down from Vicksburg and meet up with Porter and his fleet of 15 ironclads and four light vessels. They would then rendezvous with Franklin at Alexandria. Together they would head up the Red River to Shreveport and link up with General Frederick Steele's forces making their way down from Little Rock. From there, operations could be launched into Texas.

Grant was against the whole idea but this had been planned before he assumed overall command. He ordered Banks to get it over with as quickly as possible so Sherman could have his troops back for his campaign while Banks could then move on Mobile. But things were off to a bad start. Smith, having to take out the formidable Fort de Russey on March 14 had arrived at Alexandria on March 20 but Franklin would not arrive until the 25. Banks, held up by the elections would arrive the next day but he would not be alone. He was accompanied by speculators who intended to deny the Confederates of their cotton.

From the beginning nothing went right. The campaign was plagued with a lack of overall command structure and a decreasing water level. As they set out for Shreveport, the army was stretched out 12 miles along a narrow road; the rear of the column a full day's march from the front. Confederate forces attacked the leading elements at Sabine Crossroad and Banks was forced to retreat back to Pleasant Hill where he made a stand and won a tactical victory. After learning Steele had been turned back and was unable to reach Shreveport Banks called off the expedition. On their return to Alexandria they found it in flames; the supply of cotton torched by the Confederates. The expedition was a flop. They never reached Shreveport nor set foot into Texas. Mexico set up a puppet government and Sherman's men would be sent to Mississippi rather than returned to Sherman for his great march through Georgia.

When it was over the rumors began. Banks was vilified by the press. His men denounced him, saying he did not set out to defeat the rebs so much as to secure cotton. Oddly, there was no immediate call for an investigation. The Radicals knew Banks was hopeful of consideration for the presidency but there was no cause for worry, only successful generals won elections. Besides, Grant had already knocked Banks out of the equation by replacing him with General Edward Canby.

Of course, they could have used an investigation into the Red River Campaign as an excuse to test the validity of the Louisiana government. But, since the *Wade-Davis Bill* was being debated in the House there was no hurry. If it passed, there would be no need for an investigation. And if defeated, they would have to wait for a congressional reconstruction bill to be presented to Lincoln and then they could test the validity of the Louisiana elections.

As the Radicals considered what to do about Banks and Louisiana, word of the Fort Pillow massacre arrived. Fifteen hundreds rebels under the command of Nathanial Bedford Forrest had quickly overwhelmed Major William F. Bradford's small garrison of nearly three hundred black artillery troops and about the same number of white cavalry troops located on the Mississippi River just north of Memphis. Enraged by the presence of colored troops, the "Critter Company" brutally shot down many of the black soldiers who tried to surrender. Nearly three hundred, mostly black soldiers were killed during the action. The Radicals hoped to turn this tragedy into their advantage.

A cry for vengeance rang out across the North when news of atrocities was printed in the newspapers. Of course the committee, eager to persuade the public to resist Lincoln's Ten Per Cent Plan, immediately set out to investigate the tragedy. Wade and Gooch headed to Cairo where they interviewed over seventy witnesses which included soldiers who had escaped the slaughter, the surgeons who tended to the wounded, and civilians who visited the fort after the fact. Reports of the rumored atrocities now exceeded all expectations.

Stanton recognized the propaganda value of the committee's findings if they could substantiate the rumors. If Lincoln still showed leniency to the South even after the news of such atrocities then certainly, the public would insist on a candidate who would be willing to make those responsible pay for their heinous crimes against humanity.

When the committee returned to Washington to write their report, they briefed Lincoln on their findings. Lincoln in turn, called a meeting of his Cabinet to ask for their opinion regarding retaliation of the massacre. Seward, Stanton, Chase and Secretary of Interior Usher were for man-for-man retaliation while Bates, Welles and Blair opposed such extreme measures. While the debate was taking place, more upsetting news arrived in Washington. A group of northern prisoners, many emasculated to the point of death had just arrived at Annapolis. Stanton dispatched the investigative committee to Annapolis where they are appalled by the sight of the weak, fragile men whose bodies were mere skeletal frame covered by skin. Stories of starvation, torture, neglect and exposure had brought the most cynical members to tears.

To achieve the greatest shock value, the committee released both reports together. They intended to show that the massacre was not a temporary lapse of sanity but a systematic policy of savagery which the South adopted to show their contempt for the Negro soldiers and the Union. Testimony of the massacre included the senseless clubbing of women and children. The wounded, black and white alike, were said to have been beaten and bayonetted even as they pleaded for their lives while the sick, bedridden inside tents and huts were nailed to the ground by their blankets and their shelters set afire. Some living wounded were thrown into pits along with the dead and haphazardly covered with dirt.

The prisoners at Annapolis were also victims of a "...deliberate system of savage and barbarous treatment of starvation" by order of the Confederate high command. To the Radicals, these were not random unfortunate acts but proof that the South was backwards, ignorant, and primitive and in dire need of social reform. There would be no doubt now that the South would need to be totally destroyed and rebuilt.

But these reports were questionable. Testimony included that Forrest had advanced on the fort under a flag of truce which was incorrect. Bradford had prematurely abandoned his two outer lines of defense outside of his walls. It is true that the sight of the black troops enraged the rebels as they came over the wall but corresponding evidence of witnesses gave testimony that Forrest himself had stopped the further slaughter of Union soldiers. A Union gunboat captain also testified that the sick, women, and children had already been removed before the battle began. It was also thought that the black soldiers were coached while giving their testimony.

But the committee had printed 60,000 copies of their report for distribution. Northern newspaper printed the report along with eight photos of the former prisoners. Attached to their report was a recommendation of retaliation of man for man. But Lincoln had already issued the Order of Retaliation in July of 1863 when Confederate forces, under orders to take no black prisoners, refused to exchange black Union troops during prisoner exchanges. Those that did survive being captured were either forced back into slavery or executed on the spot. After the Fort Pillow massacre, Lincoln gave Stanton a directive on May 17 to notify rebel authority through proper military channels informing them that they had evidence of atrocities. Unless they would guarantee that all Union prisoners "white or colored" be treated in accordance to the laws of war then retaliation would follow. Lincoln even had 300 Confederate officers set aside for such purpose. The deadline of July 1 for a response had passed but not a word was received. Lincoln refused to execute the officers for Grant had already halted prisoner exchange on grounds that the Confederate government refused to include blacks as part of the exchange.

The report however had the desired effect on the public as well as the military but it would be temporary. Grant was now in overall command and the north believed that this would be the year of complete victory. Morale had been up and down so many times since the war began and now it was again on an upward swing. As the weather warmed the public was not going to turn their back on the president now.

Chapter 11

Disillusioned

The beginning of 1864 wasn't looking good for the South. Vicksburg and Chattanooga had fallen and the victory at Gettysburg had proven Lee could be defeated on the field and ensured that foreign intervention to aid the confederacy would not be forthcoming. Any candidate who had opposed the war was defeated in the 1863 elections and the North was prospering. The USSC had spent nearly $20 million on soldiers' relief and supplies for Union forces were endless. Although victory was imminent, the South had yet to capitulate and Lincoln continued to fret over the casualties and the cost of the war.

Lincoln followed the war closely and noticed that when the Army of the Potomac was on the march the Army of the Cumberland was idle and vice versa, thus allowing the rebel army to shift forces where needed. Even with the recent victories one thing was clear to Lincoln, Lee's and Johnston's armies were still a force to be reckoned with. Halleck remained indecisive and failed to grasp the overall picture. He often sent out contradictory orders and was remained constantly at odds with Stanton. Lincoln needed one military mind who could grasp the concept that the Southern armies must be destroyed in order to end the war.

Lincoln had never met Grant personally but the president was very aware of the general's victories. The Radicals also knew of Grant and early in the war they feared his growing reputation. Rumors had it that Grant allowed the Copperhead-leaning *Chicago Times* to circulate in his army and the general himself was under control of his subordinate Colonel John Logan, the Democratic boss of southern Illinois. To them, Grant was nothing more than another disloyal product of West Point. Fearing Grant could be a Democratic nominee, the Radicals had used the events surrounding the battle of Shiloh as a reason to investigate him. The CCW requested former Democrat General Lew Wallace to give an account of Grant. In an attempt to vindicate himself for not following orders that battle, Wallace had reported that Grant was incompetent and had bungled things greatly. Other rumors about Grant circulated in an attempt to discredit him and the harassment had reached a point where the general considered resigning during the summer of 1862. It was only after talking with Sherman that Grant decided to stay.

With continual prodding by his close friend and strongest supporter Congressman Washburne, Grant recognized which way the political winds blew and promotion was the reward for obedience. So in March of 1863, after a visit from Lorenzo Thomas, Grant embraced the radical platform and by that fall he was advocating employment of Negroes in a military capacity. Even the radical General John Palmer lauded Grant to fellow Illinoisan Lyman Trumball, saying the Republicans needed to grab him up. Lincoln himself could forgive the general for Shiloh and the rumor of intemperance, for Grant was a general who was willing to fight and he was successful.

When Congress had convened in December, 1863, Trumball presented the bill to revive the rank of lieutenant-general last held by Washington; Scott had only been brevetted this rank. The Radicals, hoping Grant would finally be the general who could and would, rid the armies of its conservative commanders, whole-heartedly embraced the idea and on March 9, Grant was officially appointed the commanding General of the Army. Halleck was now the chief-of-staff. There was no elaborate ceremony or official grandstanding for that was not in Grant's nature. Once the formalities were over Grant immediately went to work. Sherman said of Grant's promotion that after Gettysburg and Vicksburg, "...the war professionally began."

If the Radicals thought they could coerce Grant to do their bidding they were mistaken. When the committee's efforts to have Meade replaced with Hooker had failed, Chandler sent Grant a list of generals touched with "McClellanism" and a recommendation for their removal. To their surprise, and to his credit, Grant refused to play the game. Ignoring the list, Grant appointed commanders as he saw fit and thus far he was satisfied with Meade. In the West, Grant ignored Hooker and promoted Sherman (who had little respect for the volunteer soldiers) over him. This cause Hooker to complain to Senator Chandler that he was not liked by anybody and they all wanted him cashiered out of the army.

While the political intrigue continued in Washington Grant was busy preparing his Overland Campaign. After meeting with Meade at Brandy Station, Virginia on March 10, Grant decided, against the advice of Sherman, to make his headquarters in the East with the Army of the Potomac. Meade would remain in command but Grant would direct his movements. But Grant would also be starting out with a fresh army. Nearly half of the Union army would soon find their three-year enlistment ending. And the ranks were now being filled by conscription, substitutes, and bounty men. The boys of '61 branded these new recruits as burglars, thieves, and vagabonds. Grant would later say that only one in five of these men were effective soldiers. The federal government had offered $300 bounties to any soldier who would reenlist while state and local governments usually added to that amount to prevent conscription. Appeals were made to their pride and patriotism. In the end nearly half of the Army of the Potomac did reenlist while in the western armies that number was slightly higher.

Grant's grand strategy was to advance on all fronts. Meade would place his army between Lee's Army of Northern Virginia and Richmond. Butler, at Fortress Monroe would drive toward Richmond from the southeast. Sherman, now in command of the Mississippi Division consisting of the Armies of Ohio, Cumberland and Tennessee, would continue the fight in the West. Generals Crook and Averill were to operate against railroad supply lines in West Virginia; Banks, in New Orleans would head for Mobile, Alabama, and Sigel was tasked with clearing the Shenandoah Valley. After building up the cavalry, Grant gave that command to Sheridan, whose tasks it was to keep the Confederate cavalry in check. Outnumbered, Lee would have no choice but to fight or sends troops back to protect the capital from Butler. To those in secondary roles Grant told them, "Those not skinning, can hold a leg."

No longer would the confederate capital or strategic positions be the goal of the army. To Lincoln's approval, Grant made Lee's army the prize. Richmond and Atlanta would be secondary. But first, the Army of the Potomac was to be reorganized. Furloughs were recalled, officers who made Washington hotels their camp were ordered back, new clothing was issued and arms and munitions were sent to the front.

On May 4, the Army of the Potomac crossed the Rapidan kicking off the Overland Campaign. To Grant's surprise Lee took the offensive and attacked him at the Wilderness. The fighting lasted two days and both sides incurred heavy casualties but to Lee's surprise, rather than retreat as previous commanders had done, Grant ordered his army forward by the left flank. Grant intended to wear the enemy down. The next forty days would see non-stop fighting; the Wilderness, Spotsylvania Court House, Yellow Tavern, North Anna, Totopotomoy Creek, Cold Harbor, and Trevilian Station all bore a terrible price.

The North was appalled at the quickly rising number of casualties. The Radicals, still smarting from Grant's snub, were almost enjoying how the events were unfolding. Just as they did to McClellan during the Peninsula Campaign, they now began chiding Grant while they themselves remained safe in Washington. But Grant had decided to change tactics and headed south across the peninsula and approached Richmond from the east. The Radicals, who had rebuked McClellan two years earlier for taking that route, now applauded Grant for finally taking the proper course.

In Washington Senator Wade, fuming over the growing casualties, marched to the White House and blamed Lincoln for sustaining such incompetent generals and angrily demanded the removal of Grant. He concluded his verbal barrage by claiming Lincoln was responsible for the government being on the road to Hell and was about one mile from it. Lincoln quietly responded that a mile was about as far as the Capitol and Congress was.

On June 15, Union engineers who had come a long ways from the summer of '61 connected the longest pontoon bridge of the war, 2,200 feet in just seven hours allowing Grant to bypass Richmond and cross to the south side of the James. Two days later, the entire army of 100,000 had crossed to the other side and started for the railroad junction at Petersburg, the main supply base and rail depot, crucial to the entire region supplying the rebel army and Richmond. The taking of Petersburg by Union forces was essential. In doing so, it would be impossible for Lee to continue defending Richmond.

Union forces began surrounding the defenses of Petersburg on June 9, '64. As they prepared for a siege, Burnside was approached by Colonel Henry Pleasants of the 48th Pennsylvania with an idea for breaching the line. A 510 foot tunnel could be dug towards a salient in enemy lines and packed with four tons of explosives. The ensuing blast would breach the walls and allow entry inside the perimeter. Burnside had brought the idea to Meade who, although skeptical, had given his approval. The men of the 48th Pennsylvania, chosen for their experience in the coal mines, began digging on June 25 and a month later the tunnel was ready. Projects like these may have seemed impracticable but officers found the best way to keep the soldiers out of trouble was to keep them busy.

To lead the assault Burnside chose a division of black troops who had been tending to supply lines and building fortifications. They had no combat experience but they were being trained for their role. When the tunnel was ready and the explosives in place Meade, fearing reprisal if the attack failed, ordered that white troops lead the assault as opposed to the black troops. On July 30 the mine was blown, the soldiers rushed in but rather than go around either side of the crater the soldiers ran directly into it. Unable to climb the steep walls created by the blast they were caught in the deadly fire of the enemy who had regrouped. There with no chance of escape. When it was over, some 3,800 Union soldiers were casualties. Burnside immediately blamed Meade for the disaster, accusing his superior of wanting the attack to fail. Meade, wishing he had never assented to the plan, wanted to cashier Burnside for the fiasco but Grant would not allow it however, Burnside would finally be allowed to resign. A military Court of Inquiry shortly thereafter had cleared both officers of blame.

Over the next nine months Grant would put the squeeze on the city. Trench warfare would be perfected during the siege and entrenchments would eventually extend over 30 miles from the outskirts east of Richmond to around the eastern and southern outskirts of Petersburg. Numerous raids and assaults were conducted and battles fought in attempts to cut off any lines of supply and communications.

But things were not going as the administration hoped. By the end of the Overland Campaign, Grant had suffered 80,000 casualties. Most of his initiatives had failed, often because of the assignment of political rather than military generals. Butler's Army of the James bogged down against inferior forces before Richmond. Sigel was soundly defeated at the Battle of New Market in May and was replaced by General Hunter. Banks, distracted by the Red River Campaign failed to move on Mobile. Sherman was advancing on Atlanta but his progress was slowed by a tenacious and competent adversary. Crook and Averell were having the most success. They were able to cut the last railway linking Virginia and Tennessee.

While Grant was trying to contain Lee, Sherman was waging his own war. Grant had given Sherman great latitude in planning his own offensive as long as he followed Grant's general directive of breaking up Johnston's army, get into the interior and inflict as much damage as possible. Sherman had proposed the Atlanta Campaign and after convincing Grant of its practicality, began his movement.

Sherman was stationed in Chattanooga but his base of supply was located in Nashville 130 miles to the northwest. To transport all supplies to Chattanooga Sherman had ordered all trains entering Nashville to be seized. When the president of the lines complained that no cars were being returned to Louisville to continue to supply Nashville, Sherman order all cars seized from Cincinnati heading to Louisville. Ultimately, when Sherman would finally complete his march he was amused to see freight cars which followed in his wake had markings on their sides denoting their origins as New York and New England RR companies.

Sherman had in his command 100,000 troops, 35,000 beasts of burden and 254 artillery pieces. No tents or niceties would be provided for the men and officers except for those used as hospitals; and one tent per headquarters. Sherman did not exempt himself from this order; neither he nor his staff had tents. General Thomas was an exception. His headquarters consisted of several trim canvass tents and a small wagon train to haul his effects. The soldiers referred to it as "Uncle Tom's Circus."

Sherman was aware that his opponent Joe Johnston had an effective fighting force of roughly 50,000 and would not give ground easily. These veterans would contest every inch of Sherman's advance. Johnston also had a virtual army of slaves which hastily built defenses in the rear of the Confederate army which allowed the rebel soldiers to fall back upon as they stubbornly gave ground.

Sherman began his campaign using movement rather than fighting to advance and by late June he closed to within 17 miles of Atlanta. At Kennesaw Mountain however, Sherman decided to switch tactics and ordered a frontal assault which resulted in horrific casualties.

Sherman would not stray from in his strategy of flanking movements again during the campaign.

Johnston had contested nearly 110 miles of real estate but when he crossed the Chattahoochee River, the final barrier protecting Atlanta, Jefferson Davis made a major blunder. Frustrated by Johnston's lack of aggression, Davis relieved him of command of the Army of the Tennessee and appointed John Bell Hood in his place. The new commander decided to fight rather than continue Johnston's strategy of withdrawal. Johnston had incurred 10,000 casualties to Sherman's 18,000. Hood's would be much worse.

On July 22, the Battle of Atlanta was fought. Sherman overwhelmed and defeated Hood's forces defending the city but still he could not take the city proper. So Sherman settled in for a siege. In a little more than a month's time, Hood's men were forced to evacuate. They set torch to the military facilities as they departed, leaving Union forces to occupy the city on September 2. News of the capture was covered extensively by Northern newspapers which significantly boosts Northern morale. The victory would no doubt aid in Lincoln's reelection. Sherman then evacuated all civilians from the city.

In one of the battles during the campaign General James McPherson, commander of the Army of the Tennessee was killed and Sherman chose to promote General O.O. Howard to the rank of major-general and assume command. Hooker, who had served rather admirably in the Atlanta Campaign, felt slighted and became upset to the point where he asked to be relieved. He was placed in command of the Northern Department consisting of Michigan, Ohio, Indiana, and Illinois where he would remain until the end of the war. Of course, the Radicals would blame Grant for this and they would wait until after the election to wage war against him.

The Radicals hadn't liked the president's Ten Per Cent Plan or his plan to set up a state government backed by the military in Louisiana; they viewed it as playing politics. The lenient plan was proof that Lincoln would not be the man to lead the nation through the eventual reconstruction phase. They had no choice but to search for a new candidate; a rare and dangerous move to replace a sitting president during war but the Radicals were a rare and dangerous group and they wanted someone who would conform to their idea of reconstruction.

As early as 1862, the Radicals had flirted with the prospect of other candidates. Fremont, Butler, Banks, even Grant had been considered. But by early '64, things were not looking so good for the Radicals. Months earlier, they had reconsidered Grant and possibly even Rosecrans, but the latter's botched Tennessee campaign had cost him consideration. Grant's unwillingness to play the political game caused him to lose favor with them as well. The Radicals finally settled on Chase.

When it was revealed that the Radicals were backing Chase as their next possible candidate the Blair family exploded, with Frank and Montgomery Blair speaking out against the plot and defending Lincoln's stance on reconstruction. Montgomery went as far as accusing Chase of corruption. The Radicals were furious that one of their own should be so callously attacked and they demanded that Blair be ejected from the Cabinet. Thad Stevens exclaimed to Lincoln that, if Blair was not removed then they would certainly find his successor. Lincoln was unmoved however. When General Palmer wrote to Trumbull that the Western army was solidly behind the president Lincoln was relieved. Even Seward took a shot at the Radicals in a speech in his hometown in Auburn, New York where he declared that slavery would be abolished by the war but the price for readmission would be minimal. The Radicals are surprised at the sudden and violent backlash. And now, with Grant in command and the armies on the move, public support for Lincoln began to grow once again. For the Radicals, there was no time to waste.

On February 20, 1864, Chase's campaign manager, Senator Samuel C. Pomeroy made a grave mistake. In an attempt to deflate Lincoln's growing popularity, the Pomeroy Committee published the *Pomeroy Circular* which publically attacked the president. The circular claimed the current woes of the nation would continue should Lincoln be re-elected. In its summation, the circular claimed that Chase was the only candidate to possess the qualities needed to "vindicate the honor of the republic." When the circular was published, Chase immediately sought out Lincoln and denied any knowledge of the circular and offered his resignation.

The attack backfired tremendously as Republicans across the country denounced the circular and now came together in full support of the president. Even Garfield, who was no friend of the president, warned the Radicals that by alienating Lincoln, he would certainly return to the Conservative camp. A week later Frank Blair called for an investigation into the Treasury Department's trade regulation in Union-occupied territories in the South. Suddenly, not all affairs were within the authority of the CCW and they refused to investigate these allegations against their candidate's department. But the damage was done and on March 5, Chase dropped out of the race.

The Radicals were again despondent. Their latest attempt to turn the public against the president and his policies had failed. And now they watched as Chase's candidacy died a sudden death as another candidate's campaign was taking off. St. Louis' radical Germans, New England abolitionists, and angry Democrats had called for a convention to nominate Fremont. Held at the end of May in Chicago, Fremont was nominated to run as a third party candidate with General Cochrane as his running mate. Their platform consisted of amending the constitution to abolish slavery in all states in the Union and in rebellion; a congressional controlled reconstruction policy with aims to protect the freed slaves, confiscation of all property held by rebels and distributed to the soldiers and settlers, and a one term presidency. Fremont had half-heartedly accepted the nomination.

The Radicals had wanted to postpone their own party's convention scheduled for June until late summer in hopes that Lincoln's popularity would die down but that too had failed and the convention was held in Baltimore as planned. On June 7, Lincoln received the nomination, securing all the votes except those from Missouri, which went to Grant. Asa Gray had summed up Lincoln perfectly, "Homely, honest, ungainly Lincoln is the representative man of the country." Lincoln, always humble said of his nomination, "...it is not best to swop horses while crossing the stream." Their platform was for full prosecution of the war, full emancipation, and the employment of Negro soldiers.

Hannibal Hamlin was willing to run for a second term as vice-president but he was surprised that Andrew Johnson was chosen for that honor. This was a calculated move by the Republicans. As a War Democrat from Tennessee Johnson denounced secession and vigorously supported war. He had even urged Union troops to expel rebels from his beloved eastern Tennessee. His loyalty during the war was never in doubt. Johnson had the support of the southern, slave-owning, ultra-state rights advocates but to the Copperheads and other secessionist, he was a defector. With Johnson's nomination for the vice-presidency however, the Republicans had given up their identity by becoming the

Union Party. The administration wanted to show an alliance between parties in full support the war. No longer would they appear sectional but by placing a Southern Democrat on the ballot, they could now claim the North and South were united in their cause for a speedy cessation of hostility and reunification.

One more stunning blow befell the Radicals at the end of June. A squabble had broken out between Chase and a New York senator Edwin Morgan over Chase's nomination of democratic journalist Maunsell Field to replace longtime assistant-treasurer of New York John Cisco. Lincoln instructed Chase to search for a candidate satisfactory to both wings of the Republican Party in New York but Chase insisted on Maunsell who possessed no real abilities for the office. Morgan announced his opposition of the appointment to Lincoln, who in turn requested of Chase to reconsider. Once again the indignant Chase, who felt that by now he was indispensable, turned in his resignation. To his surprise and also that of the Radicals, Lincoln accepted it. Tending to his political fences Lincoln appointed Senator Fessenden as the new Treasurer.

On July 2, the *Wade-Davis Bill* laid upon Lincoln's desk. The bill was intended to counter the president's Ten Per Cent Plan. Whereas Lincoln's plan would allow readmission to each individual state which adopted his plan, the Wade-Davis bill would halt reconstruction until all fighting ceased. This new bill basically stated that former Confederate states would be admitted back into the Union only when a majority of white voters rather than ten per cent, in each state took an oath which, in effect stated they had never supported the Confederacy. Since treason should be punished, the bill would effectively strip the right to vote or hold public office from a large number of residents.

The Radicals also insisted on emancipation by a congressional edict. This was far less than what the Radicals hoped for in regards to reconstruction but it was the best they could hope for at this particular time since there was no good news regarding the war. One hour before the congressional session would adjourn Lincoln pocket-vetoed the bill, citing it exceeded constitutional authority and it would also have an adverse effect on the Southern population.

The Radicals were upset over Lincoln's veto but to make matters worse, they now believed the president was in negotiations with Southern delegates. Lincoln had received word that two confederate agents were waiting in Niagara Falls, Canada, to negotiate a peace agreement. Lincoln doubted their "authority" but he dispatched Horace Greeley to act on his behalf anyhow. If they were legitimate agents then they would be offered safe passage to Washington. Lincoln also sent along his secretary John Hay with a letter announcing his terms, the abolishment of slavery must be guaranteed before the Union could be restored. The agents turned out to be bogus and they sent Lincoln's letter to the newspapers claiming that Lincoln was unwilling to discuss peace until slavery had been eradicated. The Democrats also used the letter as further proof that the war would continue and the bloodshed was for the sake of freeing the slaves. When word got out, the Radicals were even more convinced that Lincoln was un-electable.

Another report published on the same day was about a second attempt at peace which a skeptical Lincoln permitted. Believing that J.R. Gilmore and a former Methodist college president Colonel Jacques had inside information that the Davis administration was seeking peace Lincoln dispatched the two to Richmond. Again, the Confederates balked at the condition regarding slavery.

The Radicals, again fearing Lincoln would halt the war prematurely, took advantage of his supposed waning popularity. Hoping to knock him down as top candidate they published the *Wade-Davis Manifesto* in the *Tribune* on August 5. The document was a total denunciation of Lincoln's reconstruction policy and his veto of the *Wade-Dave Bill* a month earlier. In it, they attacked his determination to reconstruct defeated Southern states by executive power and against the wishes of Congress. The proof was in his proclamation of July 8, doubting Congress had the power to enact the *Wade-Davis Bill*. It also accused the president of setting up governments in Louisiana and Arkansas merely to secure their electoral votes. It concluded by asking Republicans to refute Lincoln and his policies. This was another major miscalculation of the radicals and the repercussion of the manifesto was enormous.

So confident were the radical bosses of their deed that on August 14, Davis, Greeley and a score of other party leaders met privately at the home of attorney David Dudley Field in New York. The object of the clandestine council was to discuss the state of affairs and possibly nominate a new candidate whose views coincided with theirs. The jubilation of the radicals were short-lived however when the reviews of the manifesto became known.

Alarmed Conservatives voiced their concerns that the two authors were undermining the administration while a majority of Republican editorials denounced Wade and Davis for trying to destroy it. The *New York Times* had declared that Wade and Davis were dangerous revolutionary radicals who had sustained war "...not as a means of restoring the Union, but to free the slaves, seize the lands, crush the spirit, destroy the rights and blot out forever the political freedom of the people inhabiting the Southern States." The two were censored by many powerful abolitionists, claiming they were possibly snatching victory away from the Republicans. Even Wade's Ohio Western Reserve, the nation's strongest anti-slavery section situated in Garfield's congressional district, adopted resolutions condemning Wade for splitting the party. Garfield himself, who was thought to have a hand in the manifesto, had threatened not to re-nominate Wade. The Radicals were now on dangerous ground as Lincoln supporters made their voices heard. And the Democratic convention would seal their fate and steal their chance at finding a replacement for the head of their ticket.

At the end of August, the Democrats held their convention in Chicago and to no one's surprise, McClellan received the nomination. The most infamous of Copperheads, Vallandigham who laid out the peace platform adopted by the Democrats was named as the candidate for vice-president. The Democrats were so sure of McClellan popularity that they predicted he would secure two thirds of the soldiers' vote. In the East alone, the Army of the Potomac had 100,000 soldiers who might vote for McClellan if given the vote. But the general had been too long out of the spotlight; his popularity was waning and no important generals would openly support him.

The Democrats resorted to attacking Lincoln personally. Vallandigham had claimed "anarchy, tyranny, and Negro equality" would be ensured should the president be reelected. Another wild allegation claimed the president might be tainted with Negro blood. They also printed rumors of a conspiracy of his intent to commit Miscegenation; the sexual relations between two races.

The Republicans countered by investigating the *Sons of Liberty,* an offshoot of the *Knights of the Golden Circle,* of which Vallandigham was said to be Supreme Grand Commander. Agents had collected a long list of names and published erroneous reports of conspiracy and espionage.

To the Radicals, the team of Lincoln and Johnson would be the lesser of the two evils over McClellan and Vallandigham. But before they would pledge their support for Lincoln, the Radicals attempted to hold another convention to secure a candidate other than Lincoln. As fate would have it, word had arrived from Sherman that Atlanta had been captured. The Radicals were beaten. Lincoln would now be elevated to a level which no other candidate could reach. The Radicals had no choice but to support Lincoln but, they wanted something in return.

Chandler was now on a mission. Racing from Detroit to Washington, the Senator would attempt to convince Lincoln that, if he relieved Blair from the Cabinet, the Radicals would then convince Fremont to drop out of the race. Lincoln would then have the support of both the Radicals and Fremont's followers. On September 3, Chandler met with Lincoln and laid out his proposal and Lincoln agreed. By September 23, Blair had resigned, Fremont had dropped out and Lincoln had the full support of his party. The whole affair was a bitter pill for Wade to swallow but by the end of September even he was stumping for Lincoln in Pennsylvania; denouncing Democrats more than supporting Lincoln.

Chapter 12

Election of '64

Holding a presidential election during a civil war was unprecedented and its result would determine if the bloodshed would continue. Lincoln had never considered canceling the election, believing that, if the rebellion could cause the postponement of a national election then secession had succeeded. Besides, his opponents would interpret a cancelation as a way for the current administration to maintain power.

By September of 1864, with the election quickly approaching, political clubs began to appear across the North. One of the first, the democratic *McClellan's Legion* was opened to discharged or furlough soldiers. The Republicans responded with the *Veterans Union Club* and the *Union War Eagles of New York.* Members of these clubs would march publicly in open support of their party while the Sanitary Commission continued handing out pamphlets.

Another push for the army vote was on and Grant, who endorsed enfranchising the soldier, wrote to Stanton that guidelines should be followed. There should be no speeches, canvassing of troops or political meetings in camps. Stanton agreed and wrote out the provisions but they could hardly be upheld. By this time of the election nineteen states had allowed their soldiers to vote in the presidential election by either absentee ballots or proxy. Delaware, Indiana, and New Jersey failed to amend their state constitution to do so while soldiers from Illinois would not be given the right to vote until the following year.

Again, furloughs were granted to soldiers whose states refused them the vote from the field and where the contest in their district would be close. In Indiana Lincoln, hoping to ensure a Republican victory in the state legislature, asked Sherman for any troops not needed and send them home for the October state elections. Morton, insisting they stay for the presidential elections decided to retained all new recruits until after the election. Lincoln also asked Meade and Sheridan for assistance in the Pennsylvania election and Rosecrans for troops for Missouri. As Stanton promoted or demoted officers for the sake of Lincoln, commanders complained that the war was being put on hold for the sake of the election. To swing the predominately Democrat Irish New York State, Lincoln even donated his rough draft of the preliminary emancipation proclamation to their state's charity event.

When the election was over the results were in, Lincoln had won 212 electoral votes to McClellan's 12. Grant said of the results that this had a greater effect on the morale of the armies than a victory in the field. But did the propaganda efforts of Stanton and the Radicals succeed in influencing the vote? Morale rose and dropped with each military victory and defeat. The Conscription Act, draft riots, and political policies all had an effect. Certainly, the latest battlefield victories influenced the result at the polls. Morale was at a low point by the end of summer when news of Sherman's taking of Atlanta, Farragut's capture of Mobil Bay, and Sheridan's Ride, consisting of his string of victories in the Shenandoah Valley was announced in the North. These victories probably did more than Stanton's propaganda efforts against the Peace Democrats who advocated peace on any terms. People's beliefs were reinforced that the administration was on the right course and that the end of the war was near. The soldiers tended to distant themselves from a party that was labeled as traitorous and had intimated that the war was a failure; a lost cause in which the soldiers' sacrifice was for naught.

Lincoln had his own special way of campaigning. The president often paid visits to the numerous hospitals around the capitol and in the field where he would sit with the wounded and tell stories and jokes. After suffering military defeats, Lincoln could be found in the field visiting with the men, offering his gratitude and words of encouragement and support. He would often pardoned soldiers for minor offenses. His concern for the soldiers was genuine and he earned the trust and respect of many of them.

But emancipation was still a sticky issue with many of the soldiers. Although the purge a year earlier was an attempt to alter the composition and mindset of the army, there were still many Democrat soldiers serving in the ranks. These men were in a perilous position; they could not speak out against the administration nor could they vocally denounce emancipation or the enlistment of blacks, although they were fiercely loyal to their country and the cause. They would fight to preserve the Union and if blacks were freed in the process, so be it. Many of these soldiers hated the peace advocates who claimed the war a failure and was willing to accept a truce at any cost. They were not here on the front lines fighting, bleeding, and dying. Many detested the abolitionists who they also blamed for the president violating, in their mind, the Constitution and seeking to place the Negro on a plane equal to or higher than the whites. These soldiers may have voted for Lincoln but in letters written to their families they freely admitted they were not voting or fighting for the blacks.

Officers in fear of having their careers destroyed could not order their soldiers to vote the Republican ticket but they could certainly influence their decision to either vote for Lincoln or abstain from voting altogether. Since voting from the field was a public affair, each party's ballot was color-coded soldiers would know how their comrades had voted.

McClellan was still popular with the men but his connection with the peace platform had become an albatross. Soldiers were willing to vote for McClellan and slavery but not for a conditional peace. They detested the Peace Democrats who remained safely at home protesting the war and advocating peace at any cost while the soldiers stood on the front lines. The Emancipation Proclamation, the military defeats, desertion, and court-martials may have altered the composition of the army but not their resolve to see the war through. And Lincoln received help from Grant when he wrote that the Confederates were anxious for the election and hoping that McClellan would win.

These soldiers were not the same wide-eyed boys who had viewed the war as a grand adventure three years earlier. They were men who had seen the horrors of the battlefield. They faced the enemy and disease alike. They were underpaid, underfed, and endured hardships beyond measure. And now, the idea that their right to vote was even a debatable issue was appalling to the soldiers. Did they not earn this right through their willingness to sacrifice life and limb for the preservation of the Union? There was no doubt that the Republicans found favor with the soldiers regarding the suffrage issue. And these soldiers were fully aware of what voting for Lincoln meant; a continuance of the long, bloody struggle with full emancipation of the blacks.

But not all soldiers were consumed by the internal struggle of angst and indecision. Approximately 130,000 soldiers out of the 922,000, or about 15%, who were eligible to reenlist, did so. Those serving a three-year term could reenlist if they had less than a year remaining. For nine-month men still in service, less than three months of service remaining were required. But also, the summer leading up to the election saw more blood and carnage than the previous three year. As of July, '64 the death toll by bullet and disease now totaled 175,879.

The soldiers' vote from the field had no real effect on its outcome of the national contest. Of the more than 4,000,000 votes cast, Lincoln won the popular vote by a mere 400,000. Some historians suggest that only about 150,000 soldiers out of roughly one million soldiers serving had voted from the field. Of those, 78% or 117,000 had voted for Lincoln; the remainder went to McClellan. But is this a true representation? Only about 710,000 soldiers were actually eligible to vote. And of course, this did not mean that a large majority of those soldiers were now Republicans. But at this stage of the game, a majority of them were willing to vote the Republican ticket. Of course, there is no way of knowing how soldiers who were furloughed or convalescing at home voted.

On the state and local level however, a different story is told. If 75% of the eligible soldiers who had voted went for Lincoln and the Republican Party then, it is very likely that the soldiers' vote had affected the outcome of at least 20 of the 31 races where the victory of margin was less than 1,000 votes. The Republicans had picked up 20 seats in the House while, of the other 11, 8 remained Democrat and 3 remained Republican. That would suggest that only party adherents remained. The Radicals could now believe they had control of the military.

Because so many soldiers were willing, for whatever reason, to switch sides for this one election, politicians realized the potential of the voting bloc of the soldiers. And this would be information that they would use again in the near future.

To Sherman the only way to bring the war to a speedy and successful conclusion was to break the South's resolve to fight. During the siege of Atlanta, Sherman had devised a bold plan which he proposed to Grant; a march straight through Georgia to the sea. Forsaking his supply lines, Sherman used previous crop reports to plan his advance using routes where livestock and crop production would be prevalent, making foraging more effective. Grant was reluctant; he felt Sherman should have given chase to Hood who had, under orders of Jefferson Davis, attempted to draw Sherman out of Georgia by moving toward Chattanooga to operate against Sherman's lines of communications. But Sherman didn't take the bait and instead, he dispatched General Thomas to deal with Hood.

Sherman insisted that by heading for Savanna all that had been won so far would remain intact. He also believed the continued destruction of all war materials and liberal foraging would also have a disparaging effect on the morale of the civilian population. Lastly, by moving in Lee's rear, Grant would have the opportunity to take Petersburg. At the very least, Sherman could at least keep Southern reinforcements away from Virginia. Grant was still hesitant but after several dispatches were exchanged with Lincoln, neither of who wanted to give the direct order to do so, Grant consented.

On November 15, Sherman began his famous March to the Sea. Dividing his army into two wings, their objectives were simple; confuse and deceive the enemy while foraging and tearing up railroad tracks. One twentieth of each regiment would be used as foragers; not be confused with bummers, a term generally meant for the stragglers who disobeyed orders not to destroy, burn or pillage personal property.

By the second day of their march foragers had perfected their trade. They would set out at daybreak and head into the countryside, taking care not to wonder far from the main column. Not one farm, home and village were exempt from their craft. By nightfall they would return on horses, mules, or cattle. Oft times they drove carts, buggies, carriages and all other means of conveyances loaded with their plunder. It was dangerous work considering enemy cavalry and home militias roamed the countryside.

As they advanced, Sherman enjoyed watching the ingenious techniques used in the destruction of the rails. Here, several hundred men stood in two parallel lines facing the tracks and at a given signal, the men would stoop down and grab one end of the tie and lift it chest high. In this way a several hundred foot length of track could be lifted from the ground. Another signal and the men would jump back, dropping the heavy rails to the ground, thus loosening spikes, bolts, and rivets. From here it was easy work to detach and lay rails atop huge fires to be heated and twisted around trees. The result became known as "Sherman's neckties".

When Sherman's armies reached the outskirts of Savannah on December 10, they were unable to approach due to flooding by the 10,000 defenders. Sherman dispatched cavalry to Fort McAllister, guarding the Ogeechee River and on December 13, General William B. Hazen's forces stormed the fort. Within 15 minutes they had captured it. Now, armed with heavy artillery, Sherman was ready to take Savannah. On December 17, he sent a message into the city, calling for its surrender. The enemy decided to flee rather than surrender and three days later the city was left unprotected. The next morning, Savannah Mayor Richard Arnold, offered a proposition to surrender the city and offer no resistance in exchange for a promise of protection of the city's citizens and their property. The offer was accepted and later that day Sherman's troops occupied the city complete with about twenty-five thousand bales of cotton one hundred and fifty guns and plenty of ammunition.

On December 21, Sherman telegraphed to President Lincoln and presented him, as a Christmas gift the City of Savannah.

After the fall of Atlanta, Sherman had dispatched General John Schofield's Army of the Ohio to join General Thomas in Tennessee. Hood was right on his tail almost trapping the smaller Union force at Spring Hill but a series of blunders allowed the Union commander to steal a march on Hood. In an attempt to meet up with Thomas now at Nashville, Schofield quickly assembled a defensive line at Franklin. On November 30, the outnumbered Union forces were able to repulse repeated attacks before withdrawing and successfully linking up with Thomas in Nashville. Hood followed but was now in a vulnerable position. He had lost a quarter of his 39,000 man army including six generals at Franklin and now they were ill-equipped and demoralized. An attack would be futile but to withdraw Hood believed, would further demoralize his men.

Thomas took his own time preparing for an attack. So much so that Grant, growing impatient after repeatedly ordering Thomas to attack, was ready to personally travel to Nashville to relieve the cautious Thomas. But on December 15 Thomas was ready and with a combined army attacked Hood's depleted ranks, routed it and sent it retreating to Tupelo, Mississippi. The Battle of Nashville was the last large-scale battle in the Western Theater. The Confederate Army of Tennessee now ceased to exist as an effective fighting force.

Lincoln interpreted his re-election as proof that the only acceptable conclusion of the war should be the full restoration of the Union with the destruction of slavery. He said as much in his message to Congress in December and proposed the Thirteenth Amendment, a constitutional amendment to abolish slavery with no compensation. Congress had earlier tried to pass the bill but results of the '62 elections had prevented it. It had passed in the Senate in April but failed in the House in June. Now, Lincoln proposed it once again. He could have waited for the newly elected 39th Congress to convene but its passage now would be symbolic, it would show the country that the amendment had received bipartisan support. So, on January 31, 1865, when the bill was passed into law the chamber erupted into joyous celebration while in the galleries where they had until now been previously banned, blacks wept and laughed at the news. Congress even allowed themselves the rest of the day off to celebrate.

Wade and Chandler tried to keep the momentum up by pushing for a system of retaliation upon Confederate prisoners. Wade proposed invoking a reprisal system in an effort to halt the harsh treatment of Union soldiers in Confederate prisons. Vowing to "...make the South a desolation, and every traitor shall lose his life, unless they treat our men with humanity." Conservatives and Radicals alike were stunned by the harsh tone of his speech and the retaliation bill failed to go through.

An uneasy peace seemed to fill the air in Washington with the passage of the Thirteenth Amendment. But the joy of the Radicals would be short-lived as Lincoln had remained consistent on his reconstruction program. There would be neither punishment nor retaliation. The Radicals however, had other plans. Whereas Lincoln believed the seceding states had never left the Union then, radicals such as Sumner claimed that such states had committed "state suicide" by seceding. Stevens wanted to treat those states as "conquered territories. By now, one-third of Congress had been radicalized and that number would increase when the newly-elected officials the 39th Congress took their seats. The stage would soon be set for their next great battle. When they Radicals heard of Lincoln's latest peace negotiations, they were ready.

In late January, Lincoln had sent Frank Blair Sr. to Richmond on a fact-finding mission regarding a proposed peace agreement. As a result, on February 3, Lincoln and Seward travelled to meet with Vice-President Alexander Stephens, Senator Robert M. T. Hunter, and Judge John A. Campbell. The Hampton Roads Conference took place on a military transport anchored near Fort Monroe. When Stephens asked if there was any way to obtain peace, Lincoln's reply was the immediate disbandment of their armies and allow the national authorities to resume their functions. Regarding the question of slavery, Lincoln informed them that Congress had just passed Thirteenth Amendment. Stephens then inquired if they would be admitted to representation in Congress to which Lincoln opined that they should be but he could not promise anything at this time. When Stephens pressed the point, Lincoln informed him he could not discuss the matter with "...parties in arms against the government."

But the agents would not let the matter drop. With his patience wearing thin Lincoln finally blurted out that if he were in their shoes he would go and inform the governors of their states to recall their soldiers immediately. He would then elect Senators and members of Congress to ratify the Constitutional Amendment, if even prospectively. Whatever their views were before the war, they must now be convinced that slavery was dead.

In regards to the confiscation acts, Lincoln told them their enforcements were left entirely up to him and he assured them that he would exercise that power with utmost liberality. Oddly, Lincoln then stated he would even consider compensating the South for their slaves. Lincoln stated that there was some support for this measure in the North but he could give no assurances. But the meeting was in vain for in the end no agreement could be reached.

Two days later Lincoln met with his Cabinet to discuss recommending to Congress compensating the eleven Southern states still in rebellion four hundred million dollars if resistance to national authority would cease on April 1. This would also include the five slave states in the North. The Cabinet unanimously disapproved the recommendation.

Considering the end was so near and who made up Congress, did it come as no surprise? But had his Cabinet members had the same foresight and magnanimous attributes as Lincoln, history may have been changed. Lincoln could have possibly led the Reconstruction process thus sparing the South of the harsh period which would surely follow.

When Radicals discovered that Lincoln had entered into negotiations without informing Congress, they angrily demanded full details of the trip. They feared that Lincoln would not impose a price for readmission and possibly even backslide on the emancipation proclamation. Lincoln of course obliged, telling them of his terms but neglecting to inform them of his proposed compensation. The Radicals were relieved somewhat but, since Lincoln stood by his Ten Per Cent plan, they needed to ensure all their hard work...the protective tariff, the national banking system and the Homestead Act, would not be undone by allowing Southern representatives to take their seats in Congress. They would also demand suffrage for all freed male, adult slaves, disenfranchisement of the many whites who had taken up arms against the government and confiscation of property.

Lincoln wanted Congress to recognize the new governments established in Louisiana and Arkansas and began discussing a series of compromise with Republican leaders. The Radicals would accept the delegates only if the remaining seceding states accepted the terms of the Wade-Davis Bill. But debates on certain conditions had killed any chance of compromise between the various factions. The Radicals surprisingly accepted this defeat with grace. They knew the war would be over soon and the next elected Congress would be able to pass a harsher reconstruction program. Then they could deny Louisiana delegates from taking their seats. The Radicals pushed through Congress a resolution early in February, declaring the eleven states which were in rebellion would not be entitled to representation in the Electoral College. The Radicals believed that until those states still in rebellion had conformed; they should be placed under military control as "...conquered provinces" as Stevens had suggested previously. Lincoln relented and reluctantly signed it. The Radicals had achieved another monumental victory over Lincoln.

The Radicals had been preparing for a showdown. In December, they had turned loose the CCW on Banks to undermine its militarily imposed government in Louisiana. This time, the CCW's investigation would not be a quest to remove a general officer from command. Although the military aspect of the campaign would be the main focus, the Committee intended to scrutinize the election process of the newly formed state government. Not only would the committee call the validity of the military-imposed administration into question, it would also seek to clarify the motives of the cotton speculators.

Many in Washington that felt the election was invalid since nearly four fifth of Louisiana had been unoccupied by Union forces with less than half of the 48 parishes being represented; most of the delegates came from Alexandria and New Ecore. With the lack of a quorum, the legitimacy of its ratified constitution was questionable and Banks' retreat during the Red River Campaign had left these areas in confederate hands. There were also rumors that Banks allowed the soldiers to vote in the election.

The result of the investigation was split. Most members agreed the campaign was devoid of any military objective and conducted without capacity, discretion, or support from the government. They viewed it as one of political nature, meant to promote Lincoln's reconstruction experiment and of a commercial character, referring to the presence of cotton speculators.

To once again validate their existence, the committee decided to take on those who had not yet accepted the radical policies. Their first target was Secretary of the Navy Gideon Welles, with whom they shared a mutual distain. On February 16, Wade denounced Welles on the Senate floor, accusing him of inefficiency regarding the construction of twenty inferior monitors. Wade proposed resolution to establish a board of admiralty stood no real chance of passing but the point was clear; even the Secretary of the Navy and its branch was not safe from investigation.

The committee once again turned their attention to General Meade. In late February, '64 the committee had launched an investigation against the hero of Gettysburg based on accusations leveled by his two primary enemies; Butterfield and Sickles. The former was a good friend of Hooker's and served as his chief of staff. When Hooker resigned, Butterfield agreed to stay on until the impending danger of Lee's invasion had passed. After the battle Meade replaced Butterfield with another officer. This angered Butterfield since his association with the Army of the Potomac would be no more.

Sickles' blunder on the second day of the battle had seriously threatened the outcome of the battle. But the loss of his leg, along with his powerful political allies saved him from public scrutiny and possible court-martial. While convalescing in Washington, Sickles shared with all his heroic acts during the battle and taking credit for the successful outcome. After his recovery, Sickles returned to the Army of the Potomac in October of '64 expecting to resume command of his Third Corps but Meade refused him, stating there is no possible scenario in which there would be a place for him in the Army of the Potomac.

Outraged, both Sickles and Butterfield began to criticize Meade's generalship, For the CCW, this was a godsend. One allegation lodged against Meade for his reluctance to fight at Gettysburg. Once the battle began he had entertained the thought of retreat. Another was his failure to aggressively pursue the enemy. Still another was his failure to attack the Confederates trapped against the Potomac River at Williamsport. And lastly, they questioned his fitness to command in light of his many failures during and after the battle.

Meade's loyalty had also been suspect. Besides being a close friend of McClellan, Meade and ex-Virginia Governor Henry A. Wise wives were sisters. Furthermore, while stationed in Detroit Meade and his staff refused to obey the local authorities' resolution to renew their oaths to the Union in response to the firing on Fort Sumter, claiming that local leaders had no authority to do so. He also made a statement before the war that he did not look forward to fighting so many of his old friends. To the committee, these words were paramount to treason.

Sickles was the first of fifteen Union generals to testify claiming Meade had never wanted to fight at Gettysburg and it was he himself who brought on the battle. Doubleday, who claimed a pro-slavery clique ruled the Army of the Potomac, was seeking revenge against Meade for removing him from of I Corps on July 1. And so it went, Generals Howe, Birney, Pleasanton, and others testified against Meade until the committee was fully convinced of the general's guilt.

On March 3, Wade, Chandler and Missouri Radical Benjamin F. Loan who had replaced Covode on the CCW, met with Lincoln and Stanton to force Meade's removal. Unless Lincoln complied and placed Hooker, who had been exonerated earlier by the committee or another general agreeable to them back in command, the CCW would make public their report. Lincoln refused however based on the fact that Meade was never interviewed. Agitated, the next day Meade met with Wade who informed the general the meeting was merely to record the history of the battle and not a critique of his generalship.

Like the others before him, Meade was never made aware of any damning testimony against him. During the three hour interview Meade had given a full account of himself and his actions but the committee members were still not satisfied. Ultimately, Meade was interviewed two more times. Aware of their motives, Meade wrote to his wife, "It is a melancholy state of affairs, however, when persons like Sickles and Doubleday can, by distorting and twisting facts, and giving a false coloring, induce the press and public for a time, and almost immediately, to take away the character of a man who up to that time had stood high in their estimation." The CCW once again forced the issue upon Lincoln but by this time the president had already promoted Grant so he simply ignored their demands.

Now, scarcely a year later, when a rumor was circulating that Meade refused to arrest a Democrat who supposedly tried to pass invalid Republican ballots during the fall electoral canvass, the Radicals found their scapegoat for the "Crater" disaster at Petersburg.

Four members of the committee headed by Chandler arrived at Petersburg to conduct their interview. Dining with Grant, Julian made note afterward how they were appalled that Grant got drunk before the dinner was over. The committee then began their investigation. On interviewing Burnside, they were once again informed that it was Meade who had wanted the plan to fail and that due to his prejudice he was against using black troops.

Meade was interviewed next and he explained his skepticism of the plan but did not wish to interfere in any way. His reason for using white troops was to save the government from criticism for sacrificing black troops to such a dangerous assignment. Meade then suggested the committee interview his staff officers. The committee did and afterward, he gloomily observed the officers leaving the tent laughing, informing Meade that, as soon as they said anything critical of Burnside, they were cut off. Meade knew he was their target.

The committee then interviewed Grant. Of course, they were not happy when he supported Meade while censuring Burnside. He did agree however, that it would have been better to use the black troops only because they were trained for the operation. To be fair, black regiments had served with honor since their enlistments. The opening battle for Petersburg on June 15 saw several black regiments capture artillery pieces as they assaulted the defenses.

In February, the committee made their report. It was obvious they would assign blame to Meade for the disaster while vindicating and even praising Burnside. The committee even went as far as to distort Grant's interview to condemning Meade for not using black troops. Meade now resigned himself to the fact that he would be drummed out of service but Grant was not about to let that happen. In a letter to Meade, Grant consoled him stating the committee reported his interview out of context. But in the end the committee assigned the blame to Meade for his reversal on the decision to use black troops.

This was another instance of the damaging effect the CCW had on military leaders. If Meade had used black troops and the plan failed, he would have been blamed for sacrificing them. There was nothing positive to be gained by this investigation. With Grant's support the committee was powerless to remove Meade. With the war so near its end, the only thing to suffer would be Meade's reputation. Their annoyance over this defeat was nothing compared to what Grant was about to do next.

The members of the committee now found themselves in a peculiar position. With the war nearly at an end they become worried about the two leading military men; Grant and Sherman. Their views were not entirely aligned with that of the Radicals. Grant, who had accepted full emancipation and subjugation of the South, was still unwilling to play the political games needed to enforce harsh reconstruction. Sherman had resisted the Emancipation Proclamation, the Second Confiscation Act, and the use of black troops. He viewed the war as merely restoring the Union and nothing more. By stating that once the South surrendered and admitted wrongdoing, they should be allowed re-admission, Sherman became a marked man.

Fort Fisher, located at the end of the Cape Fear River guarded Wilmington, the last port of entry of the Confederacy to remain open. For some time Welles had wanted to take the fort. He proposed to Grant a joint army/navy venture under the young General Godfrey Weitzel and Admiral David Porter. Butler, who would supply a portion of the 6,500 troops needed from his Army of the James decided to attach himself to the expedition; much to the dismay of Grant. The project was off to a bad start as bickering amongst the army and navy officers delayed the plans. Also, the press had foolishly announced the expedition, putting the rebels on guard. Just as the operation was to be called off, Butler hit upon a scheme. He proposed floating a boat armed with explosives alongside the fort walls and detonating the charge. The blast would tear a hole in the wall into which the troops could quickly enter and take control of the fort from the remaining defenders.

Grant was skeptical but agreed to the plan and had orders drawn up with a few adjustments. When the powder boat was detonated the navy would let loose a bombardment on the fort after which the troops could quickly be landed and attack through the opening created by the explosion. But Grant ordered that if the fort could not be taken then the troops were to stay ashore and entrench. Grant gave the hand-written orders to Butler to be passed on to Weitzel. Butler however, decided that, since the idea was his so should be the glory and he never shows the orders to Weitzel.

The plan failed miserably. The boat charged with the 235 pounds of black powder had been floated up alongside the fort and detonated but the explosion failed to tear a hole in the wall. Porter quickly moved up and began his bombardment until return fire from the fort died down. It was time for Butler to land the troops. The unloading began but soon Butler had second thoughts. Believing the fort could not be taken Butler, ignoring Porter's demands to continue as ordered, quickly recalled the nearly 2,500 troops which were already ashore. Once the troops were aboard the flotilla, the fleet abandoned the mission and returned to Fort Monroe.

When news of the failed attempt on Fort Fisher had reached Washington the Radicals were afraid that Lincoln finally had reason to remove Butler, the last of their favorite sons. Not wanting Butler to share the same fate as Pope, Hooker, and Fremont, the committee had hoped to keep Butler in a powerful position which would certainly aid the Radicals in their bid to make the South pay. They quickly passed the blame to Porter and the navy. But it was too late, for Grant knew with whom the blame laid, the incompetent Butler and on January 10, Grant relieved the belligerent Massachusetts politician. Lincoln, no longer fearing Butler's political clout, was all but too happy to approve his removal.

The Radicals had wanted to go head-to-head with Grant ever since he defied their suggestions regarding appointments and Fort Fisher was their excuse. In an attempt to restore Butler to command, the Senate immediately approved a resolution to launch an investigation against Grant.

When Butler entered the lobby of Willard's Hotel he was welcomed with a standing ovation and hailed as a hero. All night the political bosses climbed up to his room to offer their support, promising that Grant and his West Point henchmen would not prevail. The next day, January 17, Butler met with the committee. In a four-hour session Butler explained how Grant had asked him to assume command of the expedition since Weitzel was young, inexperienced and feuding with Porter. He then explained that the seas became too rough after he started to unload the troops and had no other recourse other than to recall the men. Since he had technically not affected a landing, he could not be charged with dereliction of duty by disobeying Grant's orders. Additionally, since the fort could not be taken due to Porter's failure to breach the walls there were no troops ashore to entrench.

Butler answered the inquiries with long, well-prepared statements. At the end, when asked why he was relieved Butler replied that the West Point clique resented that he was the last civilian soldier who held an important command. There was no cross-examination.

Butler had prepared his defense well and when his testimony ended, the committee asked Butler if there was any other statement he cared to make. This opened the door to a tirade by Butler who had been appointed U.S. Agent of Exchange, defending his own military record while taking shots at Grant, accusing the overall commander of being "...as unjust as he is reckless of other men's lives and reputations" and blaming him for not allowing a prisoner exchange. At the end of January Butler would publically scorn Grant in the press for not enforcing a prisoner exchange. Butler also criticized the administration for their lack of adopting a retaliation system. In the end Chandler stated that Butler had done more for the war effort than any other general. Oddly, on the day Butler appeared before the committee Fort Fisher was taken.

The Radicals were jubilant over Butler's testimony but his work was not yet over. Once home in Massachusetts, Butler sent to Wade damaging evidence against Porter and a list of names that would bear witness against him. Butler then wrote to Weitzel, first patronizing and then coaching him on his testimony before the committee. He also apprised Weitzel of his political connections and influence which could secure an advanced commission for the young officer.

In order to get to the bottom of the Fort Fisher debacle, the committee felt it necessary to interview the general-in-chief himself. By ordering Grant away from his duties in front of Richmond, the committee had shown their contempt for the general. Grant appeared before the committee on February 11. Their lack of knowledge in military tactics and procedures was quite obvious as they tried to shake Grant through an intensive grilling, but Grant held his own. He informed the committee that he was against Butler joining the expedition, that his powder boat scheme was impracticable, and that Butler had deliberately disobeyed his orders to land and entrench the troops. Trying to get Grant to admit that the coastline made the landing too dangerous to effect a landing, Grant informed that was not the case; a landing was indeed practicable for it had been done and the fort was now taken. Grant informed the board that Butler's replacement Major-General Alfred Terry had taken the fort with 8,000 troops which included two black brigades.

Wade then switched his line of questioning and attacked Grant's prisoner exchange policy which had nothing to do with the Fort Fisher affair. Grant informed the committee that he had ordered Butler to halt the prisoner exchange in August of '64 because many of the rebels rejoined the ranks once they had been exchanged which prolonged the war. At the end of the session Grant departed and the committee was no further ahead. But they refused to give up and continued to call before them other witnesses; Porter, Weitzel, and any other who could somehow vindicate Butler.

Meanwhile, they continued to pressure Lincoln to appoint Butler as provost marshal of South Carolina but Grant advised Lincoln against this stating Butler had been very critical of the administration in public speeches. An attempt for Butler to gain a position in the Cabinet also failed. By the end of March, the committee decided the only way to clear Butler's name was to head to Fort Fisher personally to find the answers they needed. Due to a sudden turn of events, they would never make it.

Chapter 13

Sherman's Final Victory

Grant had wanted Sherman to move his army from Savannah to Virginia by steamers, thus tightening the noose around Lee's army but Sherman had other ideas. He wanted to continue his march north through the Carolinas, following the scorched earth policy as he had done in Georgia. His ultimate goal was South Carolina, where secession had begun. Grant must have appreciated the irony so he gave his consent.

A company consisting of 100 white soldiers and 75 black pioneers had hacked their way through the forest and swamps to build corduroy roads. This allowed Sherman's men to advance at a rate of 10-15 miles per day through the Salkehatchie swamps while Johnston, who had been reappointed as commander of the Confederates could only offer light resistance. Upon hearing of his progress, Johnston had remarked that there had been no such army in existence since the days of Julius Caesar.

By February 17, Sherman had captured Columbia, the state capital of South Carolina. Controversy as to who fired the city would continue to this day. Next, Sherman entered North Carolina which would suffer less than its southern neighbor as it was regarded as a reluctant Confederate state, having been the last to secede from the Union. Sherman's final significant military engagement was a victory over Johnston's troops at the Battle of Bentonville during the latter part of March. He then continued on to Goldsborough, North Carolina, affecting a junction with Union troops at Fort Fisher.

In regards to Lee's request for a meeting regarding cessations of hostility, Grant had requested instructions from Lincoln. His response on March 3 was that only military matters or unconditional surrender should be discussed. Lincoln however had wanted to be on hand when Lee finally surrendered which he knew would be soon so on March 24, he decided to visit Grant at Point City, Virginia. The trip also allowed Lincoln to visit his son, Robert who served on Grant's staff. The president did not wait long to witness a victory for Lee had tried to break out of Petersburg by assaulting the Union line at Fort Stedman but was easily repulsed. Two days later, Sherman arrived in camp and met with Grant and the president. Lincoln insisted on being easy on the south once they surrendered and that they should promise executive recognition of state governments if by doing so would hasten peace.

On April 1, the last railroad connecting Richmond with the lower South was taken and Petersburg and Richmond were evacuated the next day. Two days later Union forces occupied both cities. Lincoln went into Petersburg and the next day headed for Richmond where he sat at Davis' desk and ordered a glass of water. He then met with General Weitzel, commander of the occupying force and instructed him to allow the Virginian legislature to convene in order to drop their support of the war. On April 8, Lincoln climbed aboard the steamer *River Queen* to head back to the Capitol. At that same time, John Wilkes Booth was checking in at the National Hotel in Washington.

On April 9, word of Lee surrenders at Appomattox Court House had reached Washington and the Radicals were furious over Grant's lenient terms. He had placed the leading military officers of the Army of Northern Virginia on parole; effectively protecting them from punishment. The next day Julian, Wade, Gooch and Chandler, forgetting Butler and the Fort Fisher affair departed Washington for Charleston. When they made a stop in Richmond they were stunned to read General Weitzel's order calling for the Virginian legislature to convene. They did not know that Lincoln had rescinded the order. When he had returned to Washington Lincoln had met with Cabinet members who shared their concern that the order could be misconstrued as recognition of a rebel government. Lincoln agreed but the withdrawal had not yet reached Weitzel when the committee members had arrived. Immediately they headed back to Washington for another fight with the president. They would arrive at the Capitol on April 14.

The day after Lee surrendered many of the Radicals, led by Butler himself, convened on the steps of the Willard. Numerous speeches were made vigorously denouncing Lincoln and his "bribe of unconditional forgiveness." They appealed to the public not to allow the rebels to return to the Union so easily.

The following day, April 11, Lincoln gave the last speech of his life. Standing in front of a large, exuberant crowd on the lawn of the White House, the speech was more of a challenge to the Radicals as he pledged no hangings or bloody revenge. The former states in rebellion should be welcomed back into the Union and he hoped to make it easy for their return. He would not insist upon Negro suffrage but he hoped the South would give the vote to the more intelligent Negroes, and to those who had fought as soldiers. This should be of the South's own accord and without coercion from the national government.

The Radicals however were ready to accept the challenge. They enlisted the aid of the radical press once again, this time to republish reports of the atrocities committed in Southern prisons and at Fort Pillow. Alluding to Grant's lenient terms of surrender, the Radicals cried that the Confederate leaders had, if not orchestrated, then at least condoned this behavior. By allowing a military pardon to the rebels, they would be exempt of the punishment the Radicals believed they deserved.

Corporal James Tanner had lost both legs below the knees at the second battle of Bull Run. A debilitating wound for any man in those days but not for the young corporal. He displayed his wounds as a badge of honor. When he had recovered enough to travel he returned to New York, attended college and then secured a position at the Ordnance Bureau of the War Department.

"The president had been shot" echoed throughout the streets. Standing on a balcony of the boarding house located on Tenth Street a young corporal watched the soldiers as they formed a perimeter around the Petersen House. General Christopher Auger, commander of the troops in Washington was calling for a clerk who knew shorthand and immediately, the young corporal was pointed out. Armed with a short pencil and some scraps of paper, he hurried as fast as his prosthetics and the crowd allowed. It was April 14; Good Friday.

General Meigs, who was manning the front door of the Peterson House, quickly stepped aside to allow the young corporal to enter. Immediately, he heard the booming voice of Illinois Governor Richard Oglesby shouting out orders and making threats to whoever was responsible for the heinous act. Stanton was also barking out orders and did not notice the young corporal until the secretary's assistant Charles Dana a former newspaper reporter, motioned for the clerk to stand near a chair opposite of Stanton. Stanton ordered Tanner to sit and take down all testimony that was to be given and not one word should be omitted. The young clerk could only nod as he awkwardly took a chair and reached for the pen left behind on the table. His predecessor had been unable to keep up with the hurried testimony of the numerous witnesses.

It was near midnight when Stanton recalled the first witness. Alfred Cloughly, a clerk in the Second Auditor's office who had witnessed the escape Seward's attacker. Lieutenant Crawford of the Veteran Reserve Corps was next. He had seen Booth moments before he entered the entrance to the President's Box. The actor Harry Hawk, who was onstage when Booth leapt from the president's box to make his getaway, was next, followed by a neighborhood saloon keeper, James Ferguson, who claimed to know Booth well. Several more witnesses followed and Jim would often put up his hand in an effort to slow down the words which came rushing from each witness.

At 1:30 in the morning the interviews were complete. Jim was spent but wanted to transcribe his notes while the words were fresh in his mind. In the next room he could hear the wails coming from the First Lady Mary Todd. She had wanted to be near her husband but when she entered the room where Lincoln lay, she immediately broke down. Stanton ordered that she be escorted to another room and comforted.

Outside, the streets were full but the crowd, transformed into a mass of vigilance, huddled together with grim, sorrowful looks upon their faces. A constant murmur filled the air as prayers were offered up for the president and the Union. As the heavy gloom held sway over the crowd they all knew it was only a matter of time.

It was 6:45 am when young Tanner reentered the house. Activity had all but ceased inside. Making his way with a second, neater copy of his transcript to the room where Lincoln lay dying, he saw Stanton seated at the foot of the bed gazing intently. It was obvious the president was unaware of the goings-on surrounding him. He lay diagonally across the bed with his feet hanging over the edge and his head slouched over in an awkward angle in an effort to allow the wound to breathe. His usual dark complexion had now lightened due to the loss of blood and swelling began to form behind his right eye. Two doctors were keeping a close watch on the ailing president.

The room was only nine foot by seventeen foot and the men now surrounding his bed were doctors and Cabinet members. Lincoln's sporadic breathing interrupted the silence. The Reverend Dr. Gurley, who had been comforting Mrs. Lincoln, now returned to the room where Lincoln lay, surrounded by doctors who could do nothing. His long, labored breath became suddenly halting; his body jerked violently. And then, as quickly as the spasms started, they ended. As the blood drained from his face a transformation took place and a strange, relaxed look came over Lincoln's face and posture. A surreal calm now seemed to fill the room.

At 7:22 am, with Dr. Barnes touching the carotid artery and Dr. Leale, who felt the right wrist pulse, Lincoln's heart beat its last. Muffled gasps filled the room. Dr. Gurley, after moments of reverence silence, recited a small prayer; interrupted once by Stanton who had broken down and buried his face in the bed covers and sobbed. The young corporal in his haste to produce his only pencil from his pocket, broke the tip and was to unable to record the words. When Gurley finished speaking, the men in the room repeated the clergy's final word "Amen".

Stanton regained his composure, stood and announced, "Now he belongs to the *Angels*" (some sources say *Ages*) and with that he marched out of the room with several men following including young Tanner who was abruptly dismissed. Later that morning, as a drizzling rain fell, Johnson was inaugurated.

The hypocrisy of the Radicals was beyond belief. For four long years they had savagely attacked Lincoln personally and publicly through the press, committees, and on the floor of both Houses. They continually fought to undermine and sabotage his policies. The constant stress they exerted upon the slain commander in chief as he tried to guide the country through the long and bloody struggle was, if not senseless then at least selfish. Not only did it take its toll upon the president but the repercussions militarily, socially, and economically were unforgivable. And now, now, they feign outrage at the loss of their leader who had successfully guided them to a near cessation of hostility with the eradication of slavery.

There was no doubt that some Radicals believed Lincoln's demise was ordained. Chandler even wrote to his wife that God had kept Lincoln in office as long as he was useful and then placed a better man in his place. The Jacobins believed Johnson, who had used his political office to fight against secession and served on the CCW, was one their own. Not only did he adopt the radical policy on reconstruction, he even advocated it. He had just recently told Lincoln that rebel leaders should be shot. The Radicals went to extreme length to keep the new president in their circle. They had to. They needed to contain him before the Blairs got their clutches into him. On the 16, Johnson granted the Jacobins an interview. They hoped to persuade the new president to clean up his Cabinet by appointing new members.

Johnson was going to disappoint them however. They soon discovered that he would be softer on Reconstruction and tougher on civil rights issues. They would need to do something to change Johnson's mind on policy and Sherman provided that something.

Confederate General Johnston, with about 90,000 rebels at Greensboro, N.C. was still a menacing force but, with Lee's surrender, Johnston decided against the will of Confederate President Davis, to meet with Sherman at the Bennett Place in Durham to negotiate terms of surrender. They met the next day on April 18 but relations were strained as Sherman informed Johnston of Lincoln's assassination. Grant had instructed Sherman to offer the same terms as those given Lee but Johnston rejected these at the insistence of Davis who wanted resolutions regarding state government, civil rights and weapons returned to state arsenals. Sherman was aware that at Hampton Roads Lincoln was willing to end the war under two conditions, reunification of the Union and the abolishment of slavery. Knowing that Lincoln had advocated a compassionate truce Sherman agreed "conditionally" to generous terms that dealt with both political and military issues which Sherman felt were terms consistent with the views Lincoln had expressed at City Point. "Conditionally" meant that the terms must meet with Washington's approval. In a gesture of goodwill, Sherman issued rations to the starving Confederates and those who owned horses could keep them while Sherman arranged to loan horses to others to "insure a crop."

When word was received by those in Washington that Sherman agreed to recognize rebel governments and guaranteed protection of political and personal rights, the Radicals were outraged. Johnson, Stanton and the Cabinet had promptly rejected the terms and on April 21 they sent Grant, who was present at the meeting, to North Carolina to order Sherman to resume hostilities immediately. Johnston, having been informed of the rejection, ignored instructions from President Davis and agreed to purely military terms. The Confederate forces in the Carolinas, Georgia, and Florida were formally surrendered on April 26.

Sherman immediately sent a letter to Stanton explaining the incident. He had honestly believed that he was acting in accordance to the wishes Stanton had expressed when they met previously in Savannah. Sherman also explained that, although he thought it was a mistake, he had read the order given to Weitzel regarding the Virginia legislature, he was unaware however that the order had been rescinded. Feeling his case fully explained Sherman marched his troops up to Manchester on the south side of the James opposite of Richmond. While his men made camp, Sherman returned to Savannah to oversee matters there.

On April 24, even before he received Sherman's letter of explanation Stanton decided to publish in the *New York Times* his objections to the Sherman/Johnston truce while denouncing Sherman. With hints of disloyalty and sympathies for the South, Sherman was chastised for his gentle handling of the negotiations. Point by point Stanton refuted the terms and painted Sherman as a southern sympathizer. Stanton also made public a message Lincoln had sent to Grant in regards to terms of surrender. The secretary intimated that Sherman was also aware of this message. Public reaction to Stanton's letter was just what the Radicals had hoped for. Still stinging with the news of Lincoln's death the response was anticipated. Across the North Sherman, who had previously been elevated to the status of hero, was denounced publically in newspapers and speeches.

Even Halleck now in command of the Commonwealth of Virginia and headquartered at Richmond, issued a public order that no troops in Sherman's department were to obey him and should resume hostilities immediately. On his return from Savannah, Sherman was stunned when he read the order in the papers. He headed directly for Manchester where, upon his arrival, received an invitation from Halleck to join him in Richmond as his guest. Sherman of course, declined and responded that he had read the order and when he proceeded to Washington with his troops as per Grant's orders, it would be best if Halleck did not show his face for he could not be responsible for what some rash person might do.

Sherman could not let the matter go unanswered and he too published letter explaining to the public the facts which brought this all to a head. First, he had met with Lincoln, Grant and Admiral Porter at City

Point. At this meeting Lincoln had endorsed easy, conciliatory terms and never suggested avoiding discussions of civil matters. Sherman had also read Lincoln's orders to Weitzel regarding the rebel legislature. And finally, Sherman had hoped to affect a general surrender to prevent small, local bands of guerillas from forming.

His letter had satisfied the masses and once again he is revered as a hero. Sherman had turned the tables on the Radicals and now it was Stanton who was painted as the villain. Many in Washington now feared Sherman would march on the Capitol and turn his troops loose on the War Department. According to Butler, Stanton was so unnerved that he ready to resign. In an attempt to protect Stanton's job, Grant and Meade were made to appear before the CCW and testify as to the competence of Stanton as Secretary of War.

As time passed, feelings had cooled and the CCW now thought it safe to initiate proceedings against Sherman for his truce with Johnston. On May 22, the general appeared before the committee. Perhaps still apprehensive to the status of Sherman, the committee allowed the general an open forum with few interruptions in which to speak. Making no effort to hide his disgust for Stanton and Halleck, Sherman presented his case. He stated that as early as 1863, Lincoln had encouraged him to discuss civil matters. When Wade objected to this, Sherman replied that while in Georgia, Lincoln telegraphed him encouraging him to meet with Governor Brown and Alexander Stephens. He also pointed out that Stanton was aware of this and approved it on his visit to Savannah. Since Johnston and Confederate Secretary of War John C. Breckenridge both agreed slavery that was dead there was no need to include it in the article. Also, he reiterated that he felt he was acting in accordance to Lincoln's wishes when they last met at City Point.

It was at this point that Sherman observed that Stanton and Halleck's order to his subordinates to disobey orders and resume hostilities was a violation of his truce; "an act of perfidy." Furthermore, "by the laws of war and by the laws of Congress," their act was "punishable by death, and no other punishment."

The CCW had an opportunity to question Sherman on minor points regarding the surrender but thought better of it. Sherman would not be railroaded like so many others before him. To them, their job was done. In a twist of irony, the CCW which had badgered, harassed, and sabotaged West Point officers over the past three years, now find itself put into their place by a West Pointer himself. The episode with Sherman was their final chapter and in its last fight it was soundly whipped.

But for Sherman it was not over. At the Grand Review, a special viewing stand had been erected for military leader, dignitaries and the president. When Sherman ascended the stairs to take his place he shook hands with Johnson, Grant and every member of the Cabinet. When Stanton held out his hand Sherman looked at it momentarily and then turned his head. This public snub was the ultimate sign of disrespect. It did not go unnoticed.

The life of the Joint Committee on the Conduct of War had come to an end. Excepting its last fight with Sherman, committee members felt their job was a success. There was never a doubt that the one main reason for the CCW was to rid the army of what the Radicals had deemed the "undesirables." In his speech to the House on February 18, '63, Julian stated that in 1861, Democratic policy cursed this country by giving the likes of McClellan, Halleck, and Buell the three great military departments. Julian continued that they were to blame for Fitz-John Porter, General Stone, and General Nelson (possibly William "Bull" Nelson) whose sympathies with the rebels were well known throughout the country. He also lamented over the policy of favoring the Democrats with patronage in regards to appointment of general officers and assignments to the various military departments.

Article I, Section 8 of the Constitution gave Congress the right to investigate all aspects of the war and the CCW did just that. The committee did not limit their investigations to just battlefield defeats, they also investigated countless military expeditions, operations and campaigns from the Eastern coast to the Deep South, the Gulf, and the Western theatre. They inquired into matters such as ice contracts, fugitive slaves, federal contracts, convalescent camps and the treatment of wounded, trade regulations, Southern atrocities, the Fort Pillow massacre, construction of iron-clad steamers, the treatment of Negroes by General Jefferson C. Davis of Sherman's army, and the truth to questionable newspaper reports.

But the members also used the committee as a weapon; a tool by which they could rid the army of officers who they viewed as non-compliant. By using tactics of coercion, threats and public humiliation, the committee managed to manipulate a majority of the officers to either accept without question government policy or face the ignominy of dishonor and disgrace. Regardless of if they accepted these policies or not officers were still directed to instill upon their soldiers acceptance of policy.

Perhaps, the committee felt their cause was just; that the end justified the means. Working closely with Stanton, their method of interrogations was unorthodox. They had kept a checklist of the political opinions of the high-ranking officers. They had imposed their own military strategies upon the commanders and held back senate confirmation of promotions. When officers refused to reveal their plans, the committee would coerce subordinates to reveal them. During interviews they omitted witnesses sympathetic with the accused and would allow hearsay as fact.

Professionally trained officers were torn between loyalty to the government as to their West Point teachings and to their own beliefs. With their own distain for secular groups pushing radical ideologies, many felt the government imposing a national policy over a state's constitution was a matter of government overreach. The same went for many of the volunteer officers who, like the rest of the country, also had preconceived notion regarding policies i.e. the issue of slavery. By forcing these officers to accept emancipation and the enlistment of Negroes, the committee had compelled many of these officers to question their own loyalty, beliefs and integrity.

As the war progressed, so did the animosity of the committee towards the administration. In its first eighteen months of existence, the committee had enjoyed a somewhat harmonious yet tenuous relationship with the Lincoln, but the relief of Hooker and later, the president's address to Congress in December of '63, caused a rife between the two. If Lincoln refused to support their suggestions, the committee would threaten to arouse public opinion against him, or they would threaten to leak their findings to the radical press to shame the accused.

The committee had also feared McClellan's influence over the military and as it was, every commander of the Army of the Potomac had his administration either investigated or inquired into. Grant, due to his support of Meade, was no exception. Did the committee go too far? Did their contempt for the professionally trained military have a negative impact on the war as a whole? The assault on Patterson produced nothing more than to tarnish his reputation. He didn't have to answer his country's call but he did. Stone's promising career was cut brutally short because his loyalty was suspect. These men had served their country honorably, and were then discharged unceremoniously; their only crime it seemed was their conservative views. Fitz-John Porter, Franklin, and Meade were also suspect for their views. The common denominator of these three officers, all with successful military record, was a West Point education and their friendship with McClellan. But to the CCW, these officers were expendable.

But, replacing able commanders simply for their views with incompetents was also detrimental to the morale of the army. Pope, Hooker, and Burnside were not suitable commanders for such large commands. They were pressured to forego their West Point teachings and to advance at all cost. And the sabotage of McClellan's Peninsula Campaign undoubtedly had cost lives, not by battles and bloodshed alone but also by disease. McClellan may not have been as aggressive has they wanted but he possessed a genuine concern for his men. The committee's support of Pope and later Hooker over McClellan had no doubt cost lives. It could be argued that some of the committee's actions were not at all conducive to the war effort.

It is hard to know how much time, money, and resources were wasted on their mission. But the committee felt their task was justified and deemed it a success. They had forced Lincoln to accept emancipation as a war goal and restricted his plans of Reconstruction. Or had they?

Chapter 14

A Call to Arms

Thousands of spectators stacked ten deep in places lined the parade route as the victorious Union armies marched by. For two days 145,000 soldiers had marched in the great procession known as the Grand Review. Meade's magnificent Army of the Potomac, with its military air and straight-laced discipline, was one that could rival any European army in dignity and professionalism. The pride could be seen in the faces of their officers and the rigid precision of the soldiers.

Sherman's Armies of Georgia and Tennessee marched the same route the following day to no less a crowd. With long loping strides the Westerners appeared to march with a casual determination; the same unwavering yet nonchalant pace that had carried them through Georgia and up through the Carolinas. As they casted casual glances to the many well-wishers the crowd broke out singing "John Brown's Body" and soon the boys picked up the tune and the melody filled the air as the soldiers continued their triumphant march.

All along the parade route buildings were adorned with flags and bunting as a wave of patriotism filled the air. Between Fifteenth and Seventeenth Street individual states set up their own viewing stands complete with banners proclaiming such sentiments as "The West is proud of her gallant sons" and "The Pride of the Nation." But as the troops headed up Pennsylvania Avenue one banner stood out. A large strip of canvass had been suspended from, of all places, the Treasury Building. And on it was written the words "The Only National Debt We can Never Repay is the Debt We Owe the Victorious Union soldiers." The men's hearts swelled as they passed under this noble sentiment. Perhaps the cynical Colonel Charles S. Wainwright was prophetic when he hoped aloud that the public, having their minds made up that they could *never* repay, may not deem it useless to try.

The stark contrast between the two armies of Meade and Sherman was a clue as to who these men were who served in these armies. They were civilian-soldiers. The volunteers of the Army of the Potomac could stack up against any Regular regiment in their unyielding professionalism. The western armies however, with their casualness and want of adherence reflected the civilian side of the men who had fought. No less daunting in their duties, they knew of their great achievements. But these men had retained their identities and when it was over, men of both armies East and West would be veterans and soon, many of them would be headed home, prepared for their next grand adventure.

One thing missing from the great parade was the Colored units. For a war which had just freed a whole race of humanity, why was their efforts not paraded for all to see? Sherman's disdain for colored troops was well-known but it is possible that he left behind his contingent to bury the numerous dead in the wake of his march. For other Colored units whose enlistments were not up, they continued to serve in garrison duty as the occupying force throughout the South. Perhaps Johnson made the decision. A detachment of Colored troops did lead the two hour procession which carried Lincoln's remains from the ceremony held in the great East Room to the rotunda less than a month earlier. Whatever the reason it would be twenty seven years before blacks would have a chance to march along this route.

One million soldiers had stood in the ranks of the Union army when the Confederate army surrendered. Over the course of the next six months 800,000 soldiers would be mustered out of service and collecting $270,000,000 from the Treasury. Unlike the rebel soldier who made their way home on foot and penniless, most Union soldiers were sent home with their units via train, steamer, canal boat, and coach. Many a pockets were lined with an average of $250 from back pay and bounties owed them. A good many of these veterans were relieved of their earnings by swindlers and thieves as they made their way home.

Upon arrival to their hometowns and cities, most were met with much fanfare and parades. In Indiana, every unit which arrived at the state capitol heard speeches of praise and promises and an official statement from War Governor Oliver P. Morton. Even in the predominantly democratic New York City, identified as opposing the war and yet supplying over a quarter of the 450,000 New Yorkers who fought, a huge parade complete with booming cannons and a sea of bunting welcomed their heroes back from the war.

The North had flourished during the war and jobs were abundant but the industries were unable to absorb the hordes of available workers now seeking employment as the veterans returned home. Many had left for war with the promise that their jobs would be waiting for them. But the demands for materials for conducting the war had called for workers and with a steady supply of immigrants and freed slaves to fill those positions, many a veteran were now out of luck. Some could find work in the rural areas on canal and farms but when winter months set in even they were out of a job. Some took advantage of the Western lands available and, with only a small capital, could settle down to a life of farming. But for those with debilitating wounds, life would be harder.

In preceding wars, those who had returned home disabled were cared for by their local towns and neighbors but now, with so many needing assistance this was not a possibility. In an age of self-reliance and individualism the government naively believed these citizen-soldiers would return home to resume their lives which they had abruptly left. In July of '65, even Governor Oglesby claimed that veterans must now resort to their own efforts and not expect a handout from the government.

Pensions were not a new concept to America. The Continental Congress had compensated its wounded soldiers back in 1776 and it continued right up through the War of 1812 and the Mexican War. But, the country now had an army 30 times the size of the one which fought the Mexican War and, of the roughly 2.5 million soldiers who fought to preserve the Union nearly 300,000 had received debilitating wounds. Another 225,000 were discharged for ailments and disease contracted by years of poor diets, sanitary conditions, contaminated food and water supply, and emotional distress. For many, they would carry these effects of these for life.

On July 14, 1862, Congress did ratify the General Pension Law passed the previous year which would pay pensions retroactive to March 1, 1861. Top pensions of $30 a month were now paid to officers holding the rank of lieutenant-colonel and above while enlisted men could expect $8. Widows and dependents under the age of 16 would also be eligible. The pension system would be revamped two years later. Another benefit was a government allowance for amputees. This benefit entitled veterans a $50 allowance towards the purchase of a prosthetic arm and $75 toward a leg along with travel allowance to place of fitting. By July of 1866, Stanton would report the purchase of 3,981 legs, 2,240 arms, 55 hands and 9 feet.

But these measures were not enough for the disabled veteran to sustain his family. And for those veterans who had no family to care for him it was unlikely he would receive the proper care he would need. Unemployed and destitute, veterans began flocking to the cities long before the war had ended. Now however, with the mustering out of these great armies, sights of the forsaken soldiers lining the street corners and railway stations begging for alms was all too common and folks now, many claiming that army life had been ruinous to one's character, crossed the street rather than make eye contact with those seeking alms.

In New York Governor Reuben E. Fenton, who had six months earlier had promised a lasting gratitude and regards for their welfare now lamented in December of 1865, that the needs of the veterans now outweighed "the power of Executive and Legislative relief." He urged the organization of more charities and benefit fairs. Women of the North had already taken a leading role in this effort since the start of the war; their service as nurses, cooks and laundresses was indispensable. They had also organized countless soldiers' aid societies during the war to assist the suffering soldiers returning home from the war or recovering in one of the hundreds of hospitals.

Before closing its doors in the spring of 1866 the United States Sanitary Commission hosted Sanitary Fairs during and immediately after the war, raising millions of dollars. They also found employment for the disabled and assisted with their claims. The *Cooper Shop Refreshment Saloon* in Philadelphia was just one of many volunteer relief agencies which had assisted 400,000 soldiers, refugees and freedmen during the war. As the need arose, the saloon expanded into a temporary soldiers' home for the needier. Soon, other such homes were established across the country.

Other relief came from those who saw an opportunity. One example was the *Soldiers and Sailors Publishing Company* which employed physically disabled veterans to peddle history books of the late war. Another company was the *Soldiers' Messenger Corps* which also employed veterans who possessed an empty sleeve or pant leg.

In December of 1864, New York's monthly newspaper the *Soldier's Friend* was established. The publisher William O. Bourne sought to give advice to the disabled veterans, informing them to seek out white-collar jobs such as clerkships, accounting, and teaching, rather than manual labor. The paper also urged businesses to hire veterans over the "stay-at-homes." One popular feature offered was the essay-writing contest for those who had lost their writing arm. The *"Left-Handed Corps"* competed for monetary prizes from as little as $20 to a top prize of $250. The paper had even urged former enemies, North and South to unite and work towards a common goal of healing and moving forward. But this position would change over time.

In early summer of 1862, Boston established the *Discharged Soldiers' Home* and in New York, ex-governor Edwin Morgan had passed legislation in 1863 to establish a home to care for their returning heroes. The latter never materialized when residents, shocked at the notion that their promise to care for the wounded would be unfulfilled. The idea of their heroes being institutionalized was a fate they would never allow. But little did they know the second half of the war would be bloodier than the first, increasing the number of disabled veterans who would actually need care by wars' end.

The efforts of the Sanitary Commission and the other agencies had no doubt saved lives while restoring pride and self-worth in the broken soldier. They were determined to heal and rehabilitate the man; allowing him to make his own way in life. The Commission preferred generous pensions and community-based care for the veteran as opposed to Federal institutions where they feared the individual soldier would lose his identity. To the Commission it was somewhat bitter-sweet then when the *National Asylum for Disabled Volunteer Soldiers* (NHDVS) which was incorporated and passed in Congress in March of 1865 got off to a slow start.

The passage of the NHDVS act had placed the women in a secondary role since men in those days considered themselves more suited to organize and direct such Federal programs regardless of the highly successful work of the women in previous years. The first thing the men did was establish a one hundred-man *Board of Managers*, leaving the chance for a quorum highly improbable. It would be another year before this problem was rectified. Instead, it was left in the hands of volunteers led by prominent citizens but the lack of funding halted its development. Lincoln's promise of "To care for him who shall have borne the battle" in his second inaugural address was soon forgotten. And so was the state of affair regarding veterans immediately after the war.

On April 21, Lincoln's funeral train with the coffin of his son Willie also onboard departed the Capitol to begin its long, 1,654 mile circuitous trip through the northern states to Illinois. For Lincoln, the war was finally over. He left behind him a country free of armed conflict, along with the joys, pain, and suffering of his presidency. But he took with him any hope for a decided and lasting peace. His plan to "let them up easy" was not to be for Johnson was now in charge. It would not be long before he incurred the wrath of the same Radicals who had tormented Lincoln the past four years.

The Radicals, believing they had won their battles with Lincoln now had Johnson, their former comrade on the CCW, and the path would be clear to unleash their harsh reconstruction program upon the vanquished. Or so they thought. Johnson intended to block the clear path to reconstruction brought on by Lincoln's death and carry out his plan for restoration; a term he preferred to reconstruction.

Both Republican and Democratic parties were happy to see Johnson step in as president but for different reasons. Johnson was a Democrat and even though he had opposed secession he still had misgivings regarding the rights of the freedmen. The Democrats saw Johnson as a representative of the working-class who viewed emancipation as a problem child. They hoped he would be sympathetic to their plight in the South. The Republican Party outnumbered the Democrats three to one but they were divided on the reconstruction issue. The Conservatives were small in numbers but held powerful positions in the Cabinet and in both Houses. They felt the war had achieved its goal of restoration of the Union and emancipation and they advocated a speedy reunification of the country. The plentiful Moderates had favored emancipation and civil rights of the blacks but were against suffrage. Their main concern was the prevention of leading former confederates' return to power resulting in Southern Democratic control of Congress. And of course, there were the Radicals, still a minority but with their own ideas. Their plan was one of revenge. A harsh punishment upon former Confederate leaders, disenfranchisement of former rebels, confiscation, no admission until their loyalty was without a doubt, and civil and political rights of blacks.

But Johnson had a motive behind his plans. He saw the country as weary of war and wanting closure. Since the Union had been restored he saw no reason for delay. But, he also wanted to see political power transferred from the aristocracy to the working-class. By allowing blacks, who would still be bound to the former slave-powers, the right to vote, that would defeat his hopes for the political change he intended for the South. Besides, Johnson advocated the Jeffersonian doctrine of states' rights. He believed it was up to the states to decide when the enfranchisement of freed blacks would occur. Lastly, since public opinion seemed to be against Negro suffrage, by appealing to the Democrats and moderate faction of the Republican Party, he hoped to build his own coalition in which to win the presidency on his own accord in '68.

Martial law existed in the South as 200,000 Union soldiers, mostly black, maintained law and order. Initially, the South had prepared for the worst. They had lost. Although a deep hatred, mostly among the Southern non-combatants, existed for the Yankees, ex-confederate soldiers had seen enough of war and hardship to prolong the animosity anymore. Johnson began lifting restrictions on all domestic trade in Southern territories held under Union control and a month later in July he ordered all ports in the South reopened to foreign trade. By doing this, a sense of normalcy seemed to have returned as social and economic relations resumed once again between the North and the South. While few Southerners headed north to gain employment, many Northerners made their way south, taking advantage of low prices on abandoned property. Animosity between the two sections had given way as old relations were resumed, although careful to avoid topics regarding the late war.

But the South's submission would be fleeting. Treasury agents were soon invading the South to claim their prize. A two and a half cent per pound tax, later to be raised to three cents, was levied on cotton. Many of the agents saw their chance to capitalize on their position. It would not take long for the South to become defiant once again. The work of the Freedmen's Bureau didn't help. When plantation owners who fled in the face of the Union armies returned home, they wanted their lands back. But the assistant commissioner of the Freedmen's Bureau General Rufus Saxton refused them, for ten thousand black families now occupied nearly a half million acres in the coastal regions of South Carolina and Georgia.

Johnson had refused to call for a special session of Congress which was not set to convene until December. For he believed as Lincoln had, that reconstruction was the responsibility of the president. Johnson soon recalled Stanton's order for the arrests of high-ranking rebel leaders in the wake of Lincoln's assassination and was now against extensive confiscation and began returning property which had been seized. Johnson also decided to alter Lincoln's Ten Per Cent Plan. By issuing his own Amnesty Proclamation, the president had not only granted a general amnesty towards former rebels but now required them to take a qualified pledge to support all laws and decrees related to slavery. To appease the Moderates, Johnson exempted from amnesty six classes of persons, the most significant were those who had a worth in property in excess of $20,000. They would have to apply to the president for their right to vote or hold office. As for admission of rebel states back into the Union, Johnson imposed three conditions, they must officially declare the articles of secession invalid, ratify the Thirteenth Amendment, and repudiate the debt incurred during the war. Johnson's Cabinet had approved these measures but the Radicals were opposed since there left no door open to black suffrage.

Johnson also intended to recognize the militarily-imposed civil governments which had already been established during Lincoln's administration in Tennessee, Arkansas, and Louisiana; Virginia could retain their war-time imposed government. North Carolina had just begun the process prescribed by Johnson which left six states, Mississippi, Georgia, Texas, Alabama, South Carolina, and Florida. Johnson appointed loyal Union men as provisional governors in these states to oversee his reconstruction plans. Each state would hold their own conventions and elect officials. Once the three conditions were adopted, the provisional governor would be relieved and the state would be allowed readmission. But Johnson had messed up badly. By granting amnesty to former high-ranking secession leaders, 13,500 out of 15,000 who had applied, many prominent ex-confederates were elected back into position of power. Now, as delegates at their respective state conventions, they debated the constitutional legality of Johnson's program.

Johnson did try to extend the olive branch to the Radicals by suggesting to the Southern states that they consider extending "the electoral franchise to all persons of color" who could read, sign their name, or owned real estate valued at no less than $250. By doing so, Johnson explained, they could appease the Republicans and enhance their chances for quick admission to the Union. But the suggestion fell on mostly deaf ears as only six states considered black suffrage on any term. The Radicals saw right through this ruse. Contrary to Lincoln's suggestion to Louisiana's government previously, Johnson excluded suffrage to blacks who had served in uniform. With barely one black in every nine being eligible under these conditions, most Republicans saw their chance as the ruling party being taken away.

Mississippi, along with Texas failed to ratify the Thirteenth Amendment. Mississippi also joined South Carolina in refusing to repudiate their war debt while Georgia sought the right to sue for compensation for the loss of their slaves. As a result of Johnson's leniency, southern states had elected at their first election nine ex-confederates as congressmen, along with seven as state officials and numerous high-ranking former Confederate officers now held state offices. Even the former vice-president of the Confederacy Alexander Stephens was elected to the Senate. In Louisiana, ex-confederates had persuaded their provisional governor to dispose of Unionist officeholders and replace them with former secessionists.

In August, Mississippi's provisional governor William L. Sharkey even went as far as trying to form a Mississippi militia to combat the rising crime rate of assault and burglaries. But to General Henry W. Slocum, commander of occupation forces there, the militia, made up of ex-rebels, was meant to pressure the government to reduce the number of troops, mostly black, of the occupational forces there. When Slocum halted the buildup of the militia, Johnson recalled him from the state, along with General Schurz who was on an inspection tour there. To the Radicals, this was an insult to the all that fought and died in putting down the rebellion. When planters in South Carolina petitioned Johnson for the return of their property, Johnson relieved Saxton and began returning the lands to their previous owners.

Members of Congress were not happy when they reconvened in early December and listened to Johnson's impassioned speech calling for a hasty reunion of the states. The country was ready to be reunited. Remarking that the government had limited control, he stated that each state retained the right to decide when to allow the freedmen the vote. He felt the nation was ready to begin healing and to move forward. For the war-weary North, Johnson's desire for a speedy reconciliation with the South was a welcomed change. Johnson had taken the steps to restore civil governments to the Southern states and they would soon be ready to rejoin the Union. But this was not to be. What should have been a time of healing and reunification turned into another struggle over who would control Reconstruction.

The Radicals had a reason to fight for control. The Thirteenth Amendment had been officially ratified by twenty-seven states which constituted a three-fourth of the states on December 18, 1865. Slavery would be no more but another implication had grown out of the ratification. Two-thirds of the population in the South was freedmen. Previously, they had been excluded from representation but now, as citizens, each state in the South would have increased representatives in Congress. This power shift could have favorable results for the South. If the Republicans wanted to remain in power they needed to deny readmission of Southern delegates until Negro suffrage had become law.

But Johnson's December's speech was well received by the public. By now, many in the North had felt that slavery had been a source for all the country's woes. With the passage of the Thirteenth Amendment, the people would surely resist any open confrontation with the administration over Reconstruction. They were ready to move on. Johnson had the backing of the northern and southern Democrats, some Conservatives and Moderates who also believed that the war had achieved its goal of restoration of the Union and emancipation. The Radicals were very aware of the opposition so they had to proceed with caution. Besides, many of the veterans were supporting Johnson. The results of the 1864 election may have appeared that soldiers accepted emancipation but that was either because soldiers viewed it as a military necessity or they had suppressed their opinions or differences regarding emancipation and the enlistment of former slaves. Near the end of the war however, many Union soldiers stationed in the South grew apathetic towards the plight of the Negro. It is doubtful that, to many, ensuring the civil rights of freed slaves was on their minds.

Johnson, knowing a fight with the Radicals was inevitable, had hoped to decrease the margin of their majority by allowing more Southern Democrats into Congress. So, as each Southern state conformed, Johnson allowed their admission back into the Union. This of course, ran counter to the Radicals' agenda. If they were to recognize the restored civil governments, the hopes of Negro suffrage would be destroyed, along with all they had achieved over the past five years. But it was not just the Radicals who had a problem with Johnson's action. The Republican Party in general needed to work in concert lest they be voted out of office thus allowing the Democrats to regain control. And they were not about to let this happen. Just as they had with Lincoln, the Radicals were going to lead the fight with Johnson over the power to control Reconstruction. Their first move was to bar the Southern delegates from taking their seats in Congress. When they had convened in December, the Clerk of the House had conveniently omitted the names of the Southern representatives.

Former confederates were beginning to show nothing but contempt for the freedmen and loyal whites in the Southern states and tensions began to rise. Obeying Johnson's instruction to write up legislation defining specific details as to the status and rights of the freedmen, many southern legislatures began adding specific laws to their constitutions assigning Negroes to a distinct class. These laws, known as the *Black Codes,* varied throughout the Southern states but many included that freedmen were not allowed to carry weapons except after obtaining a license, they could not own land but must rent in an incorporated town, they must be employed by whites or former owner and enter into a contract with such. In South Carolina, freedmen must restrict employment to husbandry or domestic services except under a license requiring a substantial fee. If unemployed and without permanent residence they were subject to vagrancy law and sold to the highest bidder to pay off their fines. Orphans and other young dependents could be hired out to whites, which often were their former owners. Former slaves were forbidden to testify in court, except in cases concerning other blacks. Legal marriage between blacks was allowed but interracial marriage was prohibited. To the Radicals, the introduction of the *Black*

Codes in the South was a welcomed sight. They viewed them as the South attempt to snub the government as they disregarded the outcome of the war. The Radicals intended to use these laws to sway public opinion.

Reports of strained relations between poor whites and the Colored troops stationed in the South had reached Washington and Johnson sent General Schurz and two newspaper reporters, Ben C. Truman and Henry Watterson to investigate. The latter two had reported back that, while tensions did exist they believed it would ease over time and that enfranchisement of the blacks could only do more harm than good at this point. But the radical Schurz disagreed, informing Johnson black suffrage was needed to ensure that the South knew they had been defeated. He then took it upon himself to draft his findings and views in an official report and introduced into the Senate at the 39th session.

Johnson remained unconvinced and in November ordered Grant on a fact-finding mission to the South. Grant, along with Truman who had now been there 31 weeks, reported back. Both agreed that Johnson's policy was the correct path to take. Grant also agreed with Johnson's policy of pardoning established southern leaders and restoring them to their positions of power. He also recommended the continuation of a reformed *Freedmen's Bureau*, a temporary program Lincoln had authorized in March of 1865 to provide for freed slaves food, housing, legal assistance, and medical aid. Grant also advised against the use of black troops in garrisons. Grant continued, stating that the Southerners accepted their present condition but to impose at this time black suffrage against the will of the whites would only result in race wars. Their reports however, came too late as the Radicals had already accepted Schurz's position.

The fight over control of Reconstruction was on and the Radicals resorted to a familiar trick to exert their control in forming reconstruction policies. Intending to keep delegates of the former Confederate states from claiming their seats in Congress, Stevens pushed a resolution through and on December 13, the *Joint Committee on Reconstruction* (JCR) was formed. The fifteen member committee was divided into sub-committees and charged to investigate conditions in the four military districts in the South. After their investigation they reported back to Congress the horrendous treatment of Negroes and of Southern Unionists being targeted in defiance of National authority. The establishment of the *Black Code* added to the belief of the committee that the continuation of the *Freedmen's Bureau* was imperative.

In January of 1866, Senator Trumbull pushed for a two-year extension and expansion of the bureau in response to the Black Codes. Before the bill went up for consideration, it was presented to Johnson to see if he had any objections to it; he did not. But then Johnson did the unthinkable, after passage in both Houses, the bill came across his desk and on February 19, he vetoed it. While harshly rebuking the Radicals Johnson stated it was unnecessary and unconstitutional. He also added that since the eleven states were excluded from voting, its passage was illegal.

The work of the Freedmen's Bureau antagonized many of the Southerners and Johnson viewed it as detrimental to his gaining popularity in the South. He also viewed it as a ploy of the Radicals to secure the support of the blacks in the South. The next day the Senate failed to gain the two-thirds majority needed to overrule his veto. Incidentally, on the day of the failed vote to overturn Johnson's veto, the House adopted a resolution declaring no senator or representative could be admitted until Congress declared the state entitled to such.

Three days later on Washington's Birthday, Johnson had celebrated his first victory over the Radicals with fellow Democrats. From a balcony of the White House Johnson denounced the Radicals to his crowd of supporters; referring to them as traitors attempting to circumvent the Constitution. For many of the onlookers, the president's openly criticism of the Radicals whom he felt most of the Republicans were, was very unbecoming for a president.

A month later when Trumbull introduced the *Civil Rights Bill;* designed to extend Federal citizenship to the freedmen and protect them from the Black Codes. Again, Congress had let Johnson review the bill and again he gave silent approval. Once again, Johnson stunned the country by using his veto power. Johnson condemned the bill as an unconstitutional intrusion on state's rights and discriminatory against whites. But Johnson had made a miscalculation of his administration. His veto was being viewed as cozying up even more to the Southern Democrats. The Moderates, who were also concerned with losing power to the Democrats, had supported the bill and they now began joining the ranks of the Radicals. On April 9, Congress had for the first time, overruled a president's veto and the *Civil Rights* bill became law. The clash between Johnson and Congress erupted and a mass exodus of the Moderates began, rallying to the radical camp to oppose Johnson and his Democratic allies. Congress now had the power to overturn Johnson's veto of the Freedmen's Bureau in July and extend its term two years.

Continuing their work, the JCR drafted a proposition for the *Fourteenth Amendment* of the Constitution. Broken down into five parts, the first section declared that all persons born or naturalized in the United States, to include blacks would be citizens and guaranteed their civil rights. The second part would reduce House representation to any state which denied adult male citizens the vote. The third disenfranchised and made ineligible for federal office certain classes of high officials who served within the confederacy. The fourth repudiated the confederate debt while guaranteeing the national debt. Statehood could only be achieved when it accepted and ratified the amendment. The last section authorized Congress to enforce the amendment by legislation. After some discussion, the amendment passed both Houses with the necessary two-thirds majority on June 13. (Native Americans would not gain citizenship until the *Indian Citizenship Act of 1924*.

As the amendment was being debated, a bloody riot occurred in Memphis when white policemen fired upon black soldiers recently mustered out of service. An angry mob of white civilians and policemen then rampaged through black neighborhoods, killing black men, women and children. When it was over 46 blacks and two whites laid dead and 75 were injured while 100 blacks were robbed and five women raped. Nearly a hundred homes, eight schools, and four churches were burned. The riot was a result of tensions which had been building since the end of the war and was further proof to the Radicals that a harsh policy of reconstruction was needed.

While the news of the riot enraged those in the North, Johnson was unmoved and he stood firm on his policy. Johnson denounced the passage as illegal since no southern states were allowed to vote. Of course, the amendment was also denounced by all the former rebel states save one, Johnson's home state of Tennessee. They had ratified their state constitution to allow the amendment and immediately their representatives were recognized, much to the dismay of the Radicals. As it was, the amendment did not allow for black suffrage. But the Southern states had a point. As intolerable as the thought of giving blacks legal and civil equality was to them, they felt it was unfair considering the government was not forcing black suffrage upon the whites in northern states. The Fourteenth Amendment would be the platform of both parties at the '66 elections with one for and the other against.

The Radicals were gaining strength but, even though emancipation was the law, enforcing civil rights and suffrage for freed blacks was another matter. These measures were imperative if they were to gain control of state governments in the South. The Republicans now turned to the veterans in an attempt to secure their votes for the party. But forcing Negro suffrage upon the South would mean alienation of the veterans in the North. Just as they had in previous elections, the Radicals would need to condition the veterans; convince them that they must remain vigilant and not to allow the government to throw away all that they had won through their blood, sweat and tears. With congressional elections quickly approaching they needed to work fast.

But the Radicals wanted more than just votes. They intended to ask, no, to order the soldier-turned-veteran to once again pick up their arms and once again defend the Union. But this time, they would be defending it from the enemy within.

Chapter 15

Grand Army of the Republic

The ex-soldiers had grown weary of the "eternal Negro question" as they saw their own needs and concerns being ignored. To many of the veterans, the freedmen were a distraction; a threat. In the fifteen months following the surrender at Appomattox, the Freedmen's Bureau had dispensed 13 million rations, two thirds of which went to former slaves and their families while the remainder went to poor Southern whites. Although women in the North had gone to great lengths to provide for their veterans in need through numerous charitable societies, the government seemed to be halting in fulfilling their promises. There were no plans in place for adequate hospitals, housing, or care to provide for these men. The veterans felt abandoned. It was no surprise that they now supported Johnson and his policies regarding a speedy reunification.

Economic conditions, pension and bounty inequality and lack of jobs just added to the frustration of those who had already sacrificed so much. But if there was one thing the military had taught these soldiers, it was that when properly organized was there strength in numbers. Since state and federal governments seemed to ignore their plight and charitable employment bureaus were overwhelmed, veterans came together to form societies in which to offer comfort and support to those with whom they shared a common bond. By banding together as an organized body, they could make their voices heard. And their objective was clear; raise awareness of Washington's disregard to their plight. Soon, veteran organizations began springing up across the country. In New York, the *United States Soldiers and Sailors Protective Society* was just one of many societies established to raise awareness to the needs of the destitute, the poor, and the unemployed veterans.

Veteran organizations were nothing new to this country but this new organization had an agenda. As they began to march in protest to their plight the Democrats saw an opportunity. To capitalize on the frustrations of these soldiers the Democrats began charging that the blacks were now a privileged class. They told veterans that former slaves were now living in government quarters where they ate and drank for free. Their children were receiving free education while jobs that should have gone to veterans were being given to them. As they exasperated the situation, the Democrats told the veterans that the Republicans now planned to force Negro suffrage upon them. Even General Sherman unknowingly added fuel to the fire by opining that blacks were inferior and while he favored educating the Negro he did not support the 'elective franchise.'

Spurred on by the Democrats, veterans began to question officeholders and candidates on where they stood on the suffrage movement. Many of the Republican candidates were instructed not to speak openly about the issue, but behind closed doors there were many heated debates regarding the veterans' insistence that resolution committees fully accept the policies of the president. Republicans began viewing the veterans as dangerous element and tried to sidestep the issue. Undeterred, veterans pushed aside their attempts to dissuade the active participation of veterans in political activities, and began selecting their own delegates to nominating conventions. As veterans grew bolder in their demands, they now insisted that veterans appear on their respective party's tickets.

In an effort to deflect, the Republicans reminded the veterans that it was the Democratic Party, the party synonymous with treason who had tried to deny them their right to vote as they gallantly fought to save the Union. The 'true soldier' they claimed, would reject the party who fired upon them from the rear while they faced the enemy to their front. The Democrats fired back that it was the Republicans who were now in control of Congress and yet, ignored the veteran while dispensing patronage. Appointment to higher offices was usually given to officers while lower-ranking enlisted men received the menial jobs such as clerks.

As the size and strength of veteran organizations grew, many politicians on both sides of the political fence recognized their potential and they began to form their own political soldiers clubs. In September, the *Soldiers and Sailors National Union League* (SSNUL) was formed in

Washington and it quickly spread throughout the country, becoming one of the first veteran organizations to become national. L. Edwin Dudley was their national president. Although they professed no party affiliation, their character was marked with radicalism and their officers were all Radical Republicans. They supported veteran preference, bounty equalization, and an increase in pensions, high tariffs, and care for the families of the deceased. Resolutions were also passed condemning Lee and calling for military control of the South. These sentiments of condemnation for the South persuaded members to begin accepting the radical reconstruction policy.

The Democrats countered with the *United Service Society* (USS) of New York City which also gained national prominence. Its president, Colonel W.S. Hillyer openly admitted its political affiliation by stating the purpose of the club was strictly for political power. The USS would have branches in six states and boast nearly 8,000 members by November.

Although the Democrats aggressively pushed for the active participation of veterans in the political campaigns of 1865 their efforts failed. The Republicans scored a victory regardless of veteran opposition for Negro suffrage. But, they did learn their lesson and that was the veteran vote could not be dismissed.

As 1865 drew to a close the character of the veteran organizations would take a drastic change. Both camps had established successful societies which were nation-wide and organized. In addition, their officers were experienced military veterans with leadership abilities. Once used as a vessel to push for relief for the working class veterans, political leaders now viewed these organizations as politically charged voting blocs. Seeing this, one reporter for Boston's *Daily Advertiser* warned that "...unless veterans were given their share of public offices a politically powerful group would be formed, known as the soldiers' vote." This voting bloc would become one which many politicians would vie for the endorsement of.

A perfect storm was forming. Disgruntled veterans were banding together to raise awareness to their predicament while politicians agitated the situation by passing blame. All that was needed to nurture these conditions was one more element to bring it all together. This came in the form of two, very shrewd politicians.

Illinois Governor Richard Oglesby especially saw the potential of these veteran organizations; not just as a voting bloc but also as a pressure group. Oglesby's military record was secure. He fought, bled and nearly died for his country. Born in Kentucky, Oglesby moved to Springfield at age 12. He was good friends with Lincoln and came up with the slogan of, "Abraham Lincoln -the Rail-Splitter Candidate." For his gallantry at Fort Donelson, Lincoln promoted him from colonel to brigadier-general. Severely wounded at Corinth he returned to Springfield and at the encouragement of Lincoln, ran for and won the governorship of that state.

Illinois Senator John Logan was a staunch Democrat in 1861, but when war came he sought permission from Lincoln to accompany McDowell as he marched towards Manassas. Logan was anxious to get into the fight and it was at Blackburn's Ford that he observed a squad of soldiers falling back from the battle. Relieving one of the privates of his musket Logan found his place in line. The sights and sounds of the battle invigorated Logan and after the battle the senator resigned his seat to enlist; serving under Grant and Sherman. After the war, Logan returned home to Illinois but became restless. His life was somewhat anti-climactic after the excitement of the hostilities had died down. With hopes of representing Illinois in the Senate he remained silent until he could ascertain which way the political winds blew. He had tended his political fences well, even backing the radical Oglesby for governor in 1864. Logan even turned down the ministry to Mexico which Johnson offered. Together, Oglesby and Logan had formed an alliance that would soon have dramatic effects upon the country.

The two Illinois politicians had watched intently as events unfolded; and they plotted. If carefully orchestrated, a new veteran society could serve as an umbrella organization for the various smaller societies and, as one they could weld great political power. Needing to keep their hands clean they would have to find someone with a special talent for organizing and recruiting. They found him in Surgeon Benjamin Stephenson, a man who had already had plans for a benevolent veteran organization.

Dr. Stephenson's returned to Springfield, Ill. in May of 1864 after his three year enlistment had ended. He served on the examining board of surgeons at Camp Butler, near Springfield and soon had charge of the hospital where he remained until all the soldiers had mustered out. He continued his practice in Springfield and soon his reputation for taking pity on those desolated by war became well-known. He treated free of charge those with no money and hired soldiers, widows and orphans whenever possible and encouraged others to do the same. But, there was another side to Dr. Stephenson; he liked to dabble in politics.

Stephenson had formed a partnership with Dr. George T. Allen of the Surgeon-General's staff and Dr. James Hamilton, ex-surgeon of the 17th Illinois Volunteers. It was with these men that he shared his dream of forming a society where charity, loyalty, and fraternity would be its principles and caring for the destitute and less fortunate would be its mission. They would call the organization the *National Soldiers' Mutual Benefit Society.* With growing interest and support, Stephenson contacted his former messmate Chaplain William J. Rutledge, who was also excited by the idea. The two men, along with Colonel Daniel Grass who ensured the legalities of everything, studied the rituals, constitution and organizational structure of other established veteran and civic organizations. Based on those, they began drafting and detailing their own guidelines. Chaplain Rutledge suggested a meeting with Governor Oglesby for his approval. They met in the office of the governor's private secretary, Colonel John Snyder. Oglesby was impressed and suggested swearing I. N. Coltrin and Joseph Prior the proprietors of the *Decatur Tribune,* to secrecy before having the two ex-soldiers print up four hundred copies of the constitution, ritual, and rules.

With printed material in hand, their next step was to charter the first post of the new organization. Stephenson met with friends in Decatur and a committee composed of Dr. J. W.Routh, Capt. M. F. Kanan, Capt. J. T. Bishop, Maj. George R. Steele, and Capt. Geo. H. Dunning examined and unanimously approved the plans for the new organization. On April 6, 1866, the first post of what would become the most influential veteran organization of its time the *Grand Army of the Republic* (GAR) was established.

Under Oglesby close supervision Stephenson assumed the position of commander and began organizing a central department at Springfield. The Illinois governor supplied Stephenson with names of those who would be most influential in recruiting. Colonel Phelps, Jules C. Webber and others were appointed as organizers and traveled the state for the purpose of establishing additional posts and met with great success.

While Stephenson worked to build up the society Oglesby secured an appointment for Logan to lecture throughout the state on behalf of a soldiers' orphans' home. Logan, armed with great oratory skills, was a recent convert to the radical ideology and a harsh critic of Johnson. Logan infused in his speeches political rhetoric and his popularity quickly grew as the master of "waving the bloody shirt," a tactic used to stir emotions amongst the veterans and remind the people of the late war. The men of Illinois drawn in by the promotion of veterans' rights, camaraderie, and charitable traits flocked to its ranks and by October, 157 charters were issued within the state.

In April, Oglesby gained a new ally. Oliver P. Morton was the hardline war governor of Indiana and well-known as the soldier's friend for his support. He had also been a staunch supporter of Johnson's Reconstruction policies. Johnson had sent Morton on a political mission in November of 1865 but when Morton returned the following March, he assessed the political condition of the country. Johnson's veto of the Civil Rights Bill had many of the moderates fleeing Johnson's camp to join the Radicals. To revitalize Indiana's waning Republican support and ensure his own political future Morton joined them. He too looked to the veterans for support.

Intrigued by the newly forming veteran organization Morton reached out to Oglesby who shared with him the reasons for the GAR. Immediately, Morton sent Major-General R. S. Foster to Illinois to meet with Dr. Stephenson who eagerly initiated him into the new association. Upon returning to Indiana, Foster organized the first post in Indianapolis, administering the oath to Major Oliver M. Wilson and others. Elected as department commander Foster then appointed twenty men to go out among the veterans of the state to recruit.

Morton of course, was ineligible for membership but, never-the-less he became a driving force behind the movement in Indiana. He dispatched Major Wilson to Illinois to inquire about membership badges and printing supplies but Dr. Stephenson was overwhelmed by the initial success of the organization and could do little to assist. Foster however, stepped up and took the initiative. After obtaining permission to use the state senate chambers for initiation ceremonies for the increasing number of prospective members, he designed a membership badge and, once approved, began its manufacturing in Lafayette. Foster became such a dynamo that Dr. Stephenson began requesting supplies from the Indiana department.

As the GAR grew, Oglesby insisted safeguards were in place to ensure members would not give away the true intentions of the organization. The following cover story was thus given: It was during the last year of the war that messmates Major Benjamin Stephenson and Chaplain William J. Rutledge whiled away their time in camp or on the march, dreaming of reunions for soldiers after the war that would come together in mutual affection and fond memories. The society's appeal would be its declaration of principles: to preserve fraternal feelings that existed, to aid their needy and disabled comrades, to provide education and support for veteran's children and maintenance of their widows and to promote patriotism. This romanticized version was, for the most part, a fabrication, for the founders of the GAR had ulterior motives.

A ritual steeped in symbolism was then employed intended to swear the prospective member known as recruits to secrecy. In an outer room a new member was first blindfolded and a torn army blanket was draped over his shoulders. He is then led into the room by a sentry and paraded around before the other members. The recruit is then made to stand before a coffin.

Atop the coffin draped in an American flag was an open bible, crossed swords and the name of a victim of Andersonville. After much ceremony the recruit took a solemn oath to yield "implicit obedience" to his local organization and its headquarters and to never reveal the secrets of the Grand Army lest he suffered punishment as a traitor. He also promised to support his comrades for offices of "trust and profits" and extend charity to his comrades and their families.

The GAR continued to grow and soon Wisconsin Governor Lucius Fairchild heard of the growing society and sent George F. Rowell to Springfield to seek authorization to establish posts in Wisconsin. After his initiation, Rowell returned to Madison to initiate Governor Fairchild, J.K. Proudfit, Jeremiah Rusk and other leading radical veterans into the GAR. Proudfit then suggested reorganizing their branch of the SSNUL into a department of the Grand Army of the Republic. Proudfit, who was elected department commander, ordered other branches of the SSNUL to follow suit.

While the feud with Johnson was heating up over reconstruction GAR leaders decided to hold a state convention in Springfield in mid-July. To aid in recruitment invitations were extended to all veterans who were nonmembers. It was hoped they would embrace the stance of the GAR's claim to "...rights of the volunteer soldiery...morally, socially, and politically." On the agenda was the election of officers; the honor of 'Grand Commander' went to General John Palmer. Logan had been considered for the position but since his conversion to the radical program was relatively recent it was doubtful he would have received the honor. Besides, Logan had traveled to Washington instead of attending the convention to confront Johnson regarding his vetoes. A shouting match ensued and after an hour an enraged Logan promised Johnson that he would go home and make a speech and would antagonize him to no end.

During the highly advertised event resolutions were made. One resolution declared rebellion was a crime of a "most malignant nature" and, the government must take steps to deny Confederate participation in position of power. Other resolutions demanded bounty equalization and the safety of the country should override all other matters. Another resolution called for the state of Illinois to provide a soldiers' orphans' home.

Nearly three weeks after the Springfield convention a deadly riot occurred in New Orleans when blacks had gathered in support of the recalled constitutional convention regarding Negro suffrage there. Rumor had it that the Radicals in New Orleans had called for a second convention in response to the Black Codes passed by their legislature. The mayor of New Orleans, an ex-Confederate who had received a special pardon from Johnson, deemed the convention illegal since a constitution had already been accepted by the voters in that state in '65. The mayor, believing the convention was meant as a power grab by the Republicans, had received permission from the president to prohibit the convention. But the commander of the occupying forces refused to sanction the suppression of the convention and deployed troops to the area.

On the day of the convention, hundreds of blacks gathered, waiting to hear the results. They had planned on a parade as the convention broke up. Departing convention members were met by the black marchers and their band as they left the building. Unbeknownst to the marchers, a gang of anti-abolitionist Democrats mixed with ex-confederates lay in wait for the marchers. As they rounded the corner, the mob attacked. Before Federal troops were able to quell the riot over

230, mostly black were killed and 46 wounded. The city was put under martial law until Aug 3.

To counter the GAR's Springfield convention, the Democrats staged their own veteran convention in Cleveland, Ohio on September 17. At age 82, the temporary president of the convention was venerable General John E. Wool. He was one of four generals and the oldest when the war broke out. Other notables included the flamboyant General George Custer, General Gordon Granger, and Wisconsin Senator James R. Doolittle. Attendance by veterans was rather light compared to the Springfield convention. One resolution supporting Johnson's policy of Reconstruction was adopted. Another resolution proposed by an Indiana delegate with possibly the GAR in mind, warned of secret veteran societies. Oddly, since the GAR had yet to spread to the east, no one believed this organization was a threat to the administration. The resolution failed to pass.

The Cleveland planning committee had hoped to invite Confederate soldiers to attend but that idea was overruled considering the state of affairs at that time but a resolution of thanks was expressed to Forrest and other Confederates for messages received.

Leadership of the GAR executed what the New York *Tribune* called a "flank movement" in response to the Cleveland convention by urging veteran organizations in the east to host their own convention. Held in Pittsburg on September 24 the *Soldiers' and Sailors' National Union League* (SSNUL) the *Boys in Blue* hosted the affair attended by a large group of GAR from the mid-western states. Stephenson, Logan, Oglesby and Ingersoll of course were in attendance while Illinois delegates of the GAR came to the convention prepared to recruit. Indiana adjutant Wilson met with eastern delegates by appointment and supplied the necessary paperwork to organize new GAR posts.

Amidst the boisterous handshaking and speechmaking the Fourteenth Amendment was endorsed and leaders called on delegates to use their influence to urge others to endorse radical policies. General Butler, who had drafted a bitter resolution condemning Johnson, suggested appointing GAR member General Henry A. Barnum of New York to work with General T.S. Allen to consolidate the *US Service Club*, the *Soldiers' and Sailors' National Union League* of Washington, and the *Boys in Blue* club of Maryland and Michigan for campaign purposes. The result was these three societies along with any other smaller radical veteran societies would merge under a national organization of the *Boys in Blue* to work exclusively for the presidential campaign in 1868. In doing so the GAR could appear to remain non-partisan.

In contrast to the Cleveland convention which had attracted few veterans and was somewhat rambling and lacked purpose, the Pittsburg convention was labeled a huge success for it had introduced the GAR to the East. Oddly, the main draw for potential members into the society was the new membership badges being donned. It should be noted that by veterans now supporting the Fourteenth Amendment, the Radicals were achieving via the GAR what they had set out to do.

With elections approaching, radical leaders began coaching the rapidly growing GAR in an attempt to garner support of their reconstruction plan. Rallies, parades, and social balls were now being held for recruitment and to publically voice their opposition to Johnson's policy of restoration. The *Soldier's Friend,* which became an organ for the extreme faction of the Republican Party and boasting a circulation of 60,000, began writing fiery articles denouncing the administration. Logan and Oglesby instructed the posts to think of the upcoming contest as a military campaign. Their rhetoric pushed the idea that this would be a continuation of the war just fought but rather than throwing bullets veterans should cast their ballots to combat treason in the political arena.

In April Johnson's own coalition had formed the *National Union Executive Committee* (NUEC) to build support for the president's program which had been losing ground to the Republicans thanks to the tactics of the Radicals and the GAR. *Johnson Clubs* were also being organized throughout the North including the Border States while the NUEC had planned for a National Union convention to be held in Philadelphia in August. The Democrats had hoped to downplay their role at the convention but since most Republicans had already been turned off by Johnson's actions very few if any had attended. As a result, those who did attend were prominent Copperheads and former Confederates who entered the hall arm in arm. Needless to say, this did not go over well with the Republicans or the people of the North so soon after the war, especially in light of the violence taking place in the South. This was the final straw. The persistent violence, his veto of the Freedmen's Bureau and Civil Rights acts, and restoring rights to high-ranking confederates had led to three of his Cabinet members to resign.

Johnson was getting desperate and decided to do something no president has ever done before; go on a campaign tour. To add prestige to his tour, he brought along his two dedicated Cabinet members Seward and Welles, along with military heroes Grant, Custer, and David Farragut. Grant, always attentive of the political landscape, was reluctant to attend the tour.

The first leg of Johnson's 18-day, 21 stops tour known as the *Swing Around the Circle* began in the East; Baltimore, Philadelphia, New York City, West Point, Albany, Auburn, Niagara Falls, and Buffalo where he was warmly received. But as he approached the mid-west, the tour began to sour on him. Johnson was delivering the same speech at every stop and soon, pro-Republican supporters were planting hecklers in the crowd. In Cleveland one heckler yelled out 'Hang Jeff Davis' to which Johnson replied "Why don't you hang Thad Stevens and Wendell Philips?" Reminded to maintain his dignity, Johnson responded "I don't care about my dignity!" The statement was published nationwide and would contribute to his downward spiral.

At several stops the noise from the audience was so loud he couldn't even be heard and the frequent interruption caused him to lose his train of thought. In Chicago, where he attended Stephen Douglas' monument dedication, Oglesby along with members of the city council refused to attend the speech. As Johnson became flustered by hecklers he began to answer the crowd's taunts. In St. Louis, he blamed the Radical Republicans for inciting the New Orleans riot. In Indianapolis, a fight broke out between his supporters and opponents and one man's life was taken by gunfire. In Kentucky, Ohio and Pennsylvania, he was met with cheers for Congress and calls for Grant, who declined to speak.

To make matters worse, at his last stop of the tour in Johnstown, Pennsylvania, a temporary platform gave way sending hundreds of spectators 20 feet down into a drained canal. Johnson tried in vain to stop the train as it sped away towards Harrisburg, leaving the impression that he was quickly leaving the site of the disaster.

No good would come of this tour for Johnson. Rumors that he was drunk began circulating and many believed he had again disgraced the dignity of the presidency.

But Johnson's continued fight to keep the support of the veterans was futile for nothing was going right for him. When vacancies became available in various governmental departments in July, Johnson instructed department heads to give the jobs to veterans. This backfired however when so many veterans had bombarded the departments with job requests that only one out of every hundred who had applied received a job. Of course, Republicans immediately pounced, claiming Johnson was not keeping his promise.

When Congress had adjourned in September Johnson, in an attempt to garner support from the various government departments, began exercising his power of appointing pensions agents by replacing radical veteran agents with party adherents. He also enraged veterans when they learned that many of the new appointments had been opponents of the war or never served. To them, Johnson was giving Copperheads jobs over the veterans.

Johnson tried another tactic which failed miserably. Earlier in July, after several failed attempts, Republicans were finally able to push through the *Bounty Equalization Act* only after they caught the Senate trying to slip through legislation calling for pay raises for themselves. It was only then that a substantially lesser equalization bill was passed. This act entitled honorably discharged soldiers with at least three years' service $100 and $50 for those who had served at least two years or discharged with a disability. Johnson, in an attempt to take the credit for the bill away from the Republicans, tried to delay payment until after the election but obviously this tactic also backfired.

As the battle between Johnson and the Republicans raged on, radical GAR leaders continued to wave the "bloody shirt." The active participation of the GAR in the upcoming election was now becoming quite noticeable as commanders on all levels in the organization colored their speeches with political rhetoric meant to stir the emotions of the veterans. The indoctrination of GAR members was nearing completion as veterans now viewed Johnson and his allies of the South as the new enemy who would need to be put down just as the Confederacy had been.

Rumors began to spread as some radical GAR leaders laced their speeches with vague threats of violence. When some of the more boisterous officers made open threats towards the administration the newspapers were quick to investigate and report on them, adding credibility to the rumors. Leaders such as Butler openly admitted that his party would force its will upon Johnson by using the veterans. In secret correspondence, the threats were even more direct.

Johnson was now getting nervous and in October he ordered his investigator Colonel Charles O'Beirne to look into the GAR posts in Ohio, Illinois, and Indiana where more serious rumors of "military" action emanated. O'Beirne's interviews and inspections produced startling revelations. Not only did his investigation verify the verbal threats but he also discovered shipments of arms being distributed to GAR posts. He reported back that at a mass meeting held St. Louis on August 10, Logan and governors of four radical western states had discussed the possibility of appointing a dictator. O'Beirne also learned from General James B. Steedman a plan to impeach Johnson was in the works when Congress reconvened. The GAR, which should by then be fully armed and equipped, could then march on Washington in support of Congress.

One Illinois GAR leader, General John Cook was not shy about stating the GAR would use its military might if necessary to force the radical policies upon the Democrats. Even Governor Lucius Fairchild wrote to Senator Howe that, since Wisconsin's quota for arms has already been reached, perhaps Howe could enquire of Stanton the chance for 5-10,000 more rifles plus a battery. General Sol Meredith of Indiana also reported that Governors Fletcher and Oglesby had discussed disposing of Johnson and placing Grant, Sherman, or Morton as dictator in his place.

In his report O'Beirne wrote that the GAR and its kindred branches fell under the direct control of Morton and four or five other Western governors. In posts located in Indiana and Illinois, most members knew little of the posts' activities. Drawn to the society by its charitable intent, they were now sworn to secrecy and, as veterans they did not question why but merely followed orders. They drilled to the sound of the bugle and would come, armed, at a moment's notice. Echoes of these reports came from Ohio and Wisconsin as well.

O'Beirne specifically pointed out that Indiana was in dire need of reconstruction and he concluded his report by stating that he believed the Radicals would no doubt resort to violence and only the determination and fearless attitude of the president could avert any crisis. Just as the Copperheads had to be put down so did the Midwest. O'Beirne and Steedman both suggested the arms at Springfield be removed and "...the President should have at least 50,000 stands of arms at Washington."

By now Johnson had been receiving offers of "military" aid from his veteran supporters but it did not compare to what the GAR was offering. Grant informed the president that only 1,550 of the 2,224 soldiers stationed near the capitol were effective. Surprisingly, Johnson whose relationship with Stanton was shaky, ordered that, in light of the turbulent and revolutionary state of the country the secretary should take the necessary precautions to ensure the safety of Washington and "...thus discourage any attempt for its possession by insurgent or other illegal combinations." Dismissing suggestions from his fellow Democrats to direct the veterans' excitement toward England or declare war against Mexico, Johnson instead chose to remain inactive until the 1866 congressional election had taken place.

Chapter 16

40th Session

The Republicans had won an overwhelming victory thanks to the aggressive efforts of the Radicals with the assistance of the GAR or rather the Boys in Blue. Public opinion had changed over the course of the past year. A smooth and speedy reunification would have been profitable for the capitalists who had turned a tidy profit off the war. To them, the South was a land to be exploited and open relations would have certainly eased the way. But Radical propaganda coupled with Johnson's lack of tact and abilities, and the South's defiance had changed the views in the North. Convincing the public that their policy was the only safeguard to retain all that was won during the war the Radicals now felt they could safely agitate the Negro suffrage issue.

No one could deny that the GAR was a now political machine. Although leaders continued to publically deny the charges, the GAR had lost its creditability as a benevolent and charitable organization. It was no secret that veterans had been used to influence the political outcome of state and national elections. Even after the election, L. Edwin Dudley had called for a veteran army to be raised in Washington to protect the 'loyal majority' in the newly elected Congress. The Radicals however, decided it was best to lay low. Until Johnson gave them a reason to initiate impeachment proceedings, there was no reason for the GAR to remain under scrutiny in the public eye. There was no other recourse but to wait. Instructions were passed along to the GAR camps to tone down their threats of violence and talks of military takeovers.

The South would have been wise to accept the Fourteenth Amendment. As it was a harsher plan now awaited them. When Virginia and Alabama considered ratification, Johnson talked them out of it. Johnson and the South's resistance to the amendment had strengthened the Republican Party and, coupled by the work of the GAR, the Republicans gained a sweeping victory at the polls. Their large majority had now increased with the power to block any plans and could overturn any veto. When the 40th Congress convened in March of 1867, they would now be able to dictate Reconstruction policies.

The 39th Congress met for their final session in December of 1866 with the intent to peel power away from Johnson and replace his restoration program with their own. Their first order of business was to amend a Senate bill passed a year earlier which would now place all new appointments of pension agents under the scrutiny of the Senate, thus stripping from Johnson the power to appoint only party adherents. It also provided that all appointments made after January 1, 1866 must resign and new nominations should be submitted to the Senate. A few Senate members questioned the constitutionality of the bill but it passed none-the-less 117-29. Johnson, knowing his veto would be overturned, signed the bill into law. The agents, whose power would increase in later years, were now essentially under Republican control.

Congress also introduced two new bills as well. The first bill the *Tenure of Office Act* was in retaliation to a statement Johnson made during his "Swing around the Circle" tour. With Stanton in mind Johnson had stated he would fire any Cabinet member who disagreed with him. The Tenure Act was meant to prevent Johnson from removing any Senate-confirmed appointments and president-appointed Cabinet officers; Senate-approval would first have to be given. This also came under scrutiny by some senators who doubted its constitutionality since Johnson's Cabinet members were appointed by Lincoln.

The second bill was the *First Reconstruction Act* or *Military Reconstruction Act* which proposed calling for the ten states in the South to be divided into five military districts and imposing martial law. All state governments were now null and void as troops enforced Federal laws. Statehood could only be achieved when a constitutional convention, elected by eligible black and white voters, outlined a new constitution which allowed for black suffrage and ratification of the Fourteenth Amendment. Any person formally engaged in rebellion against the government would be disenfranchised and barred from holding public office.

This drastic piece of legislation was unprecedented in American history. The Republican Party, in their demand for retribution had shown their disdain for nearly the entire Southern white population. It had enfranchised upwards of a million blacks while denying political rights to hundreds of thousands of whites and subjugating millions more under military rule during peacetime. And yet, some of the Radicals still criticized the measure because it did not allow for confiscation of rebel lands for distribution to freed blacks.

Johnson countered with a modified version of the amendment calling for limited black suffrage and reinstatement of ex-Confederates but the Republicans refused. Still, an adamant Johnson vetoed both bills only to have them overturned by the Senate and on March 2, 1867, the last day of the 39th Congressional session, the bills became law.

The next day the newly elected 40th Congress convened in a special session to continue the fight. They began by outlining the duties of the district commanders which were to devise a list of eligible, registered voters and hold an election for delegates to a state convention. An election would then be held to ratify their respective constitution and, once done so, conveyed to the president. Advised by his lawyers that he had no grounds to disobey the order, Johnson reluctantly appointed Generals Schofield, Sickles, Pope, Sheridan, and Edward Ord as district commanders.

But confusion was generated over which body, the military or the legislative, held authority over the other. In the Louisiana-Texas district, Sheridan was ousting state and local officials who had supported secession. Johnson opposed this and called on Attorney-General Henry Stanbery, who gave his interpretation of the law that restricted the commander's authority over state government. Members of Congress disagreed however and when they reconvened in July and passed a supplementary Reconstruction bill which overruled Stanbery. They also added an amendment to the *Army Appropriation Act* transferring power over the army in the South from Johnson to the newly appointed General of the Army U.S. Grant. Furthermore, Johnson would not be able to relieve the General of the Army without approval by the Senate.

Republicans knew Johnson was still a force to be reckoned with. Although he promised to go along with the recent laws passed, the president could still block and obstruct the political process in the South. Wanting to wrap up the reconstruction process the Radicals again began talking impeachment. Before adjourning on their three-month recess, the Republican-led Congress appointed a judicial committee to scrutinize

Johnson's every move; looking for any possible grounds for impeachment in their absence. Congress then recessed until November.

For the next three months, Johnson was able to enjoy free reign over his administration but it would not be free of controversy. On August 5, Johnson, who had had enough of Stanton's continued intrigue against the executive program, ordered his resignation. Stanton refused on grounds that, since Congress was in recess, he should stay to keep an eye on the president. But Johnson would have none of it and he suspended Stanton. Grant, who had urged the president not to take such action, was appointed Secretary of War *ad interim* with instructions not to give up the office without first notifying Johnson. This would allow him time to appoint a new secretary so as to test the Tenure Act before the Supreme Court. Johnson does one more thing to upset the Radicals. On August 17, he relieved Sheridan whom he feels is tyrannical and insubordinate, as commander of the Louisiana and Texas district. Johnson also relieved Sickles as commander of the Carolinas as well.

Johnson's advisors warned him against making too many waves but the president thought public opinion was telling a different story. The Republicans had shied away from the issue of black suffrage during the '66 elections but this year they were now speaking out in favor of the movement. If they didn't, they would have been viewed as hypocrites but, they had misjudged the public. In 19 of the 24 Northern states where suffrage was not yet law, the issue was placed on the ballots. Democrats took a strong stance against it however, and many of the voters still rejected the idea although the margin of defeat was narrow. As result, the issue of black suffrage and talks of impeachment harmed the Republican Party and allowing the Democrats to win New York, New Jersey, and California and gained the majority in several other states. The 200,000 members of the GAR were not enough to sway this election. After the '67 election, one of Johnson's aides remarked that by forcing suffrage on the Southern states, they had lost all the Northern ones. Never one to mince words, Wade so candidly put it, "The nigger whipped us."

Out of chaos comes order and immediately after the war Federal authority was definitely needed during the early years of Reconstruction. Clashes between Southern whites and the freedmen were common and often violent. Certainly, it was more than the civil authorities could suppress. The intent of Southern occupation was to discourage violence but now a year later the Southerner's view of the occupation had changed. Defeat was humiliation enough but to promote civil rights and Negro suffrage was going too far. They now saw it as the Radicals' attempt to force the power of their party upon them via the Fourteenth Amendment. Southern Democrats would bide their time. The longer they could draw out the reconstruction process, the more they could undermine the Radicals' power.

In their attempt to enforce states to ratify the Fourteenth Amendment, district commanders and officers of the Freedmen's Bureau had their work cut out for them. Upon making their voter registration list, every attempt was made to enroll the Negro while excluding as many whites as possible. To assist the bureau was the *Loyal League*, also known as the *Union League* which got its start in 1862 to help fund organization such as the United States Sanitary Commission. Soon after the war they began establishing leagues across the South to assist the Freedmen's Bureau. These leagues were now made up mostly of blacks under the control of white Northerners known as *Carpetbaggers,* and *scalawags* who were loyal Southern whites or reconstructed ex-confederates. With the Loyal League came elements of the GAR. In Louisiana, ten posts made up mostly of black veterans had been established by July of 1867 with Governor Henry Clay Warmoth elected provisional department commander. Unofficially, they worked hand in hand with the Loyal League in organizing the constitutional conventions.

By September, 1867, approximately 735,000 blacks and 635,000 whites were eligible to vote in the ten unreconstructed states. Nearly 15% of whites had been disenfranchised while another 25-30% failed to register due to apathy or opposition to the political process. As it turned out, Negroes became the majority in South Carolina, Alabama, Florida, Mississippi, and Louisiana. In Virginia, North Carolina, Arkansas, and Texas whites held the majority and in Georgia, the numbers were about equal. But this mattered little as some conservative leaders encouraged voters to stay home thus falling short of a majority to vote on holding a constitutional convention. White landowners and employers also used economic threats to keep black voters at home. As it was, less than half the registered white voters had turned out to vote on holding the constitutional conventions and only half of those had voted in favor of it.

Nonetheless, four-fifths of registered blacks did vote making up the majority. Every preconvention election had received a majority.

About three-fourths of the delegates elected to attend these conventions were Republicans while 45% of these were Southern whites; 30% were black of which nearly all were literate, and 25% were Northerners who had since settled in the South. The constitution they meted out was far more advanced than expected. They allowed a mandate for public schooling for blacks and whites, social welfare programs and state boards of charities. The only way these ten states could receive congressional recognition was to ratify their state constitution. But there were still some democratic hold-outs who refused to see the Negro as an equal and they set out to halt ratification of the Fourteenth Amendment.

The rise of the Loyal League however resulted in the formation of a new group. The *Ku Klux Klan* (KKK) or *Invisible Empire* was established in Nashville in the spring of 1867 and it drew its membership primarily from the lower-class southerners, usually ex-confederates. Former Confederate Nathaniel Bedford Forrest would admit to a Cincinnati's *Commercial* in September of '67 that the KKK was founded to combat the works of the GAR and the *Loyal Leagues.*

The *Knights of White Camelia* formed at New Orleans was another such group and its membership consisted of the upper crust of society which included doctors, lawyers, editors and officers of the law. These groups had little effect on the first elections regarding the constitution but, by the time it went before the electorate for ratification organized opposition was in place. Even with 20,000 Federal troops still stationed in the South open acts of violence, threats, intimidation, and murder did have some effect on elections. In Mississippi for example ratification was defeated due to voter suppression. In Alabama, abstention from voting resulted in a failure to achieve a majority. Out of 168,813 registered voters only 70,812 turned out to vote for ratification while 1,005 voted against.

Republicans could not afford to have the South stall. The people wanted this business of reconstruction behind them. If the Republicans could not facilitate the restoration of the Union it would certainly hurt them in the 1868 elections. Congress made ratifications to the reconstruction acts calling for a majority of actual voters as opposed to eligible voters. As a result, by June of '68, seven of the ten states had ratified their constitution and was readmitted to the Union. Texas and Virginia however, had failed to ratify their constitution in time to be readmitted by the summer session of Congress. In Mississippi, 2,000 soldiers were unable to prevent the KKK from intimidation methods which deterred 20,000 Republicans from voting in that state. Their vote to ratify was defeated by 7,000 ballots. Even without these three states, Republicans had achieved the majority they needed and the Fourteenth Amendment was ratified on July 9, 1868.

But, ratification was not the only thing the Republicans had in mind. The feud with Johnson by now had been blown wide open and the Country once again sat on the edge of rebellion.

Chapter 17

Impeachment

When Congress reconvened in December, it was obvious that the Senate would not approve the suspension of Stanton. Johnson, bolstered by the results of the 1867 election, had informed Congress in his address that he was prepared to resist them "regardless of all consequences." The judiciary committee had since provided members of Congress with their 1,200 page report on Johnson consisting of evidence taken from testimony from individuals as high as Cabinet members to convicted felons in prison. Immediately, Massachusetts Representative George S. Boutwell offered a resolution calling for impeachment but it was obvious that no criminal act had actually been committed. By a vote of 108 to 57, the vote to impeach had failed on December 7.

Five days later, Johnson notified the Senate of his reasons for removing Stanton. Insolence, defiance and his lack of confidence in Stanton were the reasons given. The Radicals could not afford to lose such a powerful ally in the Cabinet so on January 13 they refused to approve the suspension. Grant did something which will thwart the president's plans. Grant never outwardly promised Johnson he would notify him before he gave up the keys so, when the Senate made their decision, Grant went to the War Department, locked the door to the secretary's office and gave the key to a military aide. An hour later, Stanton had once again gained access to his office. Johnson was furious and publically accused Grant of "duplicity" but Grant, tired of being exploited by Johnson, had wanted nothing to do with the feud between Congress and the president. He had told Johnson that since the Senate did not uphold the suspension, he had no choice but to return the keys.

Johnson believed that the *Tenure of Office Act* was unconstitutional, especially in the case of Stanton, who was appointed by

Lincoln. Knowing there was a chance of impeachment Johnson did something rash, on Friday, February 21, he appointed the unfortunate Adjutant-General Lorenzo Thomas as Secretary of War. Thomas immediately went to Stanton's office to present him with the order.

Over the years Stanton, who never forgave Thomas for his report on Fremont, had sent Thomas on various missions to rid his office of him. So it was with relish that Thomas delivered Johnson's orders to Stanton and allowed him time to remove his personal belongings. Stanton instead used that time to confer with Grant. When Thomas returned, Stanton informed the timid general that he would not obey the order. Thomas, being no match for Stanton's overbearing temperament quietly bowed and left the room.

Stanton had rushed a note off to the House while Johnson simultaneously informed the Senate. Radical senators had rushed to Stanton, directing him to hold his ground. With tears streaming down his cheeks Stanton vowed he would not forsake Congress. Other senators sent notes of encouragement as well. From Sumner came the note "Stick" written upon it. The senators excitedly prepared for the fight and barring their doors to the public immediately went into executive session to take a vote. The Senate had voted for impeachment. The news spread like wildfire throughout the capital city as crowds began to gather around the White House, War Department and nearby hotels. On the floor of the Senate, venomous speeches were being delivered throughout the afternoon and into the evening.

Fearing removal by force, Stanton had literally barricaded himself in his office and refused to leave. When he received word that Thomas intended to take the office by force if Stanton refused to leave by morning, Stanton swore out a warrant for Thomas' arrest to "keep him occupied." The next morning Thomas was arrested, taken before a judge sympathetic with Stanton, and released after posting $5,000 bail. Stanton would remain in his office for the next two months, leaving take a brisk daily stroll and occasionally at night to sneak home.

After his release Thomas reported back to Johnson who once again instructed him to return to the War Department and assume the duties bestowed upon him. He found Stanton, centered amidst an array of Congressmen Thomas demanded the department mail. After a heated exchange of word, the little general began to give ground. As he headed for another office across the hall in search of the mail Stanton closely followed, bellowing orders to his former subordinate. Thomas had had enough and finally gave in. Oddly, Stanton then tried to console Thomas by calling for a bottle and sharing a drink with him.

When Thomas was scheduled to appear before the magistrate Johnson ordered him to submit to imprisonment, hoping this would bring the constitutionality of the Tenure of Office Act before the Supreme Court. Thomas could then apply for a *writ of habeas corpus.* But the judge, who had been in secret conference with Stanton, was not to be taken in however, and charges against Thomas were dismissed.

Around the city rumors spread that war was coming as sectional newspapers urged action of their respective parties. One rumor had it that a Maryland militia, 10,000 strong was preparing to march on Washington. Another said Welles had offered Johnson four hundred marines stationed in the city while still another reported that Grant had been arrested. Throngs of Washingtonians gathered as the White House and War Department gathered their forces and seemingly prepared for battle.

The threat of violence was real but it would not be by the congressional combatants nor would it be incited by the factional newspapers. The peril lay in the hands of one fuming representative, the commander-in-chief of the GAR, John "Blackjack" Logan.

In November of 1866, the GAR held its first national encampment in Indianapolis and General S.A. Hurlbut was elected its first national commander. The *Great Republic* was selected as their national organ of which L. Edwin Dudley had control of the paper's GAR section. Through the *Great Republic* and the *Soldier's Friend*, instructions and information could be disseminated to the thousands of posts across the country. The message now was to advance loyalty and vindicate the rights of loyal citizens by crushing treason and protecting those in the South who had remained loyal during the war.

The GAR continued to absorb other veteran societies into its fold and as a result, they established a presence from Florida to Texas, and all the way to California. But as the GAR grew in scope, membership began to wane in the beginning months of '67. For many who had flocked to its ranks early on did so for the purpose of networking; others had sought relief or employment but over time, with their needs satisfied, many had no further use for the organization. Other members were completely turned off by the society's open partisanship. They had been drawn into the GAR by its charitable attributes only to realize the primary function was to arouse the ugly memories of the war. Others simply grew bored and were ready to move on to their next adventure.

Inefficiency had plagued Hurlbut's tenure. His adjutant-general Dr. Stephenson, severely lacking in ability, kept no records or files and either ignored or neglected to act on applications from departments for instructions and supplies. As a result, of the 21 departments across the country representing nearly a quarter million members, more than 1,400 posts were delinquent in paying dues. The lack of correspondence and organization would soon have bankruptcy threatening the society. Hurlbut even neglected to call for the annual encampment in November so one was set for January of '68. It was obvious that a leader with vision was needed and Logan, who had that vision, was elected national commander.

With conflict against Johnson increasing, Logan who was honored and respected by so many veterans, coveted his new position. And he was very aware of the collective strength of the GAR. In Illinois, 80,000 of its members had ensured his election to congress in 1866. Now, Logan intends to wield the GAR like a weapon and use it to strike a mortal blow against the administration.

The military had taught Logan the value of a central command and consolidated effort and immediately he moved the national headquarters to Washington to centralize and strengthen the working basis of the GAR. The Washington branch of the *SSNUL* had been absorbed into the GAR and its Commander Colonel Norton P. Chipman, former Attorney-General and prosecutor at the trial of Henry Wirz, was elected department commander. Seriously wounded at Fort Donelson, Chipman had resigned from the army in 1865 and settled in Washington to practice law and become a pension agent. He was highly disciplined, organized and he rigidly enforced attendance within his department.

Together, Logan and Chipman revamped the organizational structure of the GAR. District officers were abolished and the ritual was revised as well as the ranking system. Membership dues were assessed at 10 cent per man and an assessment of $1 on each of the over 2,000 posts was ordered. By mid-summer, membership has swelled to over 250,000 and with new rules and regulations strictly enforced, orders were promptly obeyed.

Before Logan had been elected to the position, the radical propaganda machine had been at work on the members of the GAR. So, when Logan and Butler strenuously contested the proposed *Southern Destitution Bill* which would aid those affected by crop failures in the South, the membership condemned any action which would aid their former enemies. The release of Jefferson Davis also caused a stir among the members. By waving the bloody shirt Logan was able to arouse GAR posts to further denounce the administration and condemn any aid to their former enemies.

When word got out that Johnson had suspended Stanton, GAR leaders ordered that circulars be sent out amongst the posts, ordering them to prepare for the coming revolution. They warned that Johnson's actions had left the administration susceptible to enemy plots of gaining control by thrusting disloyal constituencies into the government.

Hearing of Thomas' boast of possibly taking possession of Stanton's office by force was evidence enough for Logan that Johnson might use of the military to try and take control of the War Department. Logan quietly instructed Chipman to organize 'all our boys' and have them ready to march. It was to be done quickly and quietly and the order was not to be shared needlessly. If no action was needed it was Logan's intent that no one would ever know that the GAR had been on high alert.

But there was no doubt that the GAR had been activated. Logan was the last speaker to deliver his speech on the floor. As he publicly asserted Johnson was planning revolution, Chipman was forming members of the GAR into battalions and, if and when the signal was given, planned to deploy the battalions at the War Department. As it was, many of the veterans were already deployed; stationed in strategic locations around the White House and War Department. And as they stood guard, many of them never knew why they were issued arms and ammunition or what exactly their orders were.

After his speech Logan went to Stanton's office where he would stay for the next three days, sleeping on a cot at night, and informed the secretary that the GAR was prepared and now quietly patrolling the streets. It was here where he received offers from departments around the country pledging members to defend the War Department. The *Great Republic* had been advocating impeachment for a year and now the veterans had been riled to a point of action. The Missouri department offered 50,000 men for Congress to use while in New York, the *Herald* boasted they were 100,000 strong and prepared to defend the Capitol. The governors of Wisconsin, Pennsylvania, Iowa, and Illinois all promised troops to crush Johnson and his supporters.

Welles, afraid of arrest and imprisonment, asked Johnson for support of the military. Johnson could not for he had learned that General William Emory, commander of troops around Washington had recalled all his subordinate officers to duty and Emory himself openly refused to cooperate with Johnson. Sherman also refused a direct order to take command as well and fled to St. Louis to avoid further involvement. Johnson did receive offers of military aid but nothing compared to the size and scope of the Radicals. Johnson would have no other recourse but to sit and wait it out which was probably the best move he could have made.

On a stormy Monday morning, Thomas tried one last time to take control of Stanton's office but to no avail. Stanton refused and as Thomas went from office to office still trying to obtain the department's mail, Stanton haranguing him the entire time. A frustrated Thomas finally gave up and took a carriage home. The snow and cold could not deter the curious onlookers as the Washington police, heavily augmented, were ready for any emergency. A funeral procession for a prominent army major had been denied a military escort for fear that the sight of a military presence could set the whole thing off.

On February 24, a resolution to impeach on charges of "high crimes and misdemeanors" was passed by a vote of 126-47. In a dramatic move, the senators had ordered the House clock set back so the journal would record the vote for impeachment to have taken place on Washington's Birthday. The country's immediate reaction was the same as the news of Fort Sumter. As businesses shut down Sherman, writing to his brother the senator, wrote that 200,000 men in the South were against impeachment. All the while Johnson remained idle. He dared not make any move which could be misconstrued as offensive.

Just as quickly as it started, the commotion ended. Even as head of the prosecution team Senator Stevens read the eleven count indictment on February 25, the dwindling crowds continued to disperse. The first nine consisted of the Johnson-Stanton-Thomas affair which involved conspiring, obstruction, and violating the Tenure of Office Act. The tenth was Butler's idea. He had advocated impeaching Johnson for his speeches and general bad conduct since October of '66. Although the last was not an impeachable crime or misdemeanor, the Republicans accepted it nonetheless. The eleventh was a summation of the first ten articles.

Johnson's defense team consisted of Attorney-General Stanbery, who resigned his position to serve; ex-judge B.R. Curtis, W.M. Evarts, T.A.R. Nelson, and W.S. Groesbeck. It was obvious that the prosecution was no match for the judicial experience of the defense.

The trial began on March 4 and would continue for eleven weeks. The defense argued that the Tenure of Office Act was unconstitutional and even if it were it only covered civil officers and not members of the Cabinet whose terms were appointed by the president. Since Stanton had been appointed by Lincoln he was not protected by it. And technically, since Stanton still remained in office, Johnson had not violated it. Additionally, Johnson's motivation was the desire to legitimately test the constitutionality of the act. Lastly, Johnson could not be charged with "high crimes and misdemeanors" since impeachment was a political process and not a judicial process.

The trial soon became a farce and by the later stage, it was merely conducted on formality. The theme had changed from being guilty of violation of the *Tenure of Office Act* to, should Johnson be disposed because he could not get along with Congress.

The Senate was unable to secure the necessary 36 "guilty" votes needed to secure the two-thirds majority. In a vote of 35 to 19, the ten Democrats and two Conservatives senators received some unlikely allies in the form of seven Republicans who had used the time to reconsider the implications of a guilty verdict. Doubting the legal justification of impeachment which could ultimately hurt their party, the defectors now believed Johnson's promise to cease his obstruction of the Republicans' program of Reconstruction. He also promised to appoint General John M. Schofield, commander of the military district in Virginia, as the new Secretary of War. Lastly, since there was no vice-president, Wade would be next in line for the presidency, much to the dismay of many.

With Johnson's acquittal on May 16 the crisis was over. Stanton relinquished his office and General Schofield, who was agreeable to most party members, was appointed Secretary of War. After the trial Logan admitted to Johnson that, had the president sought to gain access to the War Department by force or sought control of the army, his veterans were "…ready to answer the call of their country."

The GAR had continued to agitate but as the trial wound down the order to stand down was finally given. Most members across the country reluctantly obeyed. In Philadelphia, General J.T. Owen who assigned the blame on Grimes, Fessenden, and Trumbull, had bluntly stated that if impeachment fails, it was not the fault of the GAR.

After the trial many Southern Democrats viewed it as the radical-controlled Congress's attempt to subjugate the South even further and to extend their powers by Negro suffrage.

Chapter 18

Reconstruction

Two issues were prominent in the 1868 election; the post-war economic recession caused by national banking legislation and Reconstruction. Despite their loss in the 1867 elections, the Republicans knew that Negro suffrage in Northern states was an issue which needed to be placed on the ballot. Ku Klux Klan activity in the spring of '68 had been on the rise in Tennessee, Arkansas, Louisiana, and Georgia, causing over a thousand deaths, with more than 200 political murders in Arkansas alone. Since these states were no longer in need of "reconstruction" Federal authorities were unable to impose martial law. The KKK terrorized freedmen, schoolteachers, Unionists, and voters and burnt down school houses. Nathaniel Bedford Forrest even warned that if Republican leaders intended to use the militia against the Klan, "I have no powder to burn killing negroes. I intend to kill radicals."

Klan activity in the South did affect voter turnout which gave many state governments over to the Democrats but their actions were having an adverse effect on the North where half of the electorate were Democrats. Republicans, not wanting to relinquish power to the Democrats, justified forcing Negro suffrage on the South claiming it was in the best interest "...of public safety, of gratitude, and of justice." The people the North however, reserved the right to decide on their own Negro suffrage question.

Republicans had to choose their candidate wisely. They had first considered Chief Justice Salmon Chase for the nomination. But division within their ranks on the economy and Chase's sympathetic attitude towards Johnson during the impeachment proceedings had caused them to drop the former Treasurer from the list. Grant however, never showed his political hand and Republicans were unsure where his loyalties lie. It had appeared that Grant was supportive of Johnson right up until the 1866 elections but by the spring of 1867, Grant was moving away from the administration. His support of Sheridan and the Tenure of Office Act had convinced the Republicans that Grant was their man.

But surprisingly, the GAR was divided on Grant. During the January encampment, it was business as usual. Resolutions were proposed calling for veteran preference and protection for veterans in personnel reduction in governmental departments. A proposal by the Loyal League to join forces with the GAR in the South was tabled and animosity towards their former enemies continued in the form of a resolution demanding only Union dead would be buried in national cemeteries.

Looking ahead to the presidential election many assumed Grant would be the favorite and endorsed but opposition was quickly raised by those who either disliked Grant or were opposed to the GAR being used as a political machine in general. Complaints were being made that politics were tearing apart the GAR. To rectify this, the leaders decided to not endorse Grant during their official sessions. On the last night of the encampment however, during the open meeting, it was unanimously voted to endorse Grant. Four days after Johnson's acquittal the Republican National Convention was held in Chicago where Grant's father was the honored guest as Logan announced his son as their candidate. The Republican slogan, "Let us have peace" would come from Grant's acceptance speech.

The Democrats had to scramble for a candidate to run against Grant; Johnson had too much baggage to even be considered. The War Democrats also insisted on a military candidate one of the heroes of Gettysburg, General Winfield Scott Hancock was considered. A good friend of McClellan's, Hancock "the Superb" was fortunate enough to escape the clutches of the CCW. He had replaced Sheridan in the Louisiana district and had the support of many a Southern Democrats due to his reluctance to use the military over civil courts. Some Southern Democrats were critical of his handling of the Mary Surratt trial while the Peace Democrats had opposed any military candidate.

Eventually they decided on Peace Democrat Horatio Seymour. This was a poor choice considering remarks made during the New York City riots in July of 1863 and his veto of soldier suffrage. Also, he was against a harsh Reconstruction policy, believing that southern whites should be allowed to form their own governments. To placate the War Democrats, Frank Blair Jr. had been selected as the vice-president nominee. Having converted back to his old party, he had alienated many of the veterans by denouncing the reconstruction program of the Radicals.

The Grand Army, not wanting to relive the notoriety of 1866 once again called upon the Boys in Blue to take control of the Republican campaign. Under the auspices of the GAR, the Boys in Blue, in which Chipman was the secretary, continued to wave the bloody shirt; invoking the past with its privation and sacrifices and swearing never to forgive the treason which it had caused them.

This time, the Boys in Blue added "Fighting" to their title and they would be funded by the RNC and a few state Republican committees. They travelled to cities where conventions were held to endorse Grant. They brought with them a military air; at night they would "fall into line" and with swinging lanterns they would march forward as they had during the war. Propaganda pamphlets had called on the veterans with such commands as to "Fall in! Soldiers, it is the old cause...Grant again heads the column" and "Organize then, soldiers, for another...last campaign against the Copperheads and Rebels." This time their enemies were those who would give away at the ballot box all they won during the war.

In February, the Democrats countered with their own veteran organization, the *White Boys in Blue*. Headquartered in New York City, this society, denouncing the radical policies of reconstruction, staged their own noisy rallies. A member in Brooklyn wrote that every ward in that city was represented by 9,000 members while the *New York World* announced 40,000 members marched in support in Ohio. Marching under banners reading "White Supremacy" and "No Nigger Voters" violence occasionally broke out between the two factions of the Boys in Blue.

The GAR could not stay out of the campaign altogether however. To invoke the passions of Northerners against the South a series of lectures were sponsored to raise funds for orphanages and disabled veterans. Speakers included Clara Barton, Representative Schuyler Colfax, and Former General Hugh Judson Kilpatrick who reminded the veterans of their sacrifices and privations.

Perhaps a more subtle form of propaganda appeared as Decorations Day. On May 5 Commander-in-Chief Logan issued General Order No. 11, which set aside May 30 as a day "...for the purpose of strewing with flowers or otherwise decorating the graves of comrades who died in defense of their country during the late rebellion, and whose bodies now lie in almost every city, village, and hamlet churchyard in the land."

On May 30, 1868 over one hundred ceremonies were conducted under the auspice of the GAR in the states which held the Union dead. Many of the speakers at these ceremonies stuck to the topic of their "sacred cause" and reminded those in attendance of the nation's duties to provide for the orphans and widows but of course, a few did stray from the theme, alluding to those who hindered the efforts of congressional reconstruction and remarking there was still work to do. At Washington's Arlington Cemetery, 5,000 spectators gathered as Generals Grant and Garfield, and other dignitaries gathered where 15,000 graves were decorated with small flags. Some Democrats viewed these ceremonies as another attempt to stoke the fires between the two factions for as the *New York Times* opined, they served the dead no good purpose.

Surprisingly, the election was closer than many had expected. Grant had won 26 of the 34 states (Texas, Mississippi, and Virginia had not yet been restored so they could not vote) but surprisingly, he only beat Seymour by 300,000 out of 5.7 million votes casted. Seymour had taken most of the South's white votes but the nearly 500,000 southern blacks voting in the election had possibly given Grant the victory. The Republicans again controlled both Houses. In the Senate, the Republicans won five more seats (62-12) while in the House the Republicans lost 22 seats (171-67.) Had it not been for the GAR in the guise of the Fighting Boys in Blue or had the Democrats put any pro-war candidate on the ballot the outcome may have been different.

Perhaps out of spite Johnson, who broke precedent by not attending the inauguration of Grant, pardoned a large number of ex-Confederates, including former Confederate vice-president Alexander Stevens before leaving office.

After the election, with the Democrats slowly gaining control in the Southern states, Congress now set out to ratify the Fifteenth Amendment. Only eleven of the Northern states and all five Border States still denied Negroes the vote. But Republicans controlled 26 of the 34 state legislatures and on February 26, '69, Congress voted on and passed the Fifteenth Amendment. Congress needed a three quarters of the states for a majority however for ratification. Republicans had used the delay of Virginia, Texas, and Mississippi to strengthen their numbers by requiring them to ratify both Fourteenth and Fifteenth Amendments before allowing them back into the Union. Georgia was the only hold-out. They had lost their status of statehood when state Conservatives expelled 28 black legislators on the grounds that their state constitution did not permit blacks to hold office. Under one clause of the Fourteenth Amendment however, it was discovered that those doing the ejecting were ineligible to hold office themselves! They were summarily dismissed, the blacks reinstated and Georgia ratified the Fifteenth Amendment and officially returned to the Union in July of 1869.

The Fifteenth Amendment was ratified on February 3, 1870, as the third and last of the Reconstruction Amendments and on March 30, 1870 it became law. Eventually, the Republicans' reign in the South began wane as conservatism started taking over the Northern Republican Party and by 1876, the Democrats controlled all but three of the former secessionist states, Florida, South Carolina, and Louisiana.

With continual intimidation at the polls in the South and elsewhere, three enforcement acts were passed on May 31, 1870, February 28, 1871 and April 20, 1871. The last was known as the Ku Klux Klan act which allowed legal prosecution of suspected members of the KKK in both Carolinas and Mississippi.

It is possible that the Radicals were partly to blame for the rise of the KKK. The most of the South had been willing to accept defeat but by forcing civil rights and black suffrage upon the subjugated so soon after the war was a humiliation some Southerners were unwilling to accept. Of course, the Southern leadership was also to blame. Had they been less defiant of the Fourteenth Amendment, it would seem that the Radicals would be in a weaker position to impose such strict measures. But the Black Codes and acts of violence committed by former Confederates had only strengthened the image of Southern atrocities committed against blacks and Union loyalists, an image which the Radicals had wanted to project. The Radicals had seemed unwilling to allow for a peaceful conclusion. Instead, they took advantage of the situation; hoping to exact revenge from the slave powers which had duped their countrymen into fighting their futile war.

In mid-'68 Chipman had boasted the GAR had 38 departments consisting of nearly 3,000 posts and a membership of over 400,000 veterans. The reality of the matter was that membership was at about 200,000. After the 1868 election, the Republican Party had little use for the Grand Army and the number of posts would drop to 2,050 while GAR activity in the West abruptly came to a halt. For many veterans the transition into civilian society was complete. There was no longer any need to look to the GAR for support. Others believed their mission was accomplished with the election of Grant. They had saved the country once again and now it was time to focus on family and employment.

Many other veterans were dissatisfied with the patronage which the administration had been doling out. Although many of the disabled received jobs in the customs and postal service, it was the former high-ranking officers who tended to receive the more lucrative positions while privates were awarded insignificant clerkships. In 1869, 274 generals and colonels were elected to Congress while another 1,596 held offices in state legislatures. Not one private would be elected to such a position.

Others had claimed that political partisanship had destroyed the organization. One member remarked that GAR leaders belonging to "political cliques" had abandoned the Illinois department after accomplishing their selfish purpose. Many now believed the Democrats' charge that the GAR was for promoting the Republican Party by promising veteran benefits. The Boys in Blue, dissatisfied over the lack of funding had already recessed into silent dormancy with only a few branches remaining active. But their silence would be temporary.

Another reason for the near demise of the GAR was Logan. Acting more as a dictator, he demanded strict discipline of the rank and file. He introduced the grade system which meant members would now join as Recruit and after several months of honorable membership, could be elevated to the rank of Soldier. Finally, the member could obtain the rank of Veteran and would be eligible to hold office at the department and national level. Each rise in status meant another fee to be paid. The grade system lasted about one year. He also ordered all supplies must be purchased from national headquarters at several hundred per cent mark up.

Discouraged and disappointed, the veterans began breaking away but, they would not disappear entirely. As the *Soldier's Friend* opined in September of 1869, "The Grand Army would serve as the rifle above the chimney piece, the coat of mail under the toga…The Grand Army had principles that would educate the loyal sentiment of the country…"

Veterans were not going to be left out of the 1872 campaign. This time Grant faced off against Horace Greeley, the Radicals' one-time ally who had broken with the party in the wake of scandals in the Johnson administration. Greeley had published an article in his *Tribune* in July of 1867 titled *Soldiers of Vengeance* in which he denounced the organization as being detrimental to the reconstruction effort. He did this in response to the GAR castigating him for leading the petition for Jefferson Davis's release. Greeley had the support of the some Republicans but his support of the Thirteenth, Fourteenth, and Fifteenth Amendments prevented him from rallying support of all the Democrats.

To appeal to veterans the Republican platform again consisted of making pension and bounty legislation along with care for the widows and orphans, a priority. The party, reminding the North of the South's treatment towards freed blacks, also urged strict adherence to the enforcement acts of 1871. The pains of war were still too fresh in the minds of the public not to remind the north of the KKK's existence.

Grant had easily won reelection in the '72 election (Greeley would die before the Electoral College could cast their vote although he did receive six electoral votes posthumously.) A collapsing economy and a failing Reconstruction program had handed the Republicans a loss during the mid-term election of 1874. Southern politics had allowed their states to begin controlling voting methods in their elections which allowed the Democrats to pick up 85 seats and a House majority. Corruption charges in the Grant administration also affected the country's feelings toward the administration. But it was the forgotten promises of the '72 election which had irritated veterans who had voted the Republican ticket. Their dwindling membership castrated the GAR. They were no longer the voice of the veterans; for now.

The presidential contest of 1876 was between Ohio's Governor Rutherford B. Hayes, who had served as commander of the 23rd Ohio and the reform-minded New York Governor Samuel Tilden. Hayes, who was urged by party members to run, was extremely popular with the soldiers. The idea of leaving his post while the war continued was something he thought no soldier should do. He relented however and entered and won the congressional race of 1864. His popularity amongst the veterans soared as he advocated for benefits on their behalf in Washington. When Hayes ran for governor of Ohio after the war, there was no doubt veterans had aided his election which he won by a mere 3,000 votes.

Again, the bloody shirt would wave as Republicans, who reminded veterans of their support for the soldiers during the war years again counted on the veterans to put down the Democrats who had opposed soldier suffrage during the war. During the presidential campaign veteran reunions were more like political rallies but the GAR remained inconspicuous as the Boys in Blue were again called upon to stage rallies and lead parades across the North. Even the quiet Hayes announced he would willingly bury the bloody shirt when Democrats would "...purge their party of a leprosy of secession..."

Violence and fraud ran rampant in the Southern states leading up to the election and the contest was close, 184 to 165 in Tilden's favor but 20 electoral votes were being disputed in Florida, Louisiana, South Carolina, and Oregon. Hayes had won Oregon but their governor had made a mess of the count. Democrats had won the Southern state elections by successfully suppressing the black vote however Republicans still controlled the electoral boards. Both parties claimed victory as two lists were presented.

As the controversy wore on a fifteen-member Electoral Commission made up of five senators, five representatives and five Supreme Court justices was finally established to break the deadlock. Of course Republicans and Democrats were evenly numbered and they would vote their party line; the lone Independent on the commission was Justice David Davis of Illinois. When then state's legislature had conveniently selected Justice Davis to break the senatorial deadlock between Logan and Palmer his seat on the commission went to a Republican.

A deal was struck the night before Grant's term was to expire. The *Compromise of 1877* consisted of Republicans promising to recognize Democratic control of the three contested Southern states if they gave Hayes their votes. The end result was the Federal government would pull their remaining Federal troops out of the last of the rebel states, Louisiana and South Carolina.

If the Republicans thought they had a monopoly on veteran support they were mistaken. Reminiscent of the 1866 and 1868 election, veterans were gathered to force a show down, only this time it was not the republican veterans who mobilized. Shortly after Hayes was elected the *Constitutional Democratic Veteran Legion* (CDVL) was quickly formed and began sending out a series of circulars to party adherents. The first called for all former soldiers to prepare to "...resort to force" if the current administration sought to inaugurate Hayes. A second circular requested information regarding the number of military organizations, their efficiency level, and conditions of state armories. The third circular instructed adherents to swear allegiance to the *Legion* and to obey the orders of their commanding officers. They also swore to uphold the "Constitutionally-expressed will of the people." Yet another circular urged "utmost vigilance" in selecting members and progress reports from officers. Republican newspapers reported that there was a legitimate possibility of armed confrontation.

The CDVL had support from the *Union Soldiers' and Sailors' Reform Association* which had formed in August in response to Republican propaganda that it was the party which had fought to preserve the Union. Association president General John M. Corse now sought to take the organization to the national level. Boasting a membership numbering from 100,000 to 200,000, Corse promised the society's national committee member General Palmer that these veterans would sustain Tilden if the election was stolen from him. A circular in early December sought the "...co-operation of every man who ever carried a musket." This was followed by an open letter addressed to General Sherman, commander of the army, which warned all "former officers and comrades" of a conspiracy to hold the government by military force. Unless they were to uphold the will of the people, the existence of the army would cease as an "American institution."

Rumors began circulating and Corse decided to release the circular to the press while his cohort Daniel Cameron frankly admitted that 100,000 members would march on Washington or New York and see that Tilden was inaugurated whether elected or not. Corse even told a reporter that, "...there will be fighting sure....and you will find that the army will lay down its arms." Added to this account was the report of members receiving breechloaders and were busy drilling.

Tensions mounted as more rumors circulated that McClellan and Franklin were pulling the strings in the background. As March 4 drew near the democratic press reported that while warships were being stationed in New York Harbor a buildup of troops was taking place in

Washington. As Commander of the Army General Sherman made it known that he would comply with the Republican-led Senate; the Legion continued to build up their resistance. Again the mid-West became a hotbed of activity as Ohio and Indiana began pledging troops to fight the "...flagrant acts of tyranny." The situation became so heated that a shot had been fired one evening into the home of Hayes as the family set down to supper. Not a word of this had made it to the press. It would appear that 1866 was being played out again only this time it was not the republican-led GAR who was menacing the peace.

The GAR did react only not as it had in previous years. The Republicans, accusing the Democrats of overreacting to a difficult situation, could not let on that they were nervous. The threat of violence was real, not unlike Republican reaction eighteen years previously. The 25,000 members of the GAR were trying hard to live down their partisan past. They were now a charitable organization and creditability with the public was important to them. Rather than make a scene as they accused the Democrats of doing, Colonel Drake De Kay, founder of the Boys in Blue and recording secretary of the soldiers national committee, instead used more subtle forms to secretly inform and organize campaign and veteran organizations; this included the Grand Army. Letters of information had been sent out to veterans across the country; apprising them of the crisis and instructing them to prepare but, they must do it quietly.

But, there would no need to organize further. With the Electoral-Commission bill, the loss of Justice Davis on its board, and Sherman's allegiance to the Senate, the Democrats realized the futility of pushing the matter. They finally agreed to the compromise which spared the country from another conflict. The Reconstruction Era had officially come to an end. And so it was politics as usual.

But the threat of violence had been very real. Tilden's campaign manager Abram Hewitt expressed his view that a bloody struggle was "...much nearer than was even at that time [sic] suppose." Corse appeared before a senatorial subcommittee to explain his recent correspondences. The committee was headed by none other than Morton and Logan. It is possible no blood would have ever been spilt as Tilden made it clear from the onset that he would "...never be a party to any course which will array my countryman in a civil war."

Hayes, who had admired and respected Lincoln, had disappointed his party however. He raised the issue of civil service reform believing appointments should be based on merit. To make his point Hayes went as far as firing the head of the Port of New York, future president Chester Arthur. Following a lead by Garfield, Hayes decided to help revive the Whig Party so dear to those in the South in hopes of placing "more intelligent whites" in position of power. This backfired however as hardline Southerners filled the ranks of what they referred to as Conservatives and won the Senate majority in '78 and setting back the civil rights of blacks.

The Hayes administration would have a profound impact on the GAR and the country. With Reconstruction officially over, mounting pressure, primarily from claim agents for promised pension legislation, finally resulted in the *Arrears Act* being passed in January of '79. Veterans and dependents currently receiving monthly payments would now receive a lump sum payment retroactive to their date of discharge or death rather than their date of application. It also loosened restrictions on bills to follow which would allow more veterans and dependents to become eligible for pensions. In 1880, the Treasury would pay out $57 million in pensions as opposed to $29 million in 1870. It was the Democratic-led House however, which approved the legislation of the Arrears Act before the Republican-led Senate did.

The doors of the GAR had been flung wide open. Although claim agents were primarily responsible for the new law many veterans believed the GAR had a hand in it. No longer was the GAR an exclusive organization for Republicans. Democrats began to join the ranks and the resulting political make-up of the organization would ultimately have a drastic effect on future policies and elections.

Political in-fighting had caused the Republican Party to split again into factions. The *Stalwarts* opposed Hayes and his reconciliatory policies towards the South while the *Half-Breeds* who fell more in line with the Moderates, supported the president and his policies. With Hayes content to serve just one term as president Logan, who had defeated Oglesby for a senate seat and was now a leader of the *Stalwarts*, advocated for Grant to run for a third term. No longer able to count on the black votes in the South which had been stripped away, Republicans stuck with their proven formula of a military candidate. At the Republican convention it took 36 ballots before a candidate could be chosen. Ohio Senator General James Garfield would be their nominee for the presidential bid of '80.

Garfield has been elected to Congress in 1862. Initially he was aligned with the Radicals but by 1880, after being elected to the Senate he was leaning more towards the Moderates. He would face off against another military candidate, General Winfield Scott Hancock. One of the main issues was tariffs. The Republicans favored stronger protective tariffs while the Democrats favored a "revenue only" tariff.

Not wanting to outwardly attack a fellow veteran, Republicans claimed Hancock was merely being used by the Democratic Party who now controlled the eleven former-Confederate states. But the republican press was not so generous. While claiming Hancock was a Southern sympathizer they also attacked his military record and leadership abilities demonstrated during the late war. They opined that, as a professional soldier, Hancock lacked the experience needed to hold public office. His close relationship with McClellan, his conduct during the Surratt execution and his alleged treatment of wounded Union soldiers were also being scrutinized. Newspapers even printed a few scathing remarks Grant had made about Hancock during an interview. While Grant admitted his words may have been "garbled" he never denied his statements.

Of course, the GAR could not stay out of the campaign. The veteran vote would be crucial if the Republicans were to retain power. This time Colonel De Kay, with Grant's permission, stamped the former president's signature on a circular resembling a military order and had it printed in the republican press. But Grant's endorsement did not sway all the veterans.

As expected, the contest was close. Hancock had carried the all the ex-confederate and border states while Garfield carried all but New Jersey in the North. Approximately 78% of the 9 million eligible voters went to the polls. The result was only a couple thousand votes separated the two but Garfield had won the Electoral College 214 to 155.

By September of '81, Garfield was dead. He had succumbed to his wounds after being shot by a disgruntled office-seeker two months earlier. Vice-president Chester A. Arthur, who had served honorably in the rear echelon during the war, became president. Arthur had surprised and passed the expectation of many. He had been an ardent supporter of the spoils system but, perhaps due to Garfield's assassin, he had signed into law the *Pendleton Act* which meant Federal jobs would now be appointed based on merit and not as favors being returned. He also tried to address the surplus in the Treasury which was now over $140,000 million. Republicans still wanted to protect the high tariffs while Democrats wanted them lowered. Arthur ordered a commission established to cut tariffs by up to 25%. Of course, the Republican-led House Ways and Means Committee had slashed that figure and the final result was an average reduction of less than 2%.

Republicans tried to make up for it by offering the $19 million *Rivers and Harbors Act*. While hardly making a dent in the surplus, Arthur vetoed the bill due to the narrow scope of the project. He wanted something that would benefit more Americans. Congress however, overrode his veto and celebrated the reduction of the surplus. But it was not enough to appease the Democrats. In the mid-term elections, Republicans would lose control of the House while barely hanging on to the Senate.

Arthur had hoped to gain the presidency by election but without full support of either faction of his party he saw the futility in running. When General Sherman firmly refused to head the ticket, Republicans turned away from a military candidate and settled on James G. Blaine of Maine who had supported Hayes and opposed the Stalwarts, as their presidential nominee for the 1884 election. Blaine, who had stood by Garfield's side when he was shot, was not holding any public office at the time of his nomination. Logan, who lost his bid as the presidential nominee was satisfied to be placed on the ballot as Blaine's running mate to attract the veteran vote. In their acceptance speech, both candidates endorsed a liberal pension system and veteran preference in appointments; the same promises veterans had heard before.

Their opponent would be New York Governor Grover Cleveland, known as a reformer. The Republican press was quick to point out Cleveland's faults to the veterans. They claimed he had used his office to vote against veterans' interests since the end of the war. Even though two of his brothers had served, the Republicans let it be known that Cleveland had paid a substitute to go to war for him. On the more scandalous side, he had fathered an illegitimate child while practicing law in Buffalo.

Even the new pension commissioner W.W. Dudley did all he could to ensure a Blaine victory. Before turning in his resignation, the commissioner had doubled his workforce and compiled a list of all surviving Union veteran residing in every state and territory. Concentrating on Ohio and Indiana where the election would no doubt be decided by veterans, he began to scheme. In Ohio, he increased the number of special examiners from 63 to 101. They in turn informed claimants that they would lose their claim should Democrats be victorious. In Indiana, Dudley meddled in the re-election of two Democratic incumbents by delaying pension claims they had recommended and elevating the status of those recommended by their Republican challengers.

Blaine had followed a rigorous campaign circuit but Logan was a dynamo; campaigning via a special train, enthusiastically received where ever he went, and speaking up to fifteen times a day, six days a week. Logan, who had forsaken the GAR after the 1872 election to focus on his own career, became a member once again and courted veterans at every stop. The reunions and rallies held by the GAR were meant to propagate the Blaine and Logan ticket. Although the GAR was to remain non-political this did not mean that Logan, who enjoyed the support of Grant, could not speak at their conventions which the GAR was all too happy to arrange.

Democrats again organized campaign clubs meant to appeal to the veterans by reminding them that it was their party which had passed the Arrears Act despite failing in the Republican-led Senate. The veterans were well aware of this. Republicans had made empty promises in the past. Besides, the war had been over for nigh on twenty years. Waving the bloody shirt was having less of an effect on the old soldiers. Surprisingly even leading claim agent George Lemon, owner of the for-veteran publication the *National Tribune*, sensing a Republican loss, dramatically downplayed his paper's support for the party.

Nothing was too low for either party when it came to tactics. When rumors regarding the residents of the soldiers' home in Dayton surfaced, an investigation committee discovered substantial evidence of both parties plying the old soldiers with whiskey for their support.

The election was close but Cleveland was elected by an electoral vote of 218-182 and became the first democratic president to be elected since Buchanan. The disappointments of vague promises, coupled with the influx of Democrats into the GAR were two factors contributing to so many veterans turning away from the Republican Party. Logan was devastated; he believed his veterans would not let him down. Blaine, on the other hand, blamed Negro disenfranchisement for creating a solid South. In any event, some GAR leaders used the new president's policies to incite a renewed hatred for the South.

Cleveland, who refused favors to special interest groups didn't wait long to anger the Republicans. He immediately announced that pension system was in need of review and reform. He appointed Democrat John C. Black as pension commissioner. A disabled pensioner himself and Medal of Honor recipient, Black was highly critical of the Pension Bureau declaring, "Examiners, trained in unscrupulous schools, traversed the land as recruiting sergeants for a party." Black had streamlined operations in his department which enabled him to cut cost. His first year as commissioner saw his office pay out $62,000,000 to nearly 325,000 pensioners.

Private pension measures designed to bypass the pension bureaus' examiners had been introduced by representatives eager to repay the patronage of their constituents. Not only were they fraudulent but precious time was wasted weekly reviewing these private bills. With approximately one out of every ten veterans receiving a pension, the removal of fraudulent cases would expedite the new claims coming in. Over the course of his administration, Cleveland had vetoed nearly 230 fraudulent claims out of 1,871 up for review. Although these 228 claims were obviously falsified, Republicans used them against Cleveland as being hostile towards veterans. Even with agents and Republicans angered by Cleveland's actions, many veterans applauded the president for cleaning up the rolls and keeping the pension system honorable.

Some leaders of GAR however used anything they could to rile up their members against the president. Cleveland had aroused the wrath of many veterans by fishing on Memorial Day and refusing to give a speech during his visit to Gettysburg. He also sent a letter to the unveiling of a monument for former Confederate A.S. Johnston's. His approval of the Mexican Pension Bill of which 2/3 of its recipients would be Southerners while vetoing a bill granting a $12 pension to all veterans with 90 day service who claimed their inability to work also caused dissention among GAR members. After learning of a heated debate among GAR leaders and even open threats over his possible attendance at the St. Louis encampment, Cleveland turned down the invitation. When Republicans heard of this, they used it as another example of Cleveland again snubbing the veterans.

Cleveland had even commuted Fitz-John Porter's sentence and restored his commission. The long process began with Hayes in 1878 when he honored Porter's repeated request for a military commission to review his court-martial. Headed by General John M. Schofield, Porter was exonerated for the charge of disobedience to orders and misconduct in the face of the enemy. In fact, it was decided his decision not to attack Longstreet possibly saved Pope from a greater defeat. In 1882, Arthur removed the disability which prevented him from serving in office. All the while Logan fought hard to prevent this. In the Senate, Logan spoke for a total of ten hours over the course of four days, denouncing Porter in an attempt to prevent his receiving $60,000 in back pay. Two days after his sentence was commuted and Porter's name was returned to the army rolls he resigned.

What harmed Cleveland the most with veterans was the suggestion by GAR member Adjutant General R.C. Drum to Secretary of War William C. Endicott of returning captured Confederate flags to their respective states. When brought to Cleveland's attention, the president gave verbal permission to do so. Upon hearing of it, GAR leaders exploded at the idea and used it as another excuse to attack Cleveland and the Democrats. Although Cleveland revoked the order it was too late; the tone was set for the next presidential election.

The flag issue once again gave the appearance of the GAR wanting to promote sectionalism between North and South. The democratic press began attacking the GAR for its behavior and contempt towards Cleveland; calling the society unpatriotic. But Cleveland's final annual message directed at tariff reduction now gave the Republicans new ammunition and Lemon saw his chance to rally the veterans against the president in the next election.

For the 1888 election former Ohio Senator Benjamin Harrison, a military man and supporter of liberal pension legislation would lead the Republicans back into the White House. This time the GAR would rally the troops while the Boys in Blue sat out the campaign. Reunions resembled campaign rallies as the bloody shirt was waved with a vengeance. Even the GAR's auxiliary organizations were called on for assistance. The first "camp" of the *Sons of Veterans* (SUV) appeared in Philadelphia in 1878 but it was not until 1881 that they adopted their constitution and became the official heir of the GAR. By 1888 the SUV was 56,500 members strong and eligible to vote. GAR leaders reasoned that democratic stay-at-homes had sired children during the war years, making their offspring eligible to vote in the '84 election. Now, it was the young males of the veterans returning from war who were now of age to vote.

There were other Allied Orders of the GAR which played a supportive role in the '88 election. The *Woman's Relief Corps* (WRC) and *Ladies of the Grand Army of the Republic* (LGAR) both fought for official recognition of the GAR but it was the WRC, which organized in July of 1883 that received the official recognition. Their mission was to perpetuate the legacy of the GAR, give aid and relief to veterans, widows and orphans, and to promote patriotism. These ladies had taken their mission seriously.

Cleveland however had a strong administration and his re-election was almost assured. When Democrats considered eliminating the surplus, again by lowering tariffs which advocates argued was hurting business, the Republicans saw their chance. By conveniently overlooking that three out of every ten dollars spent by the president's administration went to veterans, Republicans continued to argue that Cleveland was unfriendly towards veterans. The surplus maintained by high tariffs Republicans argued, was earmarked for pensions and to ensure no veteran should ever have to seek shelter in a county poor house or rely on private charities.

This argument, compounded by the other infractions of the Cleveland administration had won out. Although Harrison had lost the popular vote by 100,000 he did win the electoral 233 to 168. It is quite possible that the veterans had tipped the scales in favor Harrison.

Although Harrison disappointed party leaders with his Cabinet appointments he made up for it when he appointed their candidate for Commissioner of Pensions. If Democrats had worried about the surplus, they didn't need to worry any longer. Corporal James Tanner, the legless veteran who had taken notes throughout the night as Lincoln lay dying, had tended his fences well. He had served as commander of the New York's Department of the GAR and was also a member of the GAR pension committee. Tanner also had a large group of supporters who pushed for his appointment which came as no surprise. Tanner had made it clear after his appointment that he intended to "...drive a six-mule team through the Treasury." Another time he was heard to exclaim, "God help the Surplus."

So generous was Tanner in fact, that he re-rated and back-paid pensions retroactively while awarding new, fraudulent claims. Soon an investigation was called for. After a messy ordeal in which thousands of veterans rallied to his aid an agreement was reached and in September of '89, Tanner tendered his resignation. During his short term as commissioner, Tanner had awarded over $88 million, one third of the federal budget to nearly half a million veterans, widows, and dependents.

A surplus in the Treasury still existed as a result of the high tariff rates thanks to the McKinley Tariff Act being passed. So Harrison began signing appropriation bills for internal improvements, naval expansion, and subsidies for steamship lines. Spending didn't end there however. During the campaign the GAR had put together a pension committee which urged members to aggravate the pension issue. Simultaneously, the veterans had kicked off a patriotic movement across the country, endearing themselves to the public. Now, by the end of the decade a stern warning by the GAR had been sent to Congress; if a pension bill was not forthcoming then a Democratic victory in the mid-term election was guaranteed. Republican leaders listened and the continued agitation for more liberal pension legislation culminated in the costliest pension act to date to be passed; the *Dependent and Disability Act of 1890*.

It was passed by what would later be referred to as the "billion dollar congress." This new law would basically guarantee veterans claiming a disability and dependents a pension provided he had at least 90 days of continuous honorable service regardless if the disability was service-connected or not. To receive his annual $144 the claimant must show proof he was incapable of manual labor and there were many claim agents willing to attest to this. Spouses would receive benefits regardless of the cause of their spouse's death. In less than two decades nearly one billion dollars would be paid out in benefits.

But if Republicans thought a defeat of pension legislation would be ruinous to their party in the 1890 mid-term election they were wrong. In fact, its passage had the opposite effect. Many voters were disgusted with the Disability Act. Long before the end of the Harrison Administration, the surplus was quickly evaporating and Democrats blamed the McKinley Act for the waning prosperity as well. Congressional elections went stingingly against the Republicans and the Democrats gained control of the House.

Party leaders wanted to abandon Harrison although he had cooperated with Congress on party legislation. Unable to unite behind an alternative candidate, Republicans again settled on the incumbent for another match up with Cleveland.

Although the Boys in Blue again remained somewhat inactive during the campaign several leaders of the GAR forgot their instruction to abstain from political partisanship and used their encampments and rallies to send a clear message as to their candidate. Their 1892 national encampment held in Washington, D.C. was reminiscent of the one in Columbus, Ohio four years earlier. Even though national commander John P. Rea ordered that the Ohio encampment was to remain a non-political function, the great parade resembled a Republican rally as many of the 100,000 marchers carried pictures of Harrison and political banners. Although the bloody shirt waving was primarily for veterans, Republican claims of Cleveland's lack of military service and his pension vetoes were no match to the drain on the surplus. This time however the '92 encampment was a bust. Cleveland supporters had worked the crowd effectively; distributing amongst the members campaign badges resembling the GAR medal but with the likeness of Cleveland.

The damage was done. Between the costly Disability Act of 1890, the McKinley Act, the threat of the Federal Election Bill which would once again enforce black suffrage in the South, and Democrats infiltrating the GAR, Cleveland came out victorious, winning 277 of the total 444 electoral votes. His second administration would not be an easy one. Once again he turned his attention to his pet peeve; fraudulent pension claims. At the urging of former commander Rea who incidentally voted for Cleveland in the 1892 election, the president appointed former GAR advocate-general William Lochren as pension commissioner. Under his guidance nearly 2,500 pensions were dismissed and an additional 3,400 were reduced due to fraud. Needless to say, the GAR was once again in an uproar. Cleveland did make a concession. He named Lochren a Federal judge and appointed a new commissioner, D.I. Murphy. From this point on, enlistment would be proof enough that no pre-service disability existed and no pensioners would be dropped from the roll.

Cleveland also had to deal with an economic depression which led to the *Panic of 1893*, labor unrest resulting in *Coxey's Army,* made up of the unemployed workers marching on Washington, and the

Pullman Strike. With a Republican victory in both the House and Senate during the 1894 mid-term elections Cleveland declined another presidential bid in 1896.

One point of contention between the parties was the issue of free silver over gold. The country was also divided over this issue and the GAR was no different. While most members were indifferent to the issue, those in the South and West had favored silver over gold. Scrambling for a new candidate, Democrats chose Nebraska Representative William Jennings Bryan as their standard-bearer. The Republicans stuck with their trusted method of nominating another former soldier, former Ohio Governor William McKinley. Campaign manager Mark Hanna made sure the country knew of McKinley's military service. He had enlisted as a private at the age of 18, served admirably under Hayes and was promoted up through the ranks to major. McKinley played his part as well, courting the GAR and receiving dozens of visiting veterans at his home. He attended reunions and encampments, ensuring the aging soldiers their pensions were secure if paid in gold.

Rather than make more promises of pensions and preferences, Republicans merely iterated that they would enforce those laws already on the books. Also, by telling veterans that the free-sliver platform would cut the worth of their pension dollar by half, veterans rallied to his side, except in the West. But the brilliant Hanna knew how to handle the Western situation. He arranged the *"Patriotic Heroes Battalion,"* a train consisting of an engine, Pullman dining car, two private cars and a pair of sleeping coaches. These were followed by a special flatcar fitted with a portable platform, cannon, and two 30-foot collapsible flag poles. The entire train was covered with two thousands yards of bunting, portraits of the candidate and inscriptions. It also carried an entourage of notables, with the headliners being Generals Sickles and O.O. Howard and Corporal James Tanner, all amputees as a result of the war. But this was not meant as a "wave the bloody shirt" moment but rather, a show of support for the wave of patriotism which continued to flow across the country.

The train set out on its journey through the mid-western states beginning in Illinois and winding its way through eight states and ending in Ohio. The cannon would announce its arrival at each stop where the three would give speeches, expounding the virtue of country, flag and patriotism and also the dangers of free silver and the importance of high protective tariffs. When the train departed each stop, *Taps* would be played. It was a grueling trip; the train had travelled 8,448 miles and made 255 stops.

This would be the most expensive campaign to date. Hanna had spent an unprecedented $6 million in the presidential contest alone. They also sent out 1,400 speakers to campaign on behalf of McKinley.

Of course the GAR could not resist staying out of the contest and began campaigning at their national encampment held in Pittsburgh in 1894. One Republican National Committee member attended the event as a civilian in order to hand out "hard money" literature while his wife distributed pamphlets at the coinciding WRC function. So many McKinley buttons being sported left no doubt as to their choice for the presidency.

McKinley would be the last Civil War veteran to be elected to the country's highest office. It would not be a landslide victory but it was a victory. He had won by 600,000 popular votes but the electoral was 271 to 176 in McKinley's favor. Approximately 80% of eligible voters had turned out. Of those 13.6 million who had voted it is doubtful that the roughly one million veterans had any influence on the election. McKinley did not forget his old comrades either. A delegation of the GAR reminded McKinley of Cleveland's dismissal of veterans in the civil service sector so McKinley began appointing and reinstating those who had been dismissed.

When Cuba's fight for independence began to escalate, McKinley was pressured to take action on the side of the rebels. When attempts at negotiations failed, McKinley sent in the *USS Maine* to protect American lives and property. After an accidental coal bunker explosion had sunk the *Maine*, killing 267 servicemen, the press reported it as intentional; the cause due being an underwater mine. McKinley, wanting to continue negotiations, finally gave in to public pressure and turned the matter over to Congress. The vote for war was immediate.

The easy victory in the Spanish-American War which gave the US control of Guam, Puerto Rico, and the Philippines had led the nation to become a colonial power, and there was none prouder than the GAR. Oddly, the last president-elect who had fought to put down a rebellion in his own country now led that same country in a war which allowed Cuba to fight for its own independence.

McKinley had easily won the nomination for a second term in 1900 and again, he would face off against Bryan. His vice-president

Garret Hobart had passed away a year before so Theodore Roosevelt, riding high in popularity due to the victory in the latest war was named as McKinley's running mate. So sure was McKinley of victory that he did little campaigning, leaving that to Roosevelt. The result was the Republicans had won by the largest margin since the election of 1872.

In September of 1901, McKinley life would be taken by a disgruntled self-proclaimed anarchist at the Pan-American Exposition in Buffalo, New York.

Chapter 19

The Legacy

The GAR was never meant to be eternal for only those who had fought to preserve the Union would be eligible for membership but they wanted to ensure their legacy. In the early years its survival was in doubt but survive it did and flourished. These ex-warriors had learned what it meant to be called veteran. When the nation was in peril they had answered the call and served as soldiers but, when the danger had passed they were all but forgotten. But, circumstances had changed that. War had brought these warriors together and forged a bond that could not be broken. They may have felt used and neglected but they possessed the power to also demand change and respect.

The election of Grant saw the dawning of the *Gilded Age*, a term coined by Mark Twain. It was meant as sarcasm, where a gold gilt covering hid a corrupt, vile underside. The East and West had been united by a golden spike in Promontory Summit in Utah but the North and South remained divided by reconstruction. The country had entered a period of rapid economic growth controlled by greed and corruption which would play itself out time and again.

Prior to the war, a majority of Americans had worked for themselves but by the post-war era more Americans were being employed by the large factories which had once pounded out materials for the war effort. The advancement in technology had streamlined productions and as these businesses grew so did the economy. But ruthless business tactics went unchecked as the American government, tainted with corruption on every level had few regulations in place to guard against these tactics.

After the 1868 election membership in the GAR spiraled downward and by 1872 less than 25,000 members remained. They were in debt and all but defunct. But there were those who refused to see the organization die. Claim agents hoped to keep the organization alive for their own selfish interests. By gaining control of newspapers such as the *Soldier's Friend* and the *Great Republic* they infiltrated examining boards and urged surgeons to award fraudulent claims, making many of the agents rich. They also urged veterans to pledge support for candidates who backed liberal pension legislation.

Some politicians also wanted the organization to survive, believing it could still benefit their career. In an attempt to garner veteran support Senator Logan who ironically had let his membership drop, had successfully agitated a cash-bounty equalization bill in '75 which would pay $8.33 for each month of service. But to everyone's surprise, Grant, believing claim agents would be the primary benefactors, cited the current state of the financial affairs of the country as the primary reason for vetoing the bill.

Still other politicians and GAR leaders wanted to reject their organization's political partisanship altogether. In an attempt to reclaim their credibility they sought to become the benevolent society built on fraternity, charity, and loyalty which they had proudly boasted during their initial recruitment drive. In 1871, national commander Burnside ordered the remaining department commanders to remove political partisanship from its ranks. Charity and fraternity were the goals for the '70s. Reunions, known as campfires were encouraged as veterans came together in "mutual affection and fond memories" as Stephenson had envisioned. Family members and friends were encouraged to attend.

As claim agents pushed for pension legislation, the GAR turned to fund raising to aid their less fortunate of their comrades, their widows and orphans. Fairs, concerts, and lecture series were all viable ways for gathering donations; the proceeds to be doled out to members and non-members alike. In 1874 alone, nearly $46,000 was dispensed to the needy by the GAR. This work added greatly to the public's perception of the organization and soon, their credibility was reestablished as well as a surplus in its treasury.

Recruitment drives urged by several departments were being met with limited success. In the East, membership rose slightly as new recruits joined at a rate just slightly faster than those allowing their membership to lapse. In the mid-West, where the society had begun, there was barely a pulse.

One feature of the GAR which had a profound effect on its members and the country as a whole was the observance of Decoration Day. The local posts which survived despite the disappointment of the first Grant administration continued to introduce and carry on the solemn ceremony of remembering those who had fallen in the struggle to preserve the Union. All across the North many towns and cities embraced the annual event. Although the ceremony was meant to be non-political, there were still those who could not help but to revive the past; recalling the hardships endured and those who were responsible. The occasion called for decorating the graves of Union dead only and some GAR leaders made sure Confederate graves remained untouched; such was the case in 1869 when GAR members stood guard over Confederate graves at Arlington. Their reply to the criticism received was that it was meant, not for hatred of the soldier but rather their ideas in which they died.

In 1882 the observance was renamed Memorial Day and the GAR pushed to make it a national movement. By 1890, every northern state had declared it as an official day of observance. Unfortunately as time passed many Americans came to view it as a holiday; a day for personal pleasure. Although disappointed, the GAR insisted on keeping the day sacred and began inviting school children to take a more active role during the services.

But even as Decoration Day was sometimes marred by political rhetoric there were attempts to bury the bloody shirt. As early as 1875, reunions of the Blue and the Gray were being held with hopes that the healing process might begin between the former adversaries. This came to an abrupt halt when a bill was introduced in early 1876 by the Democratic-led House proposing to release all ex-confederates affected by the ban of Section 3 of the Fourteenth Amendment. Alarmed Republicans, fearing the political outcome, refused to give in. Leading the fight, presidential-hopeful James G. Blaine used the amnesty dispute to wave the bloody shirt. He gave a fiery speech on the House floor reminding all of the atrocities committed under the charge of Jefferson Davis and insisted he specifically be exempted from the proposal. This may have set the healing process back on a national level but it was temporary. By 1882, Blue-Gray Reunions were held in New Orleans and Richmond as veterans once again came together as comrades.

In hopes of attracting members, the GAR renewed their efforts to establish soldiers' homes and orphanages in Northern states. In March of '65, Lincoln had signed legislation enacting *National Asylum for Disabled Volunteer Soldiers* to care for the nearly 300,000 disabled veterans. The unwieldly 100-man Board of Managers made it nearly impossible to form a quorum. A year later the board was trimmed to twelve members with General Butler elected its president. By the end of '67 three homes had been established in Togus, Maine; Dayton, Ohio and Milwaukee, Wisconsin. General Benjamin Butler had proudly boasted that these homes, capable of providing housing and care for 3,802 disabled veterans, would be more than adequate. There was no truth to this, considering the actual number of veterans eligible to apply. The nearly five million dollars Congress had appropriated to maintain these homes somehow become tangled up in Butler's own finances which resulted in an investigation. In October of 1870, a fourth home was added in Hampton, Virginia.

In January of 1873 Congress, in an attempt to remove the stigma of images brought on by the term asylum or possibly to show that this new system was meant to be a permanent fixture so long as disabled veterans were in need, had renamed the department replacing the term Asylum with Home.

But for many veterans gaining entrance into one of the national homes meant leaving their home state where their family and friends resided. And as these homes filled to the bursting point, many of the less fortunate comrades would be turned away; their only option left was homelessness or residing in county poor houses where they received inadequate care. National GAR leaders began instructing their departments to lobby state legislatures for soldiers' homes and orphanages. Some departments such as New York for example, became frustrated when their state legislature refused to appropriate funding for such an endeavor. In 1875, the veterans made a direct appeal to the residents and within a year enough money was donated to establish their own state soldiers' home, the *Grand Army of the Republic Soldiers' Home of the State of New York*.

But GAR members did not stop there. When New York department commander General James McQuade stated during his speech at the official opening of the Bath home, "...there was not a Union veteran at the Home that would not stretch out his hand to a weary

Confederate soldier who might find his way there" this may have been a call to the organization as a whole. In the summer of 1883, the *Association of the Army of Northern Virginia* (AANV) and the *Association of the Army of Tennessee* (AAT) sought to establish a soldiers' home for needy ex-confederates in Louisiana. In a fundraising effort they received help from an unexpected source. In a two-day sham battle held at the state fairgrounds members of a local GAR post and the State National Guard "attacked a fort" defended by members of the AANV and AAT much to the delight of the 6,000 spectators. One chaplain of the AANV took to caring for the "wounded" scattered upon the field, dispensing from his "very valuable and important canteen" a miracle elixir.

On the 19th anniversary of Appomattox a large crowd made up mostly of Union veterans had assembled in the hall of the Cooper Union Institute in New York City for the purpose of raising funds for yet another soldiers' home for ex-confederates. Even a special medallion had been printed with the likeness of two former enemies shaking hands. A month later, one of the speakers Corporal Tanner hosted another such event at the Academy of Music in Brooklyn where the Reverend Henry Ward Beecher and an ex-prisoner of Andersonville both gave lectures. Over $2,000 was raised for the Lee Camp Soldiers' Home which opened in Richmond on Washington's Birthday in 1885. Even Grant had endorsed the project and reportedly made a $500 donation for the cause. If animosity was to continue to exist between the two sections, it would be agitated by the leaders and politicians. For many of the men who did the fighting, they had seen enough to last a lifetime.

The establishment of soldiers' homes popping up across the Northern states eased veterans' fear of becoming a burden on their families, or being sent to poor house to die an anonymous death and be buried and forgotten in a Potter's Field. These quasi-military old soldiers' homes would ensure tens of thousands of Union veterans would receive much better care than if they were left to their own devices. They were provided with asylum, employment, medical care, spiritual guidance, and recreation. And when a soldier answered the final roll, they were assured a proper burial complete an honor guard and a headstone to mark, not only his grave but his service to his country as well.

Whether the deceased was member of the local GAR post or not, the hall would be opened for family members. The post bible would be draped in crepe and a vacant chair would be present signifying the passing of a comrade. A detachment would escort the grieving family to the veteran's final resting place where the grave site was decorated with a floral arrangements and a U.S. flag draped over the casket. An honor guard would fire a final tribute followed by the playing of Taps.

The idea of a proper burial also led to another custom; erecting monuments. The earliest war monuments were erected by confederate forces in September of '61 on the Bull Run battlefield. Union forces in the Western theatre did likewise. By the beginning of the 1870s the idea of placing a monument, or "silent sentry" in cemeteries or near its entrance was becoming somewhat common. As the decade unfolded monuments of all shapes and sizes began to spring up in National Parks, town squares and old battlefields. Of course, this led to another matter of contention between the two sections. To see a Union monument being erected in the South was sure to cause public outcry by some. However, the same was true in the North. Confederate monuments were a rarity on the battlefields located on northern soil. Only when Gettysburg became a national park in 1895 was serious consideration being given to placing Confederate monuments upon the battlefield. Opposition was still raised however, and not just by Union veterans but by ex-confederates as well.

Encouraged by the contested election of 1876, claim agents saw their opportunity. By pushing for Democrats to join the ranks of the GAR the result would be an organization which neither party could ignore. There was some reluctance to joining at first, as they were met with opposition by republican members who expressed fears that the new members would vote for the wrong candidates. The agents, insisting there was strength in numbers convinced the nay-sayers that this was opportunity to convert those of the opposite party. The plan worked and the Democrats were begrudgingly welcomed. The GAR was no longer an acronym for "Generally All Republican." But in some instances, the plan had backfired as some departments would come under democratic control. But at this point it didn't matter as veterans of both parties began to demand that their candidates support pension legislation.

Veterans, seeing the large retro-active payments made to first time applicants of the Arrears Act legislation, saw it as incentive to apply and new claims were being made daily. With no safeguard in place against fraud it was estimated that one in four claims were illegal. So when pension commissioner John A. Bentley's proposed reforms designed to clean up fraudulent claims the *National Tribune's* George

Lemon refused to endorse the Republican Party unless Bentley was removed. Garfield dismissed Bentley in September of '80 and appointed W.W. Dudley in his place. By the end of the year, GAR membership had grown to nearly 61,000.

In 1881, the Washington-based *National Tribune,* now partnered with the GAR, urged a serious recruitment drive. The Arrears Act attracted new recruits and was the incentive for former members who had allowed their membership to drop to suddenly have a renewed interest in the organization. The work of the agents had paid off; by the summer of '85 membership had swelled to nearly 300,000 representing 36 departments. The *National Tribune* which boasted a subscription rate of 80,000 managed to have a pension bill passed which increased agents' fees from $10 to $25 a claim and of course, the paper continued to urge high tariffs to feed the Treasury.

The 1880s would be a banner decade for the GAR. By appearing to remove their political partisanship many of the northern states now welcomed the ranks of the GAR into their cities as each large metropolis vied for the opportunity to host the growing annual encampments. After weeks of preparations and tens of thousands of dollars spent on lavish floral decorations, patriotic banners and flags, veterans would take advantage of the cut-rate fares the railroads offered and converge on the selected cities. There they could stay in the tent cities erected by the army or National Guard or choose to stay with local residents who opened their homes to the old soldiers.

Newspaper coverage of the encampments not only excited the people of the North but it also served as another incentive for veterans to join the ranks of the GAR as former comrades came together to share memories and renew old friendship which time had erased. Over the course of the three day event, the organization would conduct their official business such as electing new officers, hearing the various committee reports and passing or not new proposed resolutions in secret meetings. The official meeting would also set opinions on national matters and issues of the day as well. Although they were encouraged to remain non-partisan, speakers ultimately would allude to the prevalent feelings of politicians or the veteran press. Calls for bounty or pension legislation was often heard but not always acted on. The highlight of these encampments was the much anticipated parade.

Not all was harmonious within the organization as cliques began to form. One group, still seeing the potential of the society as an outright political machine insisted on using it as such. After Cleveland's election this group began to agitate bitterness towards the president who they asserted represented the Old South. They attacked his every move and reminded comrades of his supposed hostility towards veterans. By reopening old wounds many in the organization displayed outright contempt and disrespect for the president. At one reunion of the Army of West Virginia in Wheeling, some GAR units even refused to march under a banner hanging from a balcony which bore the likeness of Cleveland. This had a detrimental effect on the harmony of the organization for not all veterans were against Cleveland and the agitation put a strain on the GAR as a whole.

Some members left the GAR to form veteran organizations in support of Cleveland while others fought the society from within. Cleveland's presence at Brooklyn's Memorial Day parade over the protest of the minority Republican faction for instance, had a reassuring effect on the president as thousands of soldiers cheered him. Well known veterans like McClellan, Rosecrans, and Slocum, had also joined the ranks of the GAR, not just for the prestige but to possibly halt the organization from once again becoming a political machine. To them it was time to finally bury the bloody shirt.

Unfortunately, not all members felt that way. For some, their status as the nation's heroes had not gone far enough. As Decoration Day was being introduced to the masses during the '70s, Union veterans often volunteered to speak at their local schools of their experience during the late war. To some, a sense of indifference from the younger generation baffled the old soldiers. They then realized that, since history had not been a part of the school curriculum until 1880, enough time had passed since the end of the war to have cooled the passion of the public. This revelation gave way to a new outlet toward sectionalism; text books.

In 1884, an Indiana post was the first to scrutinize their public schools for not teaching their classes the history of the late rebellion; its causes and ultimate victory. The GAR however, was not yet strong enough to have much influence on the matter. The subject was again approached in '86 when a Wisconsin post assembled a committee to examine a history textbook used by their state's public schools. Their report to their department the following year alleged the textbook was unreliable; written for the purpose of "…finding a market."

In an attempt to remove the book from the curriculum the post presented their report to their department's annual encampment. Another committee was appointed headed by General Fairchild to examine numerous history books used in both the North and the South. They reported that, by striving for impartiality Northern textbooks industries gave no impression of which side was right and which side was wrong. In their attempt to appear impartial, the industry seemed to condone secession. The history books of the South, on the other hand were teeming with bias and sectional slant to the point of being almost treasonous. The GAR insisted that the children learned that the North was right in their fight to preserve the Union while the South was wrong. Secession, they asserted, was paramount to treason.

In their report to the department the committee concluded that "…a broad, comprehensive, constitutional, Union-loving patriotism should be taught in our schools." Not only was this report sent to national headquarters but also to teacher associations across the country as well. The report was accepted at the '88 encampment but the fight against the textbook industry would have to wait until the fate of the *Disability Act of 1890* had been decided.

The decade of the '80s had been an eventful one for the GAR. As their membership and popularity grew they began sending delegates to every congressional session to advocate for more liberal pension legislation for veterans. And both parties knew better than to ignore the GAR.

By 1890 the GAR had reached its peak membership of over 425,000 members; about 40% of the veterans eligible to be members. With this latest pension bill being passed the GAR was ready to take up the fight against the textbook industry, insisting that only loyal history should be presented. But they would meet resistance from the *United Confederate Veterans* (UCV) which had organized in June of 1889. The UVC could not match the size and influence of the GAR; their maximum membership had peaked at about 160,000. Confederate veterans had had enough. Many had resented the recent pension legislation of which they were denied. And now to have loyalty pressed upon them and their children through the public school system, it was decided at their own encampment in 1892 on just which text books would be proper to use in their own schools. To perpetuate their *Lost Cause* ideology they preferred textbooks which included their state history. In a case of *déjà vu* it appeared a portion of the South was throwing down the gauntlet once again. The GAR of course, was willing to accept the challenge.

During the raging battles of the war, many a Union soldier had sought out the flag on the battlefields; it was their rallying point. Its appearance on the field had turned the tide of many a battle. The Union soldiers had fought, bled and died for that patriotic banner. These veterans epitomized the true definition of patriotism; a deep love and devotion for their country. Southern resistance had caused the northern section of the GAR to wage war against proponents of the rebellion. When demands from the 1890 encampment to create laws against public display of the rebel banners went unheeded, the GAR vehemently opposed Blue/Gray reunions where the "emblem of treason" was exhibited. In fact, "to maintain true allegiance to the United States of America" national commander John Palmer issued General Order No. 4 in 1891 prohibiting members from attending any function where the rebel flag would be displayed. To do so would "bring disgrace upon the order of which he is a member."

In 1888, New York's Lafayette Post, hearing of a school professor's practice of donating flags to local schools, adopted the idea. They began presenting flags to schools; the College of New York would be the first of many to receive such a gift. Before long, other posts in the state followed suit. By 1889, national commander William Warner, impressed with the practice, requested every department to instruct their posts to do likewise. As the idea caught on many departments began petitioning their state legislatures for funding and making the display of these flags mandatory. Soon flag-raising ceremonies were taking place across the country.

As the patriotic movement swept across the country veterans continued to find ways to instill in the youth of the country the same reverence and pride in the national symbol as they had. They urged the observance of Flag Day and Washington's Birthday. They also borrowed from *The Youth's Companion,* a children's magazine, the idea to sponsor essay contests on *The Patriotic influence of the American Flag when raised over the American schools.* If the South refused to accept the teaching of loyal history in their public schools then they would have to at least display an American flag.

231

This posed a dilemma for the GAR departments in the South. During the late 1860s, GAR posts in the South were too few and scattered to offer much resistance against the resentment of Southern whites. Acts of violence were reported in various departments and to openly proclaim to being a member of the GAR was an invitation to criticism, ridicule and ostracism. By the early 1870s the GAR in the South had died out. But with its rebirth, departments began to reform and over time former confederates reluctantly accepted the Northerners who moved south. No longer were they Federal officers with an agenda. These were common folks who migrated south to make a life for themselves. They brought with them no animosity and soon Blue/Gray reunions became commonplace. In some instance, Confederate graves were included during Memorial Day observances. This may have helped to heal old wounds; receiving a former enemy as a fellow American but since many places in the South recognized their own Confederate Memorial Day on April 10, it was probably of little consolation.

But one point of contention was the fact that the GAR was integrated. Its strange that Negroes were allowed to join the society even before Democrats. Records indicate integrated posts existed since its inception and all-black posts existed as early as 1867. Although many members had no problems with this, some departments in the South (where integrated posts were almost non-existent) tried to deny charters to black posts when the renewed expansion occurred. The old southern attitudes towards blacks had revealed itself once again as time had passed and many northern transplants assimilated this attitude. The issue was finally settled in 1891 when the national headquarters gave its ruling; no post could be denied a charter based on color.

Nearly 80,000 members of the GAR attended the national encampment in DC a year later. As thousands of these aging veterans retraced their steps of the Grand Review twenty-seven years before, black GAR posts were allowed to march alongside them. This act alone had provided a sense of closure for the many colored veterans who had honorably served their country.

Southern departments were forced to make a choice. To coincide harmoniously with their former enemy or to accept their "missionary duty" to "leaven this great ponderous lump of disloyalty that exists here" as one Arkansas commander put it. Enthusiastically, they chose to side with their brethren in the North and soon, the Stars and Stripes could be seen flying above many Southern schoolhouses.

By 1895, nearly 17,000 out of the 26,600 schools within the departments would have the Stars and Stripes flying above them; the animosity between North and South would not begin to diminish again until the Spanish-American War spawned a new wave of nationalism.

As the flag movement spread across the country, the GAR began teaching proper flag salutes and etiquette as directed by *Methods of Teaching Patriotism in the Public Schools* written by George T. Balch, auditor of the New York City Board of Education. It would not be until 1899 however, when the GAR would adopt the official flag salute used in schools. This consisted of the children standing and raising their right hand when the flag was either being raised outside or brought forward in the classroom. As they recited the Pledge of Allegiance, *"I pledge allegiance to my flag and to the republic for which it stands, one nation, indivisible, with liberty and justice for all,"* the hand was lowered and stretched out, palm upward and extended towards the flag. Next, the oath, *"I pledge my hand, my head, my heart to my flag. One country, one language, one flag"* was recited. In some cases the word *language* was substituted with *people*. Oft times, this was followed by the singing of *America*. Veterans were not exempt from showing their patriotic side either. In the early '90s, GAR members were encouraged to stand and salute when the Stars and Stripes had passed in review or uncover or when the first notes of *The Star Spangled Banner* began to play. This song was destined to become the national anthem in 1931 at the urging of the GAR.

With the patriotic movement came the effort, again led by Lafayette Post, to teach military instruction in schools. Concerned with the great armies of foreign nations, veterans encouraged young males to join the newly formed youth organization, the *American Guard*. This was meant to prepare the nation's youth should they be called upon to serve their country and defend their country. The idea of drill was to exercise the body, sharpen the mind, and build character. When met with opposition, Lafayette Post countered "Without being aggressive we must be prepared to defend our country's interests, whether attacked at home or abroad." By '96, 30,000 young males had become members of the guard, complete with uniforms consisting of a cap, cartridge box and a sheathed bayonet.

In a strange twist of fate, the GAR had to follow its own standard of loyalty. The economic crisis during Cleveland's administration had led to civil unrest among the unemployed and disgruntled railroad workers. When violence broke out near Chicago during the *Pullman Strike* Cleveland called out Federal troops to suppress the violence when Illinois Governor John P. Altgeld refused to utilize the state militia. The members of the GAR immediately went into action either swearing in as Federal marshals or joining local militias to help guard the mail trains; a familiar duty for many. From New York to Alaska, GAR posts were offering to help put down another "rebellion."

North and South, Republicans and Democrats all praised Cleveland's action. When Altgeld complained that Cleveland refused him opportunity to exercise state rights in how to handle the affair, the *National Tribune,* while lauded Cleveland for performing his patriotic duty blasted the governor stating that, "This was the same States Rights rot that was the cause of the rebellion..."

This was not the first occasion that the GAR would offer military aid to a sitting president. During the *Rail Road Strike of 1877* veterans took their lead from the *Soldier's Friend* who first urged veterans to support the working class shortly after the war but now warned that labor unions were detrimental to the law and order of the land. When violent mobs turned on state militias called out to suppress the strike, department leaders offered to their respective governors volunteers to help quell the labor strikes. Even national commander John C. Robinson informed President Hayes that the GAR was prepared to assist in restoring order. Although Hayes had refused the gesture, it had set the tone in years to come.

As this wave of patriotism flowed across the land, the veteran press began encouraging nationalism and strong national security. During the mid-90s the *National Tribune* urged the annexing of Cuba while denouncing McKinley's feeble response to the plight of the Cuban rebels. Soon, the GAR was urging the administration to support the Cuban rebels' fight against Spain. The alleged sinking of *The Maine* had a profound effect on the old soldiers and immediately they began to mobilize. Many offered their services in manning shore batteries while others offered to raise companies. Still others insisted their sons, many of whom already belonged to the SUV and were adept at military drill, form regiments; the old veterans would serve as their officers. Some veterans in the Western departments even offered to donate a portion of their pensions for the purpose of building a new battleship *"The Veteran."*

Although authorities did not accept their offers there was no doubt as to what length the old soldiers were prepared to go to support their country. When the brief hostility ended, it was the GAR who claimed it was their push for "inculcation of patriotism" which quickly led to a quick and decisive American victory. One thing was for sure, this latest crisis had served as reason to narrow the gap between the North and the South. The country had united for a common goal.

But the GAR could not forget the past as they compared the Nation's latest struggle with their own over three decades earlier. Just as they believed the Almighty had favored the Northern armies to abolish the evils of slavery and treason some GAR leaders proclaimed, it was divine intervention which placed the burden of rule upon the American nation in the Philippines. So it was not surprising when Lafayette Post sent 1,300 American flags down to GAR members now residing in the acquired territories to be distributed to the schools and towns. The victory in Cuba led America into the 20th century as a colonial power and the GAR laid claim to the credit for it.

The old soldiers had enthusiastically welcomed home the latest heroes but when McKinley suggested allowing the new class of veterans into the ranks of the GAR the boys of '61 to '65 drew the line. They had fought two totally different wars. The Civil War was fought to preserve the Union and ultimately free nearly four million slaves. Had it not been for those who had donned the Union Blue the country may have been destroyed. There would be no room to share their glory as the nation's saviors.

Undeterred, these new veterans began to form their own veteran organizations; the most prominent of which was the *United Spanish War Veterans.* A somewhat friendly rivalry would exist between the societies as members of the GAR reminded the younger veterans that their campaigns often lasted longer than the entire (100 day) war with Spain. When Spanish-American War veterans were allowed admittance to the State Soldiers' Home at Bath, they too were reminded that the home had been built for Union veterans and the younger veterans were merely guests.

The old veterans were not yet ready to cede their place in line to the new conquering heroes. In New York, Department Commander John

W. Kay refused to allow members in his department to march in the parade honoring Admiral Dewey when he learned that their place in line would be near the end of the procession. They had always led the processions, any procession, and they were not going to change it now but, change was coming.

The assassination of McKinley had brought an end to the Gilded Age, to the waving of the bloody shirt and the prominence of the Grand Army of the Republic. The Spanish-American War had done something which thirty-five years of peace couldn't; it brought national unity. It may have been fragile at best but it was a start.

Membership in the GAR was rapidly declining. The generous pension legislation had used up the Treasury surplus and opposition to further concessions was being made. The old soldiers were satisfied with their pensions and the accomplishments of their society as a whole and by the turn of the century only 276,000 of the nearly 700,000 surviving Civil War veterans stood in the ranks of the GAR; by 1920 that number had dropped to 103,000. Death, old age, and indifference, coupled with a growing population of eligible voters had finally castrated the great pressure group. Since the veteran voting bloc was diminishing and sectionalism could no longer be used as a tool, politicians began to look elsewhere for votes.

By 1920 the country had seen an increase in new veterans. The nearly 300,000 who had fought in the Spanish-American War and the 4.5 million who fought in the First World War would bring the total number of veterans up to just over 5 million. But a growing population, over 103 million, and the passage of the Nineteenth Amendment allowing the women the vote, and world-wide events had stifled the voice of the veteran. But circumstances would again give rise to the need of organized veteran service organizations as politicians again turned a deaf ear to the plea of the veterans.

The GAR would continue to be a fixture in American culture until 1949 when six of the last remaining sixteen Union veterans would meet for its 83rd and final national encampment in Indianapolis. And when the last Union veteran, Albert Woolston died in 1956, the Grand Army was no more. But their legacy had been ensured; the torch having been passed. As their official heirs, the *Sons of Union Veterans of the Civil War* (the Sons of Veterans had changed their name in 1925) would accept the torch with pride. But younger veteran service organizations would also accept the torch being passed on by the aging veterans who had worn the Blue.

In 1913, organizations formed by veterans of the *Spanish-American War* and the *Philippine Insurrection* began to merge with the *Veterans of Foreign Wars of the United States* (VFW) which had organized just prior to the turn of the century. Soon the VFW would have its own rival when the *American Legion* was established in November of 1919. Both organizations, modeling themselves after the GAR, shared the same desire of their predecessors; to advocate for progressive veteran benefits while promoting patriotism.

Both organizations quickly grew as they vied for new members; allowing eligible veterans of subsequent wars to join their ranks. One major difference between the two was membership eligibility. The VFW required that their members had served on foreign soil during time of war while the American Legion did not. And while both pledged to remain non-political, the Legion went a step further towards bringing the country together. At their national conventions members of both the GAR and the UCV received invitations. This was met with some objections from the aging veterans on both sides of course but for many others, the wounds continued to heal.

On Memorial Day, veterans of all wars now stood side by side to *Honor Thy Noble Dead.* No longer was this day set aside to remember those who gave all to preserve the Union. Over time all Americans who had fallen in the service of our Nation would be remembered. They may have fought in different wars and for different reasons but on this solemn occasion, they were as one. And as more members of the GAR answered the final roll the younger organizations stepped forward to conduct this humble observance.

Patriotism was just a part of the legacy left behind by the GAR but perhaps the most important lesson was that by organizing, veterans could wield tremendous power. For nearly a half a century the GAR had influenced elections and affected government policies resulting in generous pension legislation while advocating for the rights of veterans. It had been established as a political powerhouse; a virtual voting bloc created to endorse a radical agenda. Five of its members had become U.S. presidents. But as it evolved the GAR turned more of its attention to their less fortunate comrades, establishing over 30 state soldiers' homes and orphanages. They also turned to the youth of the nation and instilled in them the same love and pride for their country as they had possessed.

The VFW and the American Legion had both learned from the example set by the GAR. They were instrumental in establishing the Veteran Administration and introducing the GI Bill of Rights. The development of a national cemetery system, flag etiquette, youth programs, community service, and scholarship awards are just a few of their other achievements and proof of what can be done when veterans organize and work together.

Unfortunately, over the past few decades the American Legion and the Veterans of Foreign Wars have experienced a gradual decline in membership. The Legion currently has a membership base of roughly 2.4 million while the VFW has 1.7 million. Unlike the GAR, these organizations were meant to be perpetual but many of today's 20 million eligible veterans are turning away from the two largest veteran service organizations and forming their own. One reason given is that the former organizations appear to be outdated and unable to fill the needs of the post-911 veterans.

Today's veterans and their new service organizations must take heed. History has proven the *Divide and Rule* tactic which dates back to the time of Julius Caesar is a powerful weapon which many of today's elected officials use willingly. They wield patriotism as a tool; a device to drive deeper the wedge between the varying classes of Americans. These politicians put party before people, at all cost. This sectional divide had cost upwards of 700,000 plus lives during the Civil War while the pro-longed Reconstruction Era added heavily to that total. And today's veterans and their organizations are not exempt from this tactic.

Veterans and service members must remain on guard. Their strongest ally is their right to vote and they must exercise that right wisely for many of our elected officials do not know the meaning of words like "honor," "integrity," or "loyalty." This is hardly surprising as many of them have never donned a uniform, nor stood a post. They would rather tear asunder all that has been defended by the service of our nation's youth and instead pay lip service to our defenders while voting against their best interest.

Above all, service members past and present, must remain vigilant, united, and organized. They must heed the words of Abraham Lincoln that a house divided cannot stand. By remaining informed and involved veteran organizations can guard against the many unscrupulous elected officials who seek to capitalize on the patriotism of those who have honorably served.

Today this country is losing 20 veterans a day to suicide while countless others veterans must rely on the generosity of so-called charitable organizations and yet, politicians believe this country can afford to wage more wars. When the time comes to repay that "national debt," to properly care for our wounded and disabled warriors, they say we cannot afford it. The Veteran Administration is no longer a viable option. What a deplorable state of affairs when the American people are being solicited for donations just to provide the basic needs of those affected by war. It is quite obvious that our politicians are forsaking, not just our veterans, but all Americans. We can, however, make a difference.

Nearly 20 million veterans make up roughly 11% of the eligible voting population of 226 million. The proportion may appear disheartening but one must remember, voter turnout in the past several decades have been at an all-time low. From 1916 to 2012, voter turnout in presidential elections has wavered between fewer than 65% to a mere 49% while the turnout for midterm elections was nearly half of that. The 2014 midterms had less than a 37% turnout. If this trend continues twenty million veteran votes could have a profound effect in an election.

Americans young and old, military or civilian must hold the leaders of our nation accountable. Too many empty promises have been made to our military members in the past and it continues today. It is the duty of every American to take every politician to task and guarantee that all our wounded warriors shall never, ever want for anything. We must ensure that our elected officials heed the words of Lincoln, "To care for him whom shall have borne the battle..." and that the national debt to our veterans remains forever paid.

Bibliography

Abbot, Willis J. *Battle-fields and Campfires.* New York, Dodd, Mead and Company, 1890.

___. *Battle-fields and Victory.* New York, Dodd, Mead and Company, 1891.

___. *Battle-fields of '61.* New York, Dodd, Mead and Company, 1889.

Alotta, Robert I. *Civil War Justice: Union Army Executions under Lincoln.* Shippensburg, White Mane Publishing Company, Inc., 1989.

Beath, Robert B. *History of the Grand Army of the Republic.* New York, Bryan, Taylor and Company, 1889.

Benson, Josiah Henry. *Voting From the Field: A forgotten Chapter of the Civil War.* Norwood, Plimpton Press, 1915.

Davis, William C. *Battle at Bull Run.* Garden City, Doubleday and Company, 1977.

Dearing, Mary R. *Veterans in Politics.* Baton Rouge, Louisiana State University Press, 1952.

Donald, David. *Lincoln Reconsidered.* New York, Vintage Books, 1961.

Dunning, William A. *Reconstruction, Political and Economic: 1865-1877.* Harper and Brothers, 1907.

Ecelbarger, Gary. *Black Jack Logan: An Extraordinary Life in Peace and War.* Guilford, Lyons Press, 2005.

Foner, Eric. *Reconstruction: America's Unfinished Revolution, 1863-1877.* New York, Harper and Row, 1988.

Freedmen's Bureau Report on the Memphis Race Riots of 1866.

Gannon, Barbara A. *The Won Cause: Black and White Comradeship in the Grand Army of the Republic.* Chapel Hill, University of North Carolina Press, 2011.

Goodwin, Doris Kearns. *Team of Rivals.* New York, Simon & Schuster, 2005.

Grant, Ulysses S. *Personal Memoirs of U. S. Grant, Volume II.* New York, Charles L. Webster and Company, 1885.

Karten, Peter. *Civil-Military Relations.* Taylor and Francis, 1998.

Kelly, Patrick J. *Creating a National Home: Building the Veterans' Welfare State, 1860-1900.* Cambridge, Harvard University Press, 1997.

Linares, Claudia. *The Civil War Pension Law.* Chicago, University of Chicago, 2001.

Marszalek, John F. *Sherman: A Soldier's Passion for Order.* New York, Vintage Civil War Library, 1994.

Marten, James. *America's Corporal: James Tanner in War and Peace.* Athens, University of Georgia Press, 2014.

McConnell, Stuart. *Glorious Contentment: the Grand Army of the Republic, 1865-1900.* Chapel Hill, University of North Carolina Press, 1992.

McPherson, James M. *For Cause and Comrades: Why Men Fought in the Civil War.* Oxford, Oxford University Press, 1998.

___. *Ordeal by Fire: The Civil War and Reconstruction.* McGraw-Hill, 1982.

___. *Tried by War: Abraham Lincoln as Commander in Chief.* New York, Penguin Press, 2008.

___. *Abraham Lincoln and the Second American Revolution.* New York, Oxford University Press, 1991.

Monaghan, Jay. *Civil War and the Western Border, 1854-1865.* New York, Bonanza Books, 1955.

Ness, George T., Jr. *The Regular Army on the Eve of the Civil War.* Baltimore, Toomey Press, 1990.

Oliver, John William. *History of the Civil War Military Pensions, 1861-1865.* Madison, University of Wisconsin, 1915.

Perry, James M. *Touched By Fire.* PublicAffairs, 2003.

Pierson, William Whatley, Jr. "The Committee on the Conduct of War." *The American Historical Review,* Volume 23, No. 3 (April 1918) pp. 550-576. Oxford, Oxford University Press, 1918.

Porter, Horace. *Ulysses S. Grant.* New York, Charles Scribner's Sons, 1914.

Report of the Joint Committee on Reconstruction June 20 1866.

Rhodes, James Ford. *History of the Civil War, 1861-1865.* New York, The MacMillan Company, 1919.

Rhodes, James Ford. *History of the United States from the Compromise of 1850 to the McKinley-Bryan Campaign of 1896, 1860-1862, Volume III.* New York, The MacMillan Company, 1920.

Rosenburg, Randall B. *Living Monuments: Confederate Soldiers' Homes in the New South.* Chapel Hill, University of North Carolina Press, 1993.

Supplemental Report of the Joint Committee of the Conduct of War, Volume I. Washington, Government Printing Office, 1866.

Tap, Bruce. *Over Lincoln's Shoulder: the Committee on the Conduct of War.* Lawrence, University Press of Kansas, 1998.

Wallace, Evan Davies. *Patriotism on Parade: the Story of Veterans and Hereditary Organizations in American, 1783-1900.* Cambridge, Harvard University Press, 1955.

White, Jonathan, W. *Emancipation, the Union Army and the Reelection of Abraham Lincoln.* Baton Rouge, Louisiana State University Press, 2014.

Whiteman, Maxwell. *While Lincoln Lay Dying.* Philadelphia, The Union League of Philadelphia, 1968.

Williams, Harry T. *Lincoln and the Radicals.* Madison: University of Wisconsin Press, 1941.

___. *Lincoln and His Generals.* New York: Knopf, 1952.